AMERICA'S SOAPBOX

SEVENTY-FIVE YEARS

OF FREE SPEAKING AT CLEVELAND'S

CITY CLUB FORUM

Mark Gottlieb
Diana Tittle

FOREWORD BY DAVID S. BRODER

CITIZENS PRESS   CLEVELAND, OHIO

Published by Citizens Press, 3546 Edison Road, Cleveland, Ohio
44121, 216-381-2853

Design by Mort Epstein/Epstein Gutzwiller & Partners

For more information about the City Club of Cleveland, write to
850 Citizens Building, Cleveland, Ohio 44114 or call 216-621-0082.

Library of Congress Cataloging in Publication Data

Gottlieb, Mark.   America's soapbox.

   Includes index.
   1. Public speaking—History.   2. City Club of Cleveland—
History.   I. Tittle, Diana S., 1950-
II. Title.
PN4055.U52C554   1987   808.5'1'0973   87-14684
ISBN 0-940601-03-6

To

the

First

Freedom

I hail and harbor and hear men of every belief and party; for within my portals prejudice grows less and bias dwindles.

I have a forum—as wholly uncensored as it is rigidly impartial. "Freedom of Speech" is graven above my rostrum; and beside it, "Fairness of Speech."

I am the product of the people, a cross section of their community—weak as they are weak, and strong in their strength; believing that knowledge of our failings and our powers begets a greater strength. I have a house of fellowship; under my roof informality reigns and strangers need no introduction.

I welcome to my platform the discussion of any theory or dogma of reform; but I bind my household to the espousal of none of them, for I cherish the freedom of every man's conviction and each of my kin retains his own responsibility.

I have no axe to grind, no logs to roll. My abode shall be the rendezvous of strong—but open-minded men and my watchword shall be "informa-tion," not "reformation."

I am accessible to men of all sides—literally and figuratively—for I am located in the heart of a city—spiritually and geographically. I am the city's club—the City Club.

Creed of the City Club of Cleveland (1916)

Table
of
Contents

Acknowledgments

We wish to thank the officers and members of the City Club of Cleveland and the City Club Forum Foundation—with special reference to the initial support and continuing encouragement of Mssrs. Peter Halbin and James Huston—for giving us the opportunity to create this volume. We would also like to thank the members of the City Club editorial committee—Mssrs. Thomas Campbell, Alan Davis, Dennis Dooley and Frank Hruby—for their devotion to the project and their insightful questions, comments and suggestions, all of which added immeasurably to the quality of the manuscript. An additional acknowledgment is due Mr. Campbell for his 1963 book, *Freedom's Forum*, a history of the City Club's first 50 years, which proved an especially valuable resource at every turn.

Sincere thanks to Mr. David S. Broder, syndicated columnist of the Washington *Post* and an old friend of the City Club, for contributing the trenchant foreword to this book. Thanks also to former City Club president William Woestendiek, executive editor of the *Plain Dealer*, for helping to arrange Mr. Broder's participation and for providing access to and permitting reproduction of photographs from his newspaper's extensive collection.

We are particularly grateful to Western Reserve Historical Society library director Kermit Pike and staff members Barbara Clemenson, John Grabowski, Peg Koelble and Ann Sindelar, caretakers of the City Club archives, for their unsparing assistance and hospitality during our lengthy period of research. Heartfelt appreciation is also due the staff of the City Club for their able and cheerful responses to our spur-of-the-moment requests for documents or tape recordings. And a special word of thanks to Mrs. Betty Little for her prodigious research efforts.

We are indebted to those City Club members, Forum speakers and club staffers who gave of their time to be interviewed for this book: Lillian Anderson, Mary O. Boyle, Annette Butler, Thomas Campbell, Robert Conrad, Nancy Cronin, Alan Davis, Peter DiLeone, David K. Ford, Bertram Gardner, Peter Halbin, David Hoehnen, James Huston, Herb Kamm, Dennis Kucinich, William McKnight, Ralph Perk, Larry Robinson, Sidney Spector, Oscar Steiner, Carl Stokes, Seth Taft, David Warshawsky and Bettie J. Wiechelman.

America's Soapbox is a collaborative effort: Mark Gottlieb was responsible for the years 1912 through 1945; Diana Tittle was responsible for the years 1946 through 1986. Notwithstanding the generous assistance of the individuals mentioned above, all errors of omission or commission are the authors' own.

This book was made possible by the generous support of The Cleveland Foundation, with additional support from the Reinberger Foundation.

Foreword
by
David S. Broder

It is simply coincidence that the City Club of Cleveland reaches its 75th birthday in the same year that we mark the 200th anniversary of the Constitution of the United States. But the relationship between the two events and the two institutions is more intimate and significant than is obvious.

On its face, the Constitution is a design for government. It is mechanical in tone, almost mathematical. The great compromise that made it possible was a combination of arithmetical formulas for representation of states and people in the Senate and the House of Representatives.

But underlying the formal arrangements set forth in the Constitution is a conception of the society that could sustain the fragile Republic being created. It is this concept which has proven flexible enough to permit the expansion of the United States from the scattered seaboard settlements of 1787 to the mighty and complex continental power of 1987.

The key to that conception is embodied in the phrase "consent of the governed," the notion that government should be guided by the wishes of those it serves. That idea was rooted in philosophies nurtured in Great Britain and France, but it had never been applied to a society as untested as the United States was at its birth—or as diverse as it would become.

The challenge of such a democracy is how to discern, define and express the consensus of the public. Elections are vital mechanisms and the founders gave great weight to the frequency of election—the relative brevity of terms—of legislators and executives. But elections settle only the identity of the leaders, not the policies they will follow. Between elections many issues arise on which some means must be found to develop and then express "the consent of the governed" or what we call public opinion.

The City Club of Cleveland can legitimately claim to have served that function with courage and distinction in one of America's leading cities and states for three quarters of a century. As this history recounts, the club was formed by men who believed passionately that free and uninhibited debate was the essence of democracy. They wanted a place where all opinions could be tested—the heretical as well as the conventional. They rejected the role of being an advocacy organization. They recognized that over time, greater influence could be obtained by providing a platform for all views rather than a vehicle for advancing any particular agenda.

Because the City Club has adhered to that original conception and has become the preeminent forum in one of the nation's most important centers, it has earned an important role in national politics. Presidential candidates, Cabinet members, military, business, labor and civil rights leaders all found their way to the City Club. Long before I was ever invited as a speaker, I remember being at a press table or leaning against a wall, taking notes and watching audience reactions to one notable or another.

The audience was always a major part of the story at the City Club. Even in the more inhibited atmosphere of the 1970s and 1980s, City Clubbers found ways to make it clear whether they were sympathetic or not to what they were hearing. The audience may have grown older, with the club, but their vocabularies did not suffer. I remember walking up to one man, old enough to be my father, after Hubert Humphrey spoke to the club, and asked him what he thought. "You couldn't print what I think," he said.

I got to thinking about the City Club the other day when I was in Des Moines watching a very different kind of exercise in democracy. There, an invited audience of Democratic activists watched a televised forum of that party's presidential candidates, while holding little levers in their hands on which they could register their reactions—on a scale from one (for very negative) to seven (for very positive). Individual responses were fed into a computer, and every three seconds it merged the impulses into a composite score, displayed on offstage monitors as a continuing chart.

Basically it was an emotion thermometer for the crowd, displaying the warmth or chill with which they were reacting to the candidates' appearance and words. It was fascinating and informative in a way. But what was striking—and scary—was the instantaneousness of the process. Even before a sentence was completed, the verdict was in the computer and up on the screen. That is as perverse in its way as the *Alice in Wonderland* Queen saying, "Sentence first; verdict afterward."

It is not the City Club way, thanks be. The City Club has always allowed its speakers to have their say in full, whether or not members liked what they were hearing. The City Club has always insisted on a question period; it has recognized that any proposition, no matter how eminent the authority of the speaker, must be examined and challenged, turned this way and that to measure its substance. And finally the City Club has always understood that the reactions of its members are too diverse to be merged by any computer into a single composite "score." Indeed, the whole club concept is as much a monument to diversity and individuality as it is to consensus and community.

In that respect, too, the City Club is not only an ornament of American society; it is a perfect symbol of the nation and its underlying idea—government "by consent of the governed."

David S. Broder
Washington
July 1987

Introduction

On the afternoon of June 29th, 1916, a young man named David K. Ford was standing in the Union Depot in Cleveland, Ohio, awaiting the arrival of a train from New York City. On the train was Luis Bossero, a representative of the Mexican Bureau of Information and an unofficial spokesman for General Venustiano Carranza, the de facto leader of Mexico at the time. Bossero was coming to town that day to speak at the Forum of the City Club of Cleveland, and Ford—who had joined the City Club earlier that same year—had been asked to greet Bossero, hustle him into a waiting automobile and deliver him to 244 Superior Avenue, the club's home, in time for his scheduled appearance.

Delayed more than an hour in New York, Bossero finally arrived in Cleveland at 2:15. Ford quickly shepherded his guest to his car, and by 2:30 Bossero was addressing a few hundred City Club members on the topic "The Needs of Mexico"—a speech that was essentially a defense of his country's policies toward the United States. The audience listened attentively to the speech, asked Bossero a number of questions at the conclusion of his talk and eventually left for their respective places of business. David Ford then conveyed Luis Bossero back to the Union Depot, where he would catch a train for Washington.

Presented out of context as it is, this particular incident from the history of the City Club of Cleveland might appear to be of little interest and minimal importance. Yet it is, when viewed from the proper perspective, as revealing of the essential character of the City Club as any event in the long life of that organization. It also helps to explain the extraordinary longevity of both the club—which this year celebrates its 75th anniversary—and its Forum, the longest running uninterrupted program of free speech in the country.

Why? Because at the time of Luis Bossero's appearance at the City Club of Cleveland, hostility between Mexico and the United States was at its peak, after months of steadily growing tensions. In March, revolutionary general Francisco "Pancho" Villa had crossed the border with a band of 1,500 guerillas and shot up the little town of Columbus, New Mexico; Brigadier General John J. Pershing had been ordered to lead more than 6,000 troops into Mexico to track down Villa and his cohorts; Carranza's army, viewing this nominally punitive expedition as an invasion, had fired on and taken prisoner a number of American soldiers; domestic newspapers were printing editorial cartoons that portrayed Villa, Carranza and Mexicans in general as verminous thugs who would respond only to force; and American elected officials of virtually every political stripe were howling for blood.

On June 25th, President Woodrow Wilson issued a threatening ultimatum to Mexico which all but guaranteed an armed conflict, and by June 29th, the day of Bossero's appearance in Cleveland, relations between the two countries had deteriorated to such an extent that a formal declaration of war was expected at any moment.

Yet in the midst of this national frenzy of anti-Mexican feeling, the City Club of Cleveland not only invited a Mexican national to speak at its Forum, it *did not rescind* that invitation in the wake of Wilson's ultimatum, when many Americans were already beginning to think of Mexicans as "the enemy." For the members of the City Club, the fact that Bossero represented a country with which their own might soon be at war did not inhibit their desire to hear his point of view. On the contrary, information about a still little-known nation from one of its citizens was deemed especially valuable at such a time of crisis. And if Bossero's speech were to include elements of home-grown propaganda (as, in fact, it did), club members were confident they could pin him down to specifics during the open period of questioning from the floor—an integral part of the Forum concept—which would follow his address.

Characteristically, the members of the City Club were as pleased to welcome Senor Bossero as they would have been to welcome General Pershing himself. And that included even such club members as David Ford, who, while acting as Bossero's chauffeur that day, already knew that within a week or so he would be meeting a different sort of train—a military transport that would carry him and hundreds more newly mobilized National Guardsmen to the Mexican border, in preparation for a possible full-scale invasion.

Fortunately for David Ford—not to mention both of the countries involved—tensions soon eased and war with Mexico was averted. (Ford, incidentally, is now 93 years old and still a member of the City Club.) The crisis was, however, all too real at the time, and the City Club's response to it highlights one of the group's most enduring qualities. In fact, the best measure of the City Club of Cleveland may well lie in how faithfully it has fulfilled its own stated purpose, as delineated in the club's constitution: to maintain a nonpartisan platform for the open discussion and free dissemination of information, a platform from which any and every point of view may be expressed without fear of constraint. With but few exceptions since its founding in 1912, the City Club has done just that, inviting to its Forum speakers of every persuasion to propound, denounce, endorse or oppose the widest possible range of ideas, for the benefit of its members and—through newspaper, radio and television coverage—a community that had not only a need but a right to learn the facts.

In his decision on a 1919 case involving a question of free speech, Supreme Court Justice Oliver Wendell Holmes created a metaphor that perfectly describes this concept when he wrote of a "free trade in ideas," wherein the best test of a belief was its ability to gain and maintain acceptance "in the competition of the market." In its way the City Club has always been such a Holmesian marketplace, an institution dedicated to the exposition of ideas whose merits and demerits could be judged in relation to a broad spectrum of other ideas. But maintaining a platform of free speech has been only part of the City Club's role: By encouraging open discussion between proponents of opposing views, by bringing together candidates for office in public debate, by insisting that anyone who takes the podium to expound his beliefs must also defend those beliefs by answering questions from the floor, the club presents a neutral field against which even the most adept practitioners of sloganeering, distortion, misrepresentation and demagoguery will inevitably show themselves in their true colors.

In fulfilling the function of a marketplace of ideas, the City Club has refrained from "buying" or "selling" any of the issues its members have heard discussed in the Forum; unlike other civic organizations which endorse candidates and proposals or take stands on issues, the City Club has, in the words of its creed, stood only for "information, not reformation." Unbiased and impartial, the club endorses but one proposition—that America's first freedom, the freedom of speech, must be scrupulously maintained and jealously guarded, and that its exercise in a free and open forum is the best defense against the erosion of *all* of our freedoms.

With a self-imposed mandate to provide a platform for a wide variety of ideas, it is not surprising that among the more than 4,000 speakers who have addressed the City Club Forum in its first 75 years have been not only some of the most famous newsmakers of the 20th century, but a large number of unheralded individuals of promise, as well as a host of virtual unknowns who espoused views that might have been unpopular, poorly understood or of marginal interest at the time. Among the latter two groups, however, has been an extraordinary number of men and women who were about to attain heights that perhaps even they could not foresee. The City Club has often displayed an almost uncanny ability to find individuals of great potential, among whom could be numbered: a future President of the United States; the future presidents of the Korean, Hungarian and Czechoslovak republics; two future mayors of New York; the future heads of a national magazine-publishing empire; one of only three Americans to be buried inside the Kremlin's walls; America's most outspoken consumer advocate; America's most outspoken latter-day labor organizer; and a U.S. Air Force major general who would eventually be revealed as a central figure in the 1986 Iran-contra scandal.*

These and other Forum speakers—especially those who addressed local issues that bore on the welfare of the city itself—have generated numerous headlines and reams of copy in Cleveland's newspapers over the years, adding immeasurably to the fund of knowledge of the entire community. The newspapers (and there were four Cleveland dailies at the time of the club's founding, nearly a decade before the advent of commercial radio) have always sent reporters to cover the goings-on at the club, and quite often the results have been screaming headlines over front-page stories about fist-shaking, podium-pounding debates. In the early years especially, appearances by national and international figures—whom Clevelanders might otherwise never see or hear—also received extensive coverage, and frequently information from these stories was picked up by national news services or commented upon by editorials in papers across the country.

*Franklin D. Roosevelt; Syngman Rhee, Michael Karolyi and Thomas G. Masaryk; James J. Walker and Fiorello H. La Guardia; Briton Hadden and Henry Luce; C.E. Ruthenberg; Ralph Nader; Cesar Chavez; Richard Secord.

Of course, in the process of addressing most of the issues—both major and minor—that have affected American life over the past 75 years, City Club Forum speakers could hardly *avoid* making headlines. Many of the individuals themselves were already considered newsworthy, and often they were discussing topics of widespread current interest. (The club has always been remarkably adept at securing guests to address issues that are only a few days—sometimes a few hours—old.) There were, additionally, endless possibilities for dramatic quotes from the speakers' ad lib responses to pointed queries from the floor, in the open question periods which followed every speech.

Not all City Club addresses made waves, to be sure; some were, quite plainly, insipid. A surprising number, however, were not considered of particular note at the time simply because they took place out of context; they would be appreciated only later, because they were on subjects which were about to *become* news—within a matter of months, weeks or even days. There are numerous examples of City Club speakers forecasting future events with chilling accuracy. And there are many other examples of speakers—most considered "experts" in their fields—who made prognostications so wrongheaded and inaccurate that, even taking into account the benefit of hindsight, it is difficult now to understand how they could ever have been taken seriously.

A sounding board of its times, the City Club Forum has resonated with both the harmonious and the dissonant chords of the 20th century—virtually all of the issues which have captured the attention of America and the world over the past 75 years. *America's Soapbox* attempts to re-create those chords by bringing together excerpts from Forum addresses; biographical data about Forum speakers, to put their addresses in proper context; general historical information; interviews with City Club members and Forum speakers; and the odd bit of club memorabilia that should help to illuminate the personalities of the members over the years and the atmosphere inside the club rooms themselves. It is, in effect, a history-in-miniature of national and international affairs over nearly eight decades, and of the changing attitudes, customs, laws, manners and mores of those times.

In its home town, the City Club was and continues to be perceived as an organization that attracts as members an uncommon proportion of the most active, outspoken and civic-minded residents of Greater Cleveland. Participatory citizens, most have believed strongly in getting involved in the affairs of their community, in asking tough questions and in proposing solutions to difficult dilemmas. Many of these individuals have themselves been newsmakers, either locally or on a national stage, and not a few have achieved worldwide prominence. Even longtime current club members, however, might be surprised to learn that over the years their ranks have included men who, later in their careers, would become: the secretary of war of the United States; associate justices of the United States Supreme Court (two of these); the chief advisor in Franklin D. Roosevelt's "Brain Trust"; an assistant secretary of state and the head of the Department of Press Censorship during World War II; directors of the two largest community foundations in the country; the principal advocate for the creation of an independent Jewish state at the 1947 United Nations debate on that subject; secretary of the treasury; secretary of health, education and welfare; various mayors, governors, congressmen and senators; and even a network television talk-show host.**

That so many individuals of stature representing such a diversity of social and political viewpoints should have found mutual interests under the roof of the same club in Cleveland, Ohio, is not as surprising as it may seem. Because the founders of the City

---

**Newton D. Baker; John H. Clarke and Harold H. Burton; Raymond Moley; Harry Payer and Nathaniel Howard; Moley and Ralph Hayes; Abba Hillel Silver; Anthony J. Celebrezze; George M. Humphrey; Jack Paar.

Club envisioned an organization that would not just tolerate but thrive on the differences of its members. And it has turned out almost exactly as the founders had hoped it would, when they first sat down to invent it three quarters of a century ago.

The City Club of Cleveland was founded in 1912 as a response to the multiplying social, political and economic problems of an industrial city whose population was rapidly expanding and whose effective governance was becoming more and more difficult to achieve. As in other cities across the country which faced similar circumstances—Boston, New York, Chicago and St. Louis, for example—a group of concerned citizens came together to form an organization through which many of these problems could be studied and discussed, the ultimate goal being to disseminate information to a populace which would then be in a position to make better-informed decisions about its own destiny: decisions at home, at work and, most especially, in the voting booth.

A mere town of some 17,000 in 1850, Cleveland had grown in population to more than 360,000 by 1900. This boom was largely the result of the great waves of European immigrants who came to work in the city's burgeoning iron-ore shipping, steel-making and oil-refining industries (the latter being John D. Rockefeller's gigantic Standard Oil Company, founded in Cleveland in 1870). Unprepared to deal with such rapid growth, Cleveland by the turn of the century was faced with a raft of difficult issues: an inadequate infrastructure of roads, bridges, mass transit and city services; graft and political power-brokering; a substandard educational system; substandard housing; crime; disease; intolerance of the foreign-born.

In 1901, the voters elected a mayor who promised change. Tom L. Johnson was both a self-made millionaire and a populist reformer. His sympathies lay with the have-nots of Cleveland and against those who enjoyed the rewards of what he called "privilege," and this unique combination of values made him a remarkable municipal administrator.

Johnson was mayor for four terms, and in that time he instituted numerous efficiencies in the business of the city, created a model building code, paved hundreds of miles of streets, launched initiatives which would further improve the lot of the citizens of Cleveland and fought a lengthy war to bring down streetcar fares to three cents. Johnson's administration was so successful that Lincoln Steffens, the muck-raking journalist and author of *Shame of the Cities*, was moved to call him the "best mayor" of the "best-governed city in the United States."

It is perhaps no surprise that little more than a year after Johnson's untimely death in 1911 (he had been out of office for two years at the time), a number of his proteges, acolytes and personal friends would be among the founders and earliest members of the City Club of Cleveland. Recognizing the myriad ills that the city still faced, they believed that a local club of widest possible membership from among the community could act as a clearinghouse of ideas and a place for interested parties to meet and discuss possible solutions to some of the city's problems. Among the founders and charter members of the City Club in 1912 were such activists and political figures as Newton D. Baker, city law director in Johnson's administration, who was himself elected mayor in 1911; William Stinchcomb, the city's chief engineer under Johnson and subsequently one of the fathers of Cleveland's Metropolitan Park System; attorney Alfred A. Benesch, a former Johnson advisor who would be elected to the city council that year; and Cleveland Board of Education administrator Edward W. Doty, a lifelong Republican who was nonetheless a great friend of Johnson's.

In addition to the Johnson men who attended the birth of the City Club, exponents of a variety of different views also were involved: Daniel E. Morgan, a Cleveland city councilman and member of Theodore Roosevelt's Progressive Party; attorney John D. Fackler, another Progressive and longtime deputy tax commissioner of Cuyahoga County; attorney Carl D. Friebolin, a well-known reform Democrat who would serve for more than 60 years as a judge in bankruptcy court; Paul Bellamy, city editor (and later editor in chief) of the Cleveland *Plain Dealer*; Mayo Fesler, secretary of Cleveland's Municipal Association (precursor of the present Citizens League), who had helped to found the St. Louis City Club just a few years before; and Western Reserve University professor of political science Augustus R. Hatton, a recognized expert on municipal reform who would write a new city charter for Cleveland in 1921.

An organizational luncheon to explore the possibility of creating a city club in Cleveland was held on June 14th, 1912, in the Chamber of Commerce building on the northeast corner of Public Square. Other meetings were held throughout the summer to formulate the club's purpose and devise its bylaws. The founders eschewed the racial, religious and ethnic barriers to membership of so many other organizations of the time, opening the club to all men "of good repute." They decided to actively seek a varied membership, aiming for a group that would be truly representative of the multitude of social and political positions in Cleveland. Their club would be a platform for "the investigation, discussion and improvement of civic conditions and affairs in Cleveland." And they would keep the dues low, to ensure that anyone who wanted to join could do so.

The most important decision they arrived at was to follow the example of the Boston City Club by making their organization not only nonpartisan but non-advocatory. They would take no stands on issues and endorse no candidates for office, but remain strictly neutral on all subjects. And to guarantee a healthy dialogue between speakers and members, they insisted that every speaker who addressed the club must also make himself available to respond to an open period of questions from the floor following his speech.

On October 28th, the club was incorporated in the State of Ohio, and invitations were sent to a few hundred potential members. Two days later, October 30, 1912, the first meeting of the City Club of Cleveland was held. Mayor Newton D. Baker addressed the gathering on the importance of maintaining a nonpartisan stance for truly unbiased discussions, and of the 111 men present, 104 immediately purchased $10 "shares" in the corporation.

By November the club had elected its first board of directors: industrialist Amasa S. Mather, son of iron-ore magnate Samuel Mather; Dr. Robert H. Bishop, a prominent local physician and later director of Cleveland's Lakeside Hospital; attorneys Arthur D. Baldwin, Walter L. Flory, Daniel E. Morgan and George A. Welch; Rabbi Moses J. Gries of The Temple, Cleveland's largest Reform Jewish congregation; the Reverend Worth M. Tippy, spiritual leader of the Epworth Memorial Methodist Episcopal Church; stockbroker Edward M. Baker; Starr Cadwallader, social worker and one of the founders of the Cuyahoga County Juvenile Court; Cleveland *Plain Dealer* editor Erie C. Hopwood; and professor Augustus R. Hatton. Later in the month, Morgan was elected president, Baker vice president and Mather treasurer. Mayo Fesler agreed to serve as temporary, unpaid club secretary until that position could be filled permanently. Without club rooms of its own during its first six months of existence, the fledgling organization would hold its meetings in a variety of halls around town.

The first City Club Forum was held on December 21, 1912, and it is a measure of the club founders' reverence for Tom Johnson that they would invite as first speaker Brand Whitlock, reform mayor of Toledo, Ohio. Whitlock was one of the most able city administrators of the time, a personal friend of Johnson's and often compared to him in the effectiveness of his work as a progressive municipal leader. By inviting Whitlock to address their first forum, it was as if the founding members were trying to resurrect the spirit of their city's late, great mayor.

Whitlock spoke at the City Club on the topic of public ownership of municipal utilities, discussing his impressions of the system he had studied in Glasgow, Scotland, during a recent fact-finding tour of Europe. He could not have chosen a more appropriate subject;

public ownership had been one of Tom Johnson's pet concepts, and it has continued to be a topic of hot debate in Cleveland even to the present. In fact, many of the subjects first discussed at the City Club in the Teens and Twenties would come up again and again over the years, examples of the continuity and cyclical nature of the issues that have affected America throughout the 20th century. Club archives reveal discussions in the Twenties of American military involvement in Nicaragua, while in the Thirties there were widespread fears about passing along a huge national debt to future generations. Similarly, there were early warnings about the loss of American manufacturing capacity and industrial jobs to foreign countries, as well as debates over protectionism, immigration policy, segregation and even a 1931 proposal to hold the liquor dealer liable for any damages created by patrons under the influence of alcohol he had sold them. Among local issues in the club's earliest years were some of the first battles in a long-standing war between the city's private and public electric-power companies; the first discussion of a proposed downtown subway system, which would be debated for nearly half a century; and the pros and cons of creating a metropolitan government encompassing Cleveland and its suburbs, an issue being argued to this day.

On May 17, 1913, the club moved into its first permanent home, third-floor rooms above Weber's German restaurant at 244 Superior Avenue—the former headquarters of the local Democratic Party—where it would reside for the next three years. Forum seasons ran from the fall to the spring, and speakers appeared at Saturday noon meetings; before the advent of the five-day workweek, most club members worked a half-day on Saturday, and it was convenient for them to congregate at the club for lunch and to participate in the day's program.

Club rooms were open daily as well, and members kept up with current politics, business and social affairs over lunch. Loud and prolonged debates on various subjects were not unusual in the dining room, and sporadic shouting matches could continue well into the afternoon. Although the club accepted members without regard to racial, ethnic or economic background, the membership over the years consisted primarily of Caucasians, most of whom were politicians, judges, attorneys, physicians, educators, social workers, clergymen, newspaper reporters and editors, with a smattering of bankers, merchants and industrialists. By 1916, membership had increased to a point where the club was forced to move to more spacious quarters on the third floor of the nearby Hollenden Hotel.

By the early Twenties, two distinct factions within the club had formed their own luncheon groups: the Soviet Table, an accumulation of liberals, reformers, radicals and decidedly unrestrained talkers; and the Sanhedrin Table, a more conservative group whose original members were actually defectors from the Soviets' sphere of influence. Naming themselves after the "ancient Hebrew counsel of elders," the Sanhedrinites were known for their debating skills and subtle wit. But if the stiletto was the rhetorical weapon of choice at the Sanhedrin Table, the broadsword—wielded with joyous abandon—was the preference of the Soviet Table.

Among the most opinionated, pugnacious and partisan members of the club, the Soviets were a collection of high-profile civic activists who delighted in challenging accepted wisdom on all fronts. (The table earned its name not long after the 1917 Bolshevik revolution in Russia, which was a topic of intense interest and discussion for the group. Then club secretary Francis "Pat" Hayes one day placed a centerpiece of red roses on the table and announced, "At last you have your true colors—the Soviet Table.") Table "members" paid nominal monthly dues which afforded them the right to a seat and to have their names painted on the surface of the table in concentric circles alongside a hammer and sickle.

Jack Raper, whose satiric comments on social and political events appeared daily in his column in the Cleveland *Press*, was a charter member of the Soviet Table, along with populist attorney Edgar Byers and Ed Doty. Chief among the Soviets, however, was Peter Witt, a nationally recognized expert on public transportation who served as city clerk under Tom Johnson and was later Cleveland's traction commissioner. The most voluble member of the City Club, Witt showed up at the Soviet Table each day not to eat lunch but to debate current affairs with his comrades. (When one day the table itself collapsed, the damage was attributed to Witt's habit of pounding on it as he argued.) At various times a candidate for mayor of Cleveland and governor of Ohio, as well as a member of Cleveland's city council, Witt was vigorous in his public denunciations of political chicanery, malfeasance and shortsightedness—so much so that for 20 years he regularly arranged "town meetings," at which thousands of citizens paid a small admission charge to hear him, as he put it, "skin the skunks." Over the years other luncheon table groups—such as the Schoolmasters Table, at which educators and school-board administrators congregated—were formed, but none had the high public profile of the Soviets, whose pronouncements received almost as much newspaper coverage as the club itself.

"A social club with a civic purpose," the City Club's original albeit unofficial motto, is a fairly accurate representation of the flavor of the organization and the sense of irreverent mayhem that reigned in the earliest years. (The motto was dropped in 1927 when the club filed suit seeking a rebate from the federal government on the grounds that it had been improperly taxed as a private social club when in fact it was a non-profit "association for civic betterment.") The club rooms themselves—at the Hollenden until 1929, then in the club's own building on Vincent Avenue until 1971—were a comfortable, all-male retreat, where cigar smoke tended to displace breathable air and where members could read, play cards or pool or simply take advantage of a selection of couches and chairs for postprandial snoozing. Chess was a virtual obsession for many years, with the club staging its own tournaments and inviting chess masters to put on exhibitions. House rules decreed a decidedly casual atmosphere—so much so that, even after he had been appointed secretary of war in Woodrow Wilson's cabinet, Newton D. Baker was still habitually referred to by his fellow City Clubbers as "Newty."

The club invited visiting vaudevillians, movie stars and sporting personalities to lunch during the week, which accounts for appearances by such luminaries as New York Yankees slugger Babe Ruth, silent-movie vamp Louise Glaum and even a trained chimpanzee from a touring circus. An annual "Summer Round-up," instituted in 1919, was an excuse for the self-styled "Cityzens" to pile into automobiles (at that time still fairly rare) and drive out to the country for a day of calculated lunacy. The Round-ups were popular not only with club members but with photographers for the local newspapers, whose Sunday rotogravure sections featured numerous shots of the City Clubbers—their only concessions to informality being to remove their suit coats and high collars—engaged in softball games, horseshoe throwing, foot races and the like. As the automobile became ubiquitous and a drive into the country was no longer considered a great adventure, interest in the Round-ups waned; in 1928 the event was cancelled, and no further attempts to revive it were made in succeeding decades.

Each year the club's membership elected new officers and a board of directors, and from the nominating process for these elections came the Candidates' Field Day. An annual special session inaugurated in 1918 and continuing through the early Sixties, the Field Day was an excuse for aspirants to club office—along with their "managers"—to present mock campaign speeches and skits, often augmented by elaborate props and costumes. Employing everything from low comedy to subtle wit, candidates lampooned themselves and each other in performances so entertaining that the papers regularly reviewed them as they did new vaudeville shows.

The Field Day was actually the second of the club's forays into show business, however. In 1913, an entertainment portion of the club's first annual meeting included an informal roast of those members who were politically prominent in town. The following year the club instituted a "Stunt Night," a scripted though still informal playlet written by and starring club members, that poked fun at the machinations of local politicians. One of the actors in the first Stunt Night was bankruptcy judge Carl D. Friebolin, who was to impersonate Mayor Newton D. Baker. Friebolin thought his lines were not particularly funny and said so; challenged to come up with something better, he sat down and wrote what amounted to a whole new play. Friebolin's show was such a hit that for the next half century he would be called upon to be the principal author of virtually every script for what soon became known as the Anvil Revue.

A full-scale production presented on the stage of a local theater or, later, at Cleveland's Public Auditorium, the Anvil Revue grew into one of the most popular annual entertainments in the city. Filled with wicked satire on local, national and international affairs and personalities, Friebolin's revues were directed, designed, choreographed and performed largely by club members, for presentation to club members and their guests—the latter most often being the very objects of the satire. But the whole town looked forward to each year's Revue, which was always preceded by weeks of publicity stunts (a fake bomb planted in the club rooms, or the "theft" of the show's script) dreamed up by members and dutifully reported in Cleveland's newspapers. The Revue itself was given extensive coverage, including full reproduction of the scripts by the local papers. Friebolin and his longtime collaborator, Joe Newman—co-owner of a local sporting goods store (and uncle of actor Paul Newman), who wrote the song lyrics beginning in 1921—became so well known that by the Forties even the *New York Times* was sending a drama critic to cover the show.

Although certainly meant to amuse, the Anvil Revue was fundamentally an exercise in free speech: an opportunity to hold up to the light of public scrutiny the follies and foibles of the powerful, which included mayors, governors, senators and Presidents. (As author Friebolin put it in his curtain speech in 1937: " 'It's all in fun,' as Nero said to the early Christian martyrs.") Remarkably enough, the shows' "goats" were, for the most part, willing to take their lumps with equanimity. Maurice Maschke, for some 20 years the most powerful behind-the-scenes politico in Cleveland, was mercilessly lampooned in Revues throughout the Twenties and Thirties, yet each year he sat in the front row—laughing, it was said, until the tears ran down his cheeks. A version of the Anvil Revue—performed as an old-fashioned radio broadcast—survives to this day, although it is regarded now more as an entertaining diversion than a penetrating social satire. Other traditions of the club, however, continue to thrive in much the same form, and with much the same impact, as when they originated. In its earliest years the City Club began the practice of inviting local congressional candidates to debate in the closing weeks of the campaign, and before long this idea was expanded to include mayoral, gubernatorial and senatorial candidates, as well as those running for seats on the city school board. These debates have proven to be of significant value over the years, primarily beause they are often the only time during the campaign when the candidates confront each other face to face. The performances of the candidates—and especially their ability to deal with hostile questions, whether from opponents or from club members—have often resulted in front-page news in the waning days of a campaign and have provided voters with a deeper understanding of their choices in upcoming elections. Not long after regularly scheduled radio coverage of Forum sessions was instituted in 1928 by Cleveland radio station WGAR, the club broadened the scope of the debates even further by taking phone-in questions from listeners.

Questions themselves—often cogent, sometimes hostile, almost always thought-provoking—constitute one of the fundamental values of the City Club Forum. If the Forum provides a platform for a speaker to propound his ideas, so too it forces that speaker to defend his ideas in the face of a none-too-friendly inquisition from the membership. In this way, phrasemongering and propaganda might indeed pour forth from the podium, but a few pointed questions from the floor can usually bring the discussion back in balance. Every speaker invited to address the City Club Forum agrees in advance to answer questions at the conclusion of his speech, and early on this proviso earned the club a reputation as one of the toughest audiences in the country. The speaker who came unprepared to defend his ideas, or whose arguments were easily punctured, would inevitably be exposed by the most damning evidence of all—his own words.

Throughout its history the City Club has always tried to find speakers who could offer both information and provocation: that is, facts to be considered *and* new ideas to be argued. It was, therefore, typical of the club that in 1928 it would stage a debate between a Presbyterian minister and the originator of the then shocking concept of companionate marriage, or that in 1932 the club would be the platform for the first full public exposition of Technocracy, a "rational" economic system that, it was hoped, would end depressions for all time. In 1975 the club had to request police protection to ensure the safety of Stanford University professor William Shockley, who had previously been denied numerous other platforms for espousing a theory that blacks are intellectually inferior to whites. And pickets protested the 1967 appearance of avowedly segregationist presidential candidate George C. Wallace, as well as the 1982 speech of Equal Rights Amendment opponent Phyllis Schlafly.

The propriety of inviting these and similarly controversial figures has often engendered heated debate within the club, and not a few members have resigned or threatened to resign in protest. For the most part, the Cityzens have responded well to the challenge of keeping their Forum open to all ideas, even those which they personally find abhorrent. This was not the case in 1923, however, when the club issued an invitation to a soft-spoken, unassuming Indianan named Eugene V. Debs.

Three times Socialist Party candidate for President, Debs had been arrested in 1918 in Canton, Ohio, for making a public speech in opposition to the drafting of young men for military service. Tried and convicted under newly devised sedition laws, he was sentenced to a lengthy term in the federal penitentiary in Atlanta, but his sentence was commuted in 1922. By that time Debs was widely perceived as not only a dangerous radical but a traitor to his country. Nonetheless, some members of the City Club—most notably Peter Witt, a personal friend of Debs's—raised the possibility of inviting the aging socialist to speak at the Forum.

Beginning in 1919, at the height of the great Red Scare that immediately followed World War I, the City Club began holding what it called "extension" forums in neighborhoods around the city. These gatherings served the dual purpose of bringing speakers and debates to a larger audience outside the club and of reaching out to an otherwise feared and neglected immigrant population, many of whom were widely mislabeled as subversives and anarchists. Given the tenor of the times, the club displayed no small measure of courage in sponsoring the extension forums, but that courage was apparently in short supply when it came to the question of Debs.

Internal discord threatened to destroy the club as many members—including the president and some directors—ex-pressed outrage at the thought of providing a platform for a man of Debs's record. Yet despite the resignations of some club members, the board of directors issued an invitation. At the height of the internecine warfare, Debs—having been told of the situation—gracefully declined the invitation in a letter which explained that he did not want to cause undue hardship for the club by appearing. Most of the members who had resigned subsequently renewed their memberships, but it was impossible to deny that the club had come close to reneging on its own fundamental principle of free speech. In the end, the invitation to Debs was not rescinded, but the bitterness engendered by the incident has to this day served as a reminder to some club members that even in their most open of houses the twin demons of fear and intolerance can at times hold sway.

Throughout its first three decades, the City Club provided honoraria to speakers directly from its own operating funds, but after barely surviving the Depression years of the Thirties—when many members were forced to resign because they simply could not afford the dues—the club realized a new system had to be found. In 1940, a drive spearheaded by then president Philip W. Porter, executive editor of the *Plain Dealer*, resulted in the creation of the Forum Foundation, a fund of separate monies that would be used solely to underwrite the cost of forums. Through annual contributions, gifts and endowments, the foundation has continued to grow over the years, providing much-needed stability for the Forum program even during periods when membership has declined.

The original stated purpose of the foundation was to permit "non-members, radio listeners and women," as well as active club members, to participate in underwriting forums, which points up one of the club's most obvious blind spots about itself. Through its first 60 years the City Club—an organization sufficienty idealistic that since its inception it had always been open to black and Jewish members, when other local organizations were unabashedly restricted—was a solely male preserve. This was, perhaps, understandable in its first decade, given that the club was founded eight years before women won the vote, and even for years after, given the realities of contemporary standards. But it was not until 1972 that the question of admitting women as members was voted on and approved, and at that it was argued vehemently. Today, of the club's 1,400 members only some 300 are women, and only two women have served as president.

Much of the argument over the admission of women took place in the letters column of *The City*, the weekly members' newsletter that was founded in 1916 and continues to this day. An informative, amusing, though at times unduly chatty publication, *The City* was created by the club's first full-time, paid secretary, Ralph Hayes, who had been assistant secretary under Mayo Fesler. The quintessential bright young man of the Teens, Hayes was intelligent, witty, capable and handsome, a Gatsby-esque character who had ventured forth to Cleveland's Western Reserve University from the little town of Crestline, Ohio, only after shedding his real name—Alphonso Lamont. Author of the City Club's creed, Hayes would eventually leave the club to serve as Newton D. Baker's personal secretary in Washington, and in later years he would become a vice president of the Pulitzer family's Press Publishing Company, director of the New York Community Trust (then the second largest community foundation in the country, which was modeled after the pattern established by The Cleveland Foundation) and vice president and treasurer of the Coca-Cola Company.

Ralph Hayes was followed as secretary of the club by Francis T. "Pat" Hayes, who would organize the first Summer Round-ups and many other such activities. The club reached its all-time high in membership under Pat Hayes's stewardship, with some 3,000 members in 1920. He left in 1923 to become legal counsel for the Cleveland Citizens League and was followed by Charles B. Ryan, who presided over the club until 1931. Toward the end of Ryan's tenure, as the Depression deepened, even the most provocative Forum programs were not sufficient to staunch the flow of resignations forced by economic necessity, and the dismal possibility had to be faced that the City Club would meet the same fate as the much larger (and more financially secure) Boston City Club, which had collapsed in 1930.

A windfall of nearly $50,000 from the successful resolution of the tax-refund lawsuit initiated in 1927 helped the organization enormously, but the real savior of the club was its new secretary, John J. "Jack" Lafferty. A former automobile and insurance salesman, Lafferty put his charm and selling skills to good use in a membership drive that increased the club's ranks from its all-time low of 668 in 1935 to nearly 1,000 by May of 1937. Often going without pay so that other staffers could be assured their wages, the genial Lafferty managed to keep the club humming through some of its darkest hours. He was ably assisted in his endeavors by assistant secretary Hilda Snyder, who refused salary increases through many of the worst years and who would stay with the club until her retirement in 1972.

By the advent of the Sixties, the impact of the five-day work week and the wholesale migration to the suburbs of former city dwellers forced the club to move its traditional Saturday Forum to Friday. At the same time, a tendency to focus less on local issues in the Forums than on topics of international interest—which were already being covered in depth by radio, television and a rapidly growing network of instantaneous global communications—took its toll on club membership. In 1965, longtime member Peter DiLeone became president and acted as unpaid secretary until the appointment of Peter Halbin. Together DiLeone, Halbin and Halbin's successor, Fred Vierow, began vigorous membership campaigns and brought balance back to the Forum by giving equal weight to its role as a platform for discussion of both national and local issues.

Current City Club Executive Director Alan Davis (the title of secretary was changed in 1971, shortly after Davis was named to the post) has been a driving force behind a number of innovations that have further broadened the scope and audience of club activities. Radio broadcasts of Forum programs, for example, were originally heard only on Cleveland-area stations; today, forums are broadcast via satellite to a network of more than 140 stations in 38 states by Cleveland's WCLV-FM, which has presented the Forum live since 1970. (By way of contrast, the National Press Club's weekly broadcasts are carried by a network of fewer than 50 stations.) And the club regularly receives requests for tapes of particular Forum programs from listeners as far away as Alaska.

In 1977, Cuyahoga Community College began videotaping Forum sessions, and these programs are now carried weekly by Cleveland's Public Broadcasting Service affiliate, WVIZ-TV. A variety of new programs within the club have also been instituted. A host of midweek Forums have made programming a year-round affair, and each week 40 high school students from Greater Cleveland schools are invited to attend the Forum and to hold their own seminar with the day's speaker at the conclusion of his appearance. Since the mid-Seventies the club has underwritten a program that brings inner-city senior citizens to lunch on Forum days. And the former Schoolmasters Table is now the Issues Table, where on various days throughout the month such topics as politics, sports or the arts are informally discussed with local guest experts.

In 1971 the City Club was forced to leave its longtime Vincent Avenue home to make way for the construction of a new bank building. It moved into joint quarters with the Women's City Club in the Women's Federal Savings and Loan Association headquarters—next door to the building that in 1912 had housed the club's first home, Weber's Restaurant. In 1982 the two clubs again moved (this time to make way for construction of the Standard Oil Company's new headquarters) to the Citizens Building, on Euclid Avenue at East Ninth Street, which is still their joint home. While some members bemoan the loss of the crusty, casual atmosphere of the old, all-male accommodations, none would deny that the association with the Women's City Club has brought financial stability to both organizations.

Despite the many surface differences between the City Club of today and the City Club of 1912—differences which reflect the vastly altered society in which it has grown—the club remains, in many respects, essentially the same organization as when it was founded 75 years ago. It is an institution whose *raison d'etre* was and continues to be the exercise and maintenance of free speech. It is mere coincidence that the City Club's 75th anniversary falls in the same year as the 200th anniversary of the Constitution of the United States, but it is an entirely appropriate circumstance. For the First

Amendment of that Constitution, the one that guarantees to all citizens the freedom of speech, has been the guiding principle of the club since its inception so long ago.

"I am the city's club" reads the last line of Ralph Hayes's City Club creed, and the organization has indeed been credited with playing an important role in the history of its home town. The source waters of a constant stream of information that has enriched nearly every part of its community, the club has also been a congenial retreat for some of the city's brightest minds, a place in which the mutual exchange of ideas among individuals concerned about the vitality of their city has often resulted in actions which—whether tangibly or intangibly—have affected that city.

There are those—among them some senior members of the club—who express disagreement with that assessment, minimizing the ability of a given Forum speaker to change a listener's mind on a subject or downplaying the effect that discussions within the club might have on the world outside its walls. There is, it would seem, validity in both points of view: Some local issues, for example, have been argued at the club for decades without resolution; at the same time, former Cleveland mayor Carl B. Stokes credits his Forum appearances with helping to establish the legitimacy of his candidacy when he was starting on the road to becoming the first black mayor of a major American city.

Ultimately, the true value of the City Club of Cleveland may best be discerned from the first line of the club's creed, which begins, "I hail and harbor and hear men of every belief...." The City Club has indeed welcomed men and women of every belief, and, most importantly, it has provided them with a place to be heard when others may not have been so open or secure. Whether or not an individual Forum speaker's words ever reached beyond the confines of the club itself, whether or not a particular idea or theory or argument advanced there had an impact or effect on the world at large, could certainly be debated. But the very fact that the City Club has for 75 years maintained its free and open Forum—guaranteeing the *opportunity* to be heard—means that its principal function continues to be fulfilled.

Explanatory Note

America's Soapbox is divided into eight chapters, each of which is further divided by year. Each year begins with a short introduction that provides a measure of historical context for the information to follow. Introductions are presented in boldface type.

Following each year's introduction, individual items are presented chronologically. All items begin with a month and day, also in boldface type. Material quoted directly from a Forum speaker's remarks, as well as newspaper or magazine accounts of Forum addresses that may or may not include quotations, are presented in Roman type. Newspaper or magazine items that have some bearing on the City Club, as well as interviews with past or present City Club members and Forum speakers, are presented in italic type. Timeline information delineating specific historical events appears in boldface italic.

All individual items end with source identifications. Forum speakers who appear more than once are identified fully the first time they appear and not thereafter.

Cleveland newspapers cited as sources are denominated as follows: *Citizen, Edition, Leader, News, Plain Dealer, Press* and *Times*. All other newspapers cited include their city of origin in the citation.

Archaic spellings of certain words (e.g., "aeroplane") from source materials have, for the sake of consistency, been changed to reflect currently accepted form.

1912-1918

Coming Into the World

The progressive ideals of Tom L. Johnson (center) lived on in City Club co-founder Newton D. Baker (right) and club activist Peter Witt.

1912

The population of the United States approaches 100 million with the admission of New Mexico and Arizona as the 47th and 48th states. More and more people have left the farm to take up new lives in the city, and major urban centers are choked with slums, poverty, disease and racial and ethnic intolerance. Nationwide, influenza, pneumonia and tuberculosis are by far the leading causes of death.

Former President Theodore Roosevelt announces his intention to seek the Republican nomination for President by coining the phrase, "My hat is in the ring." Rebuffed by the Republicans, who nominate incumbent President William Howard Taft, Roosevelt forms the Progressive Party and is chosen its standard-bearer. Both men will be defeated in November by Democrat Woodrow Wilson. It will be another year before a federal income tax is instituted and before senators are elected by popular vote, rather than by their state legislatures. It will be another eight years before women can vote.

A continuing flood of European immigrants seeking work in America's manufacturing industries has further accelerated the growth of many cities. In Cleveland, the population exceeds half a million, making it the sixth-largest city in the country. But with rapid growth come problems never before encountered, and Clevelanders elect a commission to frame a new city charter to address those questions. One place where the issues are debated is a new organization of concerned citizens, social reformers, politicians and civic gadflys—the City Club.

OCTOBER 30

FORM FORUM CLUB
FOR PUBLIC DEBATE
Cleveland Men to Discuss Questions
From Nonpartisan Standpoints
The City Club of Cleveland [has come] into active existence....
More than 100 men signed as members of the new organization, and afterward went into session in the first stockholders' meeting....

Article 2 of [the] constitution explains the purpose of the club and its future method of procedure: "The objects of the organization...shall be the investigation, discussion and improvement of civic conditions and affairs in Cleveland; the maintenance of club rooms, library and other facilities of a social club for the use of men desiring to cooperate in the furtherance of these objects, and the arrangement of frequent meetings at which speakers may be heard and questions of civic interest may be discussed; provided, however, that the organization, as such, shall not endorse nor oppose any individual or measure."
—Plain Dealer

Brand Whitlock

NOVEMBER 19 *Discussion of the proper field of work for the City Club of Cleveland, at a dinner in the Chamber of Commerce club rooms..., brought suggestions that selection of the new charter which Cleveland may devise and adopt next year was by far the most important topic.... The feeling was expressed that the field for the club's discussion was as broad as municipal activity itself, and that the obtaining of a truly representative membership was as essential to the club's success as any other factor....*
—Plain Dealer

DECEMBER 21 Municipal ownership of utilities [in Glasgow, Scotland] is such an old and well-established thing that there is no longer discussion of it. The city owns tramways, lighting, gas, abattoirs, schools and museums. Here we are too generous. We give away everything....
—Brand Whitlock, *reform mayor of Toledo, Ohio, recently returned from a study trip of European municipal governments, speaking at the first City Club Forum*

1913

Responding to the nation's growing fear of the continuing tide of immigration, Congress attempts to restrict the influx of the foreign-born by enacting a literacy test for immigrants, but the bill is vetoed by the President. In Mexico, civil war and sporadic border incidents are setting the stage for eventual American armed intervention. Domestic labor unrest is rife, and the activities of unions—especially the Industrial Workers of the World, or "Wobblies"—only aggravate the widespread distrust of "radicals" and "foreigners" that will bear bitter fruit by decade's end.

Cleveland's new charter, municipal ownership of city utilities (a subject that will be debated throughout the century) and the need for child-labor laws are discussed at the City Club, which moves into its first permanent home: third-floor rooms above Weber's German restaurant, at 244 Superior Avenue.

JANUARY 25 **Hopkins:** Three-cent fare on [streetcar] lines is what has prevented the [proposed] subway from being in operation now. If a subway is not built in Cleveland you will not have three-cent fare for even five years longer.
Witt: Three-cent fare is here to stay. It is a paying proposition, and the street railway company has surplus instead of deficits. ...The trouble with Cleveland people is that they are overeducated in the street railway business. They never will be satisfied.
—Debate between William R. Hopkins, president of the Cleveland Underground Rapid Transit Company, and Peter Witt, Cleveland street railway commissioner

FEBRUARY 15 Ohio is in the van. Your state has taken the lead in all legislation affecting the child.... Heretofore, the

1913

working child has been the last to receive attention. You now recognize that he or she needs the attention of the state as [much] as the orphaned and the delinquent. ...[And] the very day Ohio writes 15 years as the [minimum] age limit for [the employment of] boys and 16 years as the age limit for girls, that very day Ohio fixes a new standard and we will all go out and work for that.
    —Owen R. Lovejoy, *secretary of the National Child Labor Committee, speaking shortly before the Ohio legislature passes the state's new child-labor law*

MARCH 15   The only argument left against public ownership [of municipal utilities] is in the fear that [the potential for] graft makes it best to leave operation of utilities to private enterprise. The answer to this is that no one says we should turn the police force over to operation by a detective agency or the fire department to the insurance companies, or abandon public education.
    —Delos F. Wilcox, *chief of New York City's Bureau of Franchises and a nationally respected expert on municipal utilities*

APRIL 5   In the matter of city planning, New York with all its greatness and wealth...[is] taking a lesson from [Cleveland's Group Plan to erect public buildings around a series of open malls].... You have, in fact, set many such examples.... Only two weeks ago I sent one of our engineers here to study your plant for the incineration of refuse. He comes back to me with the word that we cannot do better than to accept your plant as the model for what we propose to do upon a larger scale....
    —George McAneny, *borough president, Manhattan*

OCTOBER 10   ***The Panama Canal opens to ocean-to-ocean ship traffic.***

1914

Women across the country are marching to demand the right to vote, while an "army" of thousands of unemployed men, led by Jacob Coxey of Massillon, Ohio, marches on Washington to demand a federal jobs program. Mexico is an on-again, off-again hot spot, but a much larger altercation grabs the nation's attention in August. After months of saber rattling, the German invasion of Belgium sparks war throughout Europe, but President Wilson's proclamation of neutrality is a reassuring note for most Americans, who want nothing to do with Old World fights. The City Club hears comparatively few local issues discussed, as national and international questions come to the fore.

FEBRUARY 7   People in all sections of the country are trying to solve the perplexing problem of what to do with the city boy.... Present statistics show that the city boy spends an average of five hours a day on the streets or alleys. In Gary [Indiana] we

Theodore Roosevelt

have overcome this situation in considering proper facilities for play and study in their right proportion, so the boy—instead of trying to avoid going to school—expresses disappointment when the schools are closed.

We teach boys arithmetic by letting them work out batting averages on the World Series baseball games.... We take newspaper reports of baseball games and compare the English of the language used by the writers. With a map in front of them, the boys followed the [1913-1914 world exhibition] tour of the Giants and the Sox. What better geography lesson could you have?

—**William A. Wirt,** *superintendent of schools in Gary, Indiana, and a nationally known innovator in public education*

FEBRUARY 18   The limitation of foreign immigration into this country to 5 percent annually of those already naturalized is the solution of the so-called "yellow peril" problem, according to Reverend Sidney L. Gulick [former Congregationalist missionary in Japan and lecturer at Kyoto's Imperial University]....

"Such limitation would allow a normal immigration from northern Europe, cut down the undesirable influx from southern Europe, and admit but a comparatively small number from Asia."

—Leader

APRIL 4   There is too much moral sense in America to listen to the argument that [the Panama Canal] is *our* canal. It is not our canal. We hold it in a trust as sacred as any trust ever created, and we are trustees to use it in such a way that all nations shall be treated with entire equality.

—**John H. Clarke,** *Cleveland attorney (who will be named a justice of the U.S. Supreme Court two years later), supporting President Wilson's demand for complete neutrality in America's stewardship of the canal*

JUNE 28   Austrian Archduke Franz Ferdinand is assassinated in Sarajevo; in little more than a month, all of Europe is at war.

SEPTEMBER 28   The only way to give woman a square deal is to let her go through the educational courts of full citizenship. I hope Ohio will take the step [of enfranchising women] this year that has been taken by Illinois.... A number of my conservative friends tell me that if women vote it will break up home life. Home life is going on very well in Illinois, thank you.

You know why I am in [Ohio]. I have come here to appeal with all my heart and strength for [Progressive Party candidate for governor James R.] Garfield and [Progressive candidate for U.S. Senate Arthur L.] Garford.... If you elect Mr. Garfield and a Progressive legislature you know just what you will get. If you don't, nobody knows what you will get, except that it won't be good.

—**Theodore Roosevelt,** *former President of the United*

1914

States and now nominal leader of the national Progressive ("Bull Moose") Party

"I'm glad to see you looking so well," [City Club member] John D. Fackler, deputy state tax commissioner, remarked to [Roosevelt after his speech].

"I feel just as fine as I look," responded Roosevelt with a broad smile. "You couldn't kill me with a club."

—Plain Dealer

OCTOBER 10   Allen: There are more than 200,000 women taxpayers in Ohio and 400,000 women wage earners.... We are being taxed without representation and that is tyranny. We are hindered in obtaining laws that protect us, and without the ballot have no way in which to force recognition.

Price: The majority of the women do not want the vote.... The suffragists are placing all their emphasis on political rights. They do not figure that women can do more good for the race by not becoming political factors and therefore divided against themselves.

You get the right kind of public opinion from people who are not enfranchised....

—*Debate between Florence E. Allen, Cleveland attorney and executive-board member of the Ohio Woman Suffrage Association (who in 1923 will become the first woman justice of a state supreme court and, 11 years later, the first woman appointed to a U.S. Court of Appeals), and Lucy Price, representative of the Association Opposed to Woman Suffrage*

1915

To some Clevelanders the European conflict—while capturing headlines daily—still seems far removed from the more immediate problems of municipal government. The City Club, for example, hears one of its own advocate the city manager plan and a council elected by proportional representation, a rarely used method of voting in which candidates in at-large elections earn preference points as the first, second or third choice of voters. But club members also want to learn more about Germany's position in the war, and they invite a former German colonial minister to speak. His appearance in May will prove to be a test of the club's policy of providing a free and open forum of ideas, no matter how controversial or unpopular the subject. And as Germany continues to spread terror on the high seas, club members are reminded of an old but very appropriate maxim.

JANUARY 9   If I had furnished such reeking, chlorinated stuff as the city has furnished for drinking water during the last eight years, I would have been hanged.

—**Samuel Scovil,** *president of the Cleveland Electric Illuminating Company, using the city-owned water system as an argument against municipal ownership of utilities*

Theodore E. Burton

JANUARY 30 Dr. Karl H. Kumm, British explorer...who has spent more than 20 years in Africa, described it as richer in natural resources than the other...continents combined and inhabited by a "child race," whose development along the wrong lines would lead to the greatest conflagration the world has ever seen.

Dr. Kumm urged the support of Christian missions in Africa, declaring Mohammedanism was spreading rapidly, developing a fanaticism boding ill for the Christian races. Conversion to Christianity and education [are] the only successful weapons to combat the spread of this cult among the millions of ignorant and savage peoples of Africa....

—Leader

FEBRUARY 27 You have in Cleveland the most advanced conception of a modern [public] hospital of any city in the world.... [But] I have never seen a hospital where both [public and private] patients are taken, in [which] the private patient does not get a little the better of it.

—Dr. John A. Hornsby, *nationally recognized health-care expert and superintendent of the University of Virginia Hospital, urging that paying patients no longer be admitted to Cleveland's public City Hospital*

MARCH 13 I had hoped to spend the year in travel [abroad], but...suppose a boat were to be sunk with a loss of life, and thousands would rise up and demand war. In such a time as that I would not want to be away from the United States.

—Theodore E. Burton, *Republican senator from Ohio, recently retired from Congress where he had served for 22 years*

APRIL 23

NOTICE!
Travelers intending to embark on the Atlantic voyage are reminded that a state of war exists between Germany and her allies and Great Britain and her allies...and that travelers sailing in the war zone on ships of Great Britain or her allies do so at their own risk.

IMPERIAL GERMAN EMBASSY
Washington, D.C.
—*Advertisement run in dozens of U.S. newspapers, including Cleveland's*

MAY 2

OCEAN STEAMER NEWS
Sailed

Steamer	Port
NIPPON MARU	*MANILA*
SAXONIA	*LIVERPOOL*
LUSITANIA	*NEW YORK*

—Plain Dealer *shipping news*

1915

MAY 3   Dr. Bernhard Dernburg, former German minister of the colonies and at present one of Germany's leading representatives in the United States on the war situation, will address the members of the City Club at luncheon Saturday, May 8.... Dr. Dernburg...has been active in the movement to protect the German interests in...this country...[and] has recently been publicly criticizing the position of the United States on its attitude toward neutrality.
    —Plain Dealer

MAY 7   A German submarine torpedoes the British liner** Lusitania **off the coast of Ireland. Of the nearly 1,200 lost more than 100 are Americans, which results in a nationwide outcry for action against Germany.

MAY 8   Before an audience representing all Cleveland's municipal, business and professional interests, Dr. Bernhard Dernburg pleaded Germany's case in an address on "Conditions of Permanent Peace from the German Viewpoint".... It was a difficult position the speaker occupied, made even more so by the freshness of the *Lusitania* disaster, but he carried his audience of 500 or more, being stopped frequently by applause....

"...It cannot be proved and is not true Germany has sought world power or world dominion. She is the only nation on earth that has had a peace record of 44 years. ...What we demand for ourselves as well as every other nation on earth is a free sea. It exists in law and it must exist in fact.... Germany wants an open door and rights and duties in foreign ports equal to those of other nations.

"We can never think of any terms of peace that cannot be accepted and lived under for a very long time...."
    —Plain Dealer

NOVEMBER 13   I don't believe the people ought to elect mayors. We should have a council chosen by the proportional representation plan, and council should appoint the mayor.
    —Augustus R. Hatton, *professor of political science at Cleveland's Western Reserve University and member of the city's charter-writing commission*

DECEMBER 4   We must have men prepared for war. Let us approach that fact fearlessly. Let us have compulsory military training. Let us, incidentally, overcome one great weakness in the American character and teach how to obey authority. I am for moral sense in the nation—but keep your powder dry.
    —Charles H. Grasty, *Associated Press war correspondent, recently returned from nearly a year in Europe*

1916

Despite the *Lusitania* outrage, isolationist America reelects President Wilson on his avowed promise to keep America neutral. In March, General John J.

Pershing leads American troops into Mexico to chase Pancho Villa and his guerillas. Margaret Sanger opens the country's first birth-control clinic in Brooklyn, New York, five more states vote themselves "dry" (to bring the total to 24) and, coincidental to the looming specter of nationwide prohibition, General John T. Thompson invents the Thompson submachine gun.

Consistent with its expanding size and growing stature in the community, the City Club takes up residence in a new, more permanent home: spacious rooms on the third floor of the Hollenden Hotel. There the bitter rivalry between Cleveland's private and public electrical-power suppliers erupts into a shouting match between partisans. The club also hears the first expression of what will prove to be a recurring internal argument—the "imbalance" between the number of liberal and conservative thinkers invited to speak.

MARCH 4 *For more than 14 years I have held office in this old city hall.... As I am about to take my place again in the ranks of the legal profession, in an endeavor to earn an honest living, I can't help but express my love for all of you whom I have met in the years of my sojourn in this city. I should like to get better acquainted with you—especially those of you who may have need of the services of a lawyer. The love of David for Jonathan, Damon for Pythias or Roosevelt for office is as sounding brass and tinkling cymbals compared with my love for everyone of you with litigating possibilities.*

—Carl D. Friebolin, Cleveland attorney and charter member of the City Club, impersonating former Cleveland Mayor Newton D. Baker during a club "Silly Session" (an annual event that will evolve over the next four years into a fully staged theatrical satire called the Anvil Revue)

MARCH 7 *Newton D. Baker is nominated for the post of secretary of war by President Wilson.*

APRIL 24 *Irish nationalists lead the Easter Uprising against British rule; within days most of the rebels are arrested and many are eventually executed for treason.*

JUNE 29 Speedy cavalry was the only suitable sort of force to send after a fleeing bandit..., and when the United States began to send slow-moving infantry, ponderous artillery, airplanes and machine guns, grave suspicion was aroused that the pursuit of the bandit was not the only object of the invaders.

The Mexican people, who have not the educational facilities nor the newspapers which the people of the United States possess, can judge Americans only by what they see of them, and they see nothing but...troops.

—Luis Bossero, *representative of the Mexican Bureau of Information, explaining his country's objection to the*

1916

"invasion" of American troops seeking to capture bandit Pancho Villa

OCTOBER 10 It has taken more courage to keep this country out of war 10,000-fold than it would to put it into a base and ignoble war.... Any man who would plunge the country into unnecessary war would be the grossest traitor that ever occupied the presidential chair.
　　—**William G. McAdoo,** *secretary of the treasury, praising his boss (and father-in-law), President Wilson*

OCTOBER 13 *Rumblings of internal trouble in the City Club, with Republican members aroused at the preponderance lately of Democratic speakers and the club's seeming swing toward the Wilson side, could be heard plainly....*
　　Ralph A. Hayes, club secretary, admitted Friday that the club's speakers lately have been limited to Democrats or pro-Wilsonites, but insisted it is not the club's fault. "We have tried every means possible to obtain good Republican speakers," declared Hayes.
　　—News

OCTOBER 14 *The City Club...announced the engagement of three Republican speakers....*
　　—Leader

NOVEMBER 4 Judge [Pierre A.] White, of the municipal court, shook his finger in the face of Councilman [Harry C.] Gahn after the latter had intimated the adoption of unfair business methods by the Cleveland Electric Illuminating Company to gain its ends in the past. The two were debating the proposed $1.75 million bond issue for extension of [Cleveland's] municipal lighting [system].
　　"I say it right to your face, that you should either follow up such a charge by prosecution or should refuse to give tongue to such a scandal," declared Judge White, who was speaking against the bond issue.
　　"The municipal light plant has succeeded despite attacks by the Illuminating Company," councilman Gahn asserted. "...It has lowered rates throughout the city [and] is paying for itself...."
　　—Leader

Ralph A. Hayes

NOVEMBER 15 There is no better tribute to American autohypnosis than that process by which an utterly godforsaken spot on the plains of Kansas deludes itself into the belief that it is the soul and center of the earth. Take any spot out there—call it Aridia, Kansas, if you please—and you will find a commercial club, shouting slogans, bedecked with buttons and publishing maps showing the rest of the country arranged in concentric circles around Aridia....
　　—**George Edgar Vincent,** *president, University of Minnesota*

NOVEMBER 18   William Judson Kibby, founder of the Kibby Institute of Character Analysis and Vocational Guidance, described from charts the generalizations which, he declared, thousands of analyses had taught him regarding the reading of character through physiological and psychological traits.... The high-arched nose, he stated, indicated aggressiveness; the perpendicular forehead, reflectiveness; the receding forehead, rapid but not sustained thought....
   —Plain Dealer

1917

The war in Europe seems permanently stalemated, but by spring circumstances have conspired to bring America into the conflict. With the declaration of war, exclamations of patriotic fervor and virulent anti-German tirades become commonplace, even at the "unbiased" City Club, which will invite no anti-war speakers for the duration of the conflict. And as Cleveland's industries gear up for war production, a new wave of immigrants—Southern blacks—pours in to work in the city's humming mills and factories. By decade's end, Cleveland's black population will increase by some 300 percent, to nearly 35,000.

The city-manager plan is still a hot topic in Cleveland, as is the growth of aviation, the possibility of national prohibition, women's suffrage and the Russian revolution. Meanwhile, Sigmund Freud publishes his *Introduction to Psychoanalysis*, and bobbed hair becomes a political, as well as a fashion, statement.

MARCH 7   I am convinced that with a proper city manager the plan approaches the ideal of city government. For it places the responsibility on the shoulders of one man.

Boards are irresponsible. As we say in the army, they are "long, narrow and wooden." My idea of first principles of organization of any group of men...is one in which one man in charge is vested with full power and responsibility.
   —George W. Goethals, *U.S. Army major general, builder of the Panama Canal and current consulting engineer of New York City*

MARCH 11   *Revolutionaries overthrow the Russian government.*

MARCH 24   A fleet of airplanes could destroy a city like Cleveland in a single night. Cleveland should have a fleet of hundreds of airplanes. Each craft should have powerful guns mounted on it....

...The day of the skeptic who says the conquest of the air is a dream has passed. We shall come to realize finally that a country's military power will be measured by her air strength as it is now judged by the number of battleships and the size of her army.
   —Robert E. Peary, *U.S. Navy rear admiral, first man*

1917

to reach the North Pole (in 1909) and current chairman of the National Aerial Coast Patrol Commission

APRIL 6   Citing continuing unrestricted submarine warfare against American shipping, the United States declares war on Germany. Within months Congress enacts legislation granting the federal government drastic powers in dealing with incidents of espionage. subversion and even domestic opposition to the war.

APRIL 28   As governor of this great state, I voice here and now what I sense to be the overwhelming feeling of Ohio, that we are for conscription.... We must have no patience with the pacifists. We can't make war with powder puffs. ...The street-corner bums who have been consuming and not producing are going to disappear from Ohio like a June frost. Those who will not work are going to be taken to farm detention camps.

I give you this solemn assurance, that if treason raises its head in Ohio, with all the power of the government and all the wrath of a great citizenship, I'll stamp it out as I would a snake.

—James M. Cox, *Democratic governor of Ohio, issuing a war-preparedness message to a cheering City Club crowd*

MAY 12   Thousands of court cases to test the rights of conscientious objectors to war in connection with the conscription law to be passed by Congress were predicted...by Roger N. Baldwin [of] St. Louis, associate secretary of the American Union Against Militarism [precursor of the American Civil Liberties Union] and a conscientious objector himself on "ethical grounds."

Mr. Baldwin pleaded that the constitutional rights of conscientious objectors be kept inviolate even during the stress and tension of war.... The army [conscription] bill now before Congress... provides exemptions for members of well-recognized religious sects [but] does not take into account individual objectors—those who object on broadly humanitarian and ethical grounds, radical Socialists and Industrial Workers of the World [union] members. Instead of jailing such persons for refusing to bear arms, it would be far better to have them do farm work, Mr. Baldwin declared....

—Plain Dealer

James M. Cox

JULY 2   War has become a world habit and the sooner we acquire that habit the better it will be for ourselves and our allies....

Strip away the glamour and war is a business. America's middle name is business. We are the masters of standardization. The moment destruction is standardized, the allies will have the great advantage.

—Isaac F. Marcosson, *special writer,* Saturday Evening Post

AUGUST 22 It will be the duty of American women to marry disabled soldiers when they return from [Europe]. In the full strength of American manhood they will want to marry and surely if anyone deserves the love and comfort that only wife and children can give it is these heroes of ours. They will be fit for marrying, with the exception of a small proportion, and the women of the country ought to marry them, even if it be a sacrifice.

—**Julian W. Mack,** *Chicago juvenile court judge and author of the pending Soldiers' and Sailors' Dependency Act, which would provide life insurance for men taken into the military under selective service*

SEPTEMBER 24 An airplane is the most perfectly controllable machine in existence. The higher one goes, the safer. If the craft should upset at a high altitude, the driver has time to right it before the machine crashes to earth. It is not half as dangerous to drive an airplane over Cleveland as it is to drive an automobile through the streets.

—**Charles F. Kettering,** *founder of Ohio's Dayton Engineering Laboratories Company (Delco), inventor and member of the board of the General Motors Corporation (which purchased Delco in 1916) who will become co-founder in 1945 of New York's Sloan-Kettering Institute for Cancer Research*

OCTOBER 6 The action of some of our authorities in forbidding free discussion of our war aims by peaceably assembled citizens, in suppressing newspapers and magazines for the expression of opinions which are unpopular...have made it difficult for men like myself to engage in war work with undivided aim and untroubled spirit.

...It were better that we incurred some risk of giving consolation to the enemy by our freedom of criticism than that we fastened upon our own nation the repressive spirit and institutions of the autocracy we seek to crush....

—**John Spargo,** *former Socialist leader who left the party over its stand against American participation in the war*

OCTOBER 13 Cooperation in a movement to make intelligent citizens will solve the Negro problem confronting Cleveland [according to L. Hollingsworth Wood, chairman of the National League on Urban Conditions Among Negroes].... A trained Negro social worker should be selected to head all activities among colored folks. There must be a central point to which all Negroes may be referred for information about amusements, positions, churches, recreation and houses to rent....

"Playground facilities must be provided," [said Wood]. "...Public baths must be erected in the district where colored folks congregate; colored policemen and policewomen are an advantage.... And above all, make these new residents feel that they are not here purely as a war measure, but that Cleveland has something in store for them after the war."

—Plain Dealer

1917

OCTOBER 17   *The Boston City Club today discharged 20 employees, mostly waiters, because they were enemy aliens. ...Someone discovered that there were Germans employed in the house. Then came a roll call. Waiters, firemen and bellboys were required to tell their birth places and the discharges followed.*
—Leader

OCTOBER 26   **The Bolsheviks overthrow Russia's provisional revolutionary government and Vladimir Ilyich Lenin is appointed premier.**

NOVEMBER 2   **Perkins:** Men of Ohio wanted women to vote—otherwise the [state] legislature would not have passed the bill [granting women's suffrage in presidential and municipal elections, pending approval in a statewide referendum]. We must not forget the meaning of democracy. If it is worth dying for in France, it is worth voting for in Ohio.

     Bronson: A suffrage speaker in New York said the anti-suffragists must accept one of two horns of a dilemma—either we don't believe in democracy or we do not believe men and women are equal. But we believe in both. It is the suffragists who do not believe in democracy. If they did, they would be turning heaven and earth to prevent the question [from being] voted on by the people.

     —Debate between Mrs. Roger Perkins, chairwoman of the Cleveland Suffrage Party, and Minnie Bronson, general secretary of the National Association Opposed to Woman's Suffrage, over the upcoming referendum on the suffrage bill (which will be defeated)

DECEMBER 29   Postmaster General [Albert] Burleson is an autocrat who is sacrificing efficiency, service and consideration for the workers to make the department show a profit. He is the Kaiser at Washington; a quarter million postal employees sneeze when Burleson takes snuff.

     Postal employees receive no pensions and they do not get sick leave.... Unskilled laborers are getting more than carriers. I worked in a rolling mill before I got to wanting a white-shirt job. Then I went into the postal department. So hard have the carriers been driven to make the department show a surplus that I often thought I'd like to go back to the rolling mill for a rest.

     —Edward J. Gainor, *president, National Letter Carriers' Association*

1918

Gruesome tales of German atrocities feed the wartime hysteria that grips the nation, yet astute businessmen are realizing that war and its aftermath will prove to be highly profitable. Postmaster General Burleson orders the burning of copies of the *Little Review* containing installments of James Joyce's *Ulysses*, and early in the fall, the first cases of Spanish

Jane Addams

influenza presage an epidemic that will kill millions.

At the polls in November, Ohio voters decide to take the state dry. Six days later, at the 11th hour of the 11th day of the 11th month, the Great War comes to an end. Europe is a depleted, smoking ruin, but two decades of immigration have brought America's population from 76 million in 1900 to 103.5 million. The nation, it seems, is poised for prosperity.

JANUARY 19   I have been among cannibals and headhunters, but I must state that I have never seen nor heard of anything as concerns the treatment of captives that compares with the damnable and diabolical manner in which the Germans treat their prisoners, including women and children. One young Belgian's nose and ears were cut off and his tongue torn out for trying to save a young girl from German soldiers. On another occasion, [the] eyes of a group of Belgians were burned out for the same reason.

...One German soldier we captured was seen to drop a small package. It consisted of two baby hands, wrapped in a handkerchief. He was saving them as a souvenir. I am not going into details as to what we did to him.

—Ivor Thord-Gray, *commander of the Northumberland Fusileers, British Expeditionary Force*

FEBRUARY 3   Will H. Hays is elected chairman of the Republican National Committee.

MARCH 2   The necessity for feeding our allies is laying the foundation for a new type of internationalism, which will continue after the war ends. Commercial control of importing and exporting food may never reappear. ...[The new international system] would free the seas to all countries as far as the movement of food is concerned.

—Jane Addams, *social reformer and founder in 1889 of Chicago's Hull House neighborhood settlement house*

MARCH 9   The Germans are educated [in] the doctrines that power in itself is the supreme thing in the universe; that God is a God of power and not of justice, truth and mercy; that the Germans are God's chosen people, a superior race without moral obligations to act justly toward persons of other races.... It is [an] American fallacy to suppose that Germany is prostrate, will not be able to recover and will cease to be a menace to mankind.

—John Grier Hibben, *president, Princeton University*

APRIL 19   A new time is coming with a new concept of social and industrial justice, freedom, democracy and brotherhood. And like all great blessings of humanity, it's coming in a baptism of blood.

—Samuel Gompers, *president, American Federation of Labor*

1918

JUNE 1   If I read the future aright, the financial center of the world will be shifted from London to New York. ...Wall Street is [already] the very center of the financial and business interests of the country. There is in it the highest type of honesty as well as the lowest type of scalawag. [But] the dishonest broker found there is fired out quickly.

> **—Theodore E. Burton,** *former senator from Ohio now president of the Merchants National Bank of New York*

Thomas G. Masaryk

JUNE 15   The Czecho-Slovaks have been betrayed and oppressed by the Hapsburg rulers of Austria-Hungary. That is why, at the outbreak of the present war, I declared myself on the side of the Allies. Holding that position, I could not remain in Bohemia.

...Independence for Bohemia, Poland and other Slavic nations will form a natural barrier against pan-German plots to occupy eastern Europe. ...If Austria can keep the Slavic nations under her rule, Germany will have a clear road to the east, through her control of Austria. And if Germany can get her hands on the east, it will only be a question of time until she is trying again to conquer England, France and America.

> **—Thomas G. Masaryk,** *exiled provisional president of Bohemia, known as the "father of Bohemian independence"*

JUNE 30   *Eugene V. Debs, four-time Socialist Party candidate for President, is charged with violating the wartime espionage and sedition laws for an anti-government speech at the Socialist state convention in Canton, Ohio. In September he is convicted and sentenced to 10 years in the federal penitentiary in Atlanta.*

NOVEMBER 11   *The armistice ending the World War is signed. Three days later Thomas G. Masaryk is confirmed as president of the new Czechoslovak republic.*

1919-1929

Whose

Side

Are

You On?

Eugene V. Debs, imprisoned for speaking out against American involvement in the war, sparked the club's fieriest debate.

1919

In Versailles to help draft a treaty of peace, President Wilson urges creation of the League of Nations, but American participation is opposed at home by those who would avoid "foreign entanglements." Steelworkers and coal miners strike for higher wages, and the time has finally come for ratification of a national prohibition amendment—the latter thanks in no small part to the efforts of one of the City Club's guests this year, one of a number of distinguished international figures who address the club.

Bred by fear engendered by the Bolshevik revolution and widespread distrust of labor unions, foreign-born nationals and Socialists, the great Red Scare seriously threatens the freedoms of speech and assembly. Recognizing the danger, the City Club holds a number of "extension" forums around Cleveland, an attempt to include the otherwise neglected immigrant population in the mainstream processes of democracy and to open to wider discussion some of the important questions of the day.

JANUARY 16　　The 18th Amendment, prohibiting the manufacture and sale of intoxicating liquors, is ratified. Actual enforcement of Prohibition under the Volstead Act begins the following year.

MARCH 28　Bolshevism is the most fundamental menace of the time. But it will have no power in America unless by restricting the freedom of speech and the freedom of the press we create bitterness that will not be satisfied with less than the overthrow of our democratic institutions.

　—Raymond Robins, *head of the American Red Cross mission in Russia, social economist and chairman of the 1912 Progressive Party national convention*

APRIL 5　The Bolsheviki never will engulf all of Russia....
　—Count Ilya Tolstoy, *son of Russian novelist Leo Tolstoy*

APRIL 12　During the life of the 65th Congress [March 4, 1917 to March 4, 1919], we appropriated $57 billion, a sum more than twice as great as the total expenditures of our government in peace and war from the first inauguration of George Washington up to and including the second inauguration of Woodrow Wilson. Investigation of expenditures of the war will be one of the big problems of the next Congress. The American people are entitled to know where their money went.

　—Nicholas Longworth, *Republican congressman from Cincinnati (and husband of Theodore Roosevelt's daughter Alice)*

MAY 1　　May Day riots break out in most major American cities. In Cleveland, soldiers and policemen

attack paraders carrying red flags, leaving one dead, dozens injured and the local Socialist Party headquarters demolished.

MAY 8   *The City Club will be asked to hold double the number of "open meetings" planned for various sections of the city to debate the question "Is America Sound?"*

Carl D. Friebolin, former club president, said he will ask for the extra meetings to follow up the first "extension forum" held Tuesday night at East Tech [High School].

Men and women were present. Soldiers were sprinkled through the crowd. Some workers were there with left-wing Socialist manifestos in their hands. Friebolin, opening the forum, invited "heckling to get at the truth...." Questions rooted in Bolshevism, Socialism, single tax, religious freedom, the theory of direct action and obstructionism were fired at the speakers....
—Press

MAY 17   [Cuyahoga County Democratic State Senator Howell] Wright called attention to a provision of the [pending Ohio prohibition act] under which dwellers in apartments over stores would not be permitted to have private stocks of liquor as dwellers in other apartments and those occupying detached houses may have.

"People who live in mansions may possess, furnish or give away liquor to friends, while those who live in tenements cannot. It's fine for Euclid Avenue, but hard on the Haymarket."
—Press

MAY 19   Rise 7 a.m. Stand in middle of room, raise arms slowly overhead, take deep breath and say, "Damn the government," lowering arms in attitude of despair. Ten times.

Extend body flat downward on floor, cover eyes with hands, kick heels, think of the railroads and weep. Till dry.

Kneel, wring hands, meditate upon the labor question and groan 150 times.

Assume sitting position, hands on hips, sway gently to and fro and concentrate on [Postmaster General] Burleson until a generous frothing at the mouth sets in. Till exhausted.

Collapse on floor. Grovel vigorously, think of the income tax and gnash teeth as in anger. Ad lib.

Note—Observe this simple regimen every morning before breakfast and you will reach the office with most of the cares and troubles of the day already out of your system.
   —Theodore H. Price, *editor and publisher of the weekly New York financial newspaper* Commerce and Finance, *prescribing morning exercises for the tired businessman*

JUNE 8   One fourth of the [American Expeditionary Force] was ...unable to read and write.... Weaknesses of local school systems have made America a nation of sixth-graders. [The] present deplorable conditions demand federal supervision to keep the

1919

nation from sinking to a lower level of illiteracy.
  —Frank E. Spaulding, *superintendent of Cleveland Public Schools and member of the A.E.F.'s Educational Corps Commission*

JUNE 28   A peace treaty demanding heavy reparations from Germany is signed at Versailles. France's General Ferdinand Foch declares, "This is not peace, it is an armistice for 20 years."

JULY 4   Jack Dempsey takes the heavyweight boxing crown from Jess Willard at Toledo, Ohio.

SEPTEMBER 30   *Platforms were announced when the candidates [for City Club directorships and] their managers were presented to the members at a dinner. ...Some candidates took matters in their own hands [while] some managers submerged their candidates and insisted on occupying more than the five minutes allowed each pair....*

When the toastmaster called upon [Bankruptcy Court Judge Carl D.] Friebolin as manager of [Press columnist] Jack Raper's campaign, Raper leaped to his feet and shouted, "Judge Friebolin is fired. I heard an hour or two ago that [he] was...entangling me in dangerous alliances...." Raper said that he was...treading in the footsteps of that "eminent American," Jess Willard, who also had appeared without a manager. He was interrupted here by shouts from the audience, who asked him if he knew what had happened to Willard....

H.P. Boynton, campaign manager for Karl Lemmerman, had just finished a solemn speech in behalf of his candidate when he was interrupted by E.A. Pettingill. "I have here Mr. Lemmerman's campaign card," heckled Mr. Pettingill. "It has no union label. I cannot support a candidate who does not use a union label...."

"There's no debate on that subject," declared Boynton, coming to the defense of his candidate. "[But] I'll test your unionism. Is there a union label on your trousers?"

"Yes," declared Pettingill.

"Show us," demanded Boynton....

  *—*Leader *account of City Club board of directors Candidates' Field Day*

Eamon De Valera

OCTOBER 7   [Eamon] De Valera was greeted by a great crowd at University Circle on his arrival in Cleveland.... There was waving of green, white and orange flags, the emblem of the Republic of Ireland. The unrecognized republic which he represents was formed by himself and others elected in Ireland as members of the parliament of the United Kingdom of Great Britain and Ireland. They refused to take their seats in parliament....

"Ireland is a nation and there is no test of nationhood which Ireland doesn't respond to. She has struggled against giving up

William Jennings Bryan

that sovereignty of state which has been under subjection during the last seven and one-half centuries.... We claim the right to govern ourselves whether or not we do so in a worse form than others could govern us.

"The proposition has been advanced to divide Ireland from the parts of Ulster favoring alliance with England. In these parts 40 percent of the people are opposed to Ireland. What are you going to do about this minority? ...If we are going to let a minority veto the act of a majority, democracy ends....

"If Ireland is given independence there will be no religious question. You will find there will be no trouble on that score."

—Plain Dealer

OCTOBER 16   The League of Nations covenant represents the greatest thing that has happened to the world west of the Ganges since the Crucifixion. And the man who is responsible for it, if it becomes a reality, is the President. But if it is not adopted, the blame can be placed on the same man—President Wilson. ...He is killing it, slowly and surely. While he was in France in the peace conference he did wonderful work. But...he is too secretive, too furtive. He doesn't take anyone in his confidence. He does not know how to do team work.

I believe the President is sincere, believe he is honest, and I think he has a great mind. But he has made a hundred blunders.

—William Allen White, *editor of the Emporia (Kansas)* Gazette *and special correspondent at Versailles*

OCTOBER 21   The saloon will sell the virtue of any woman and the valor of any man.

...What I am trying to accomplish in this tour of Ohio in the interest of Prohibition is the conversion of the businessman. At the start of the fight for the abolition of the saloon, the farmer was the hero. It was in the rural districts that Prohibition first gained headway. But we now want the businessman to join in this last fight to make the nation dry.

Enlarging the dry area makes enforcement easier. State prohibition is more easily enforced than local prohibition, and national Prohibition will be easier to enforce than state prohibition.

—William Jennings Bryan, *three-time unsuccessful candidate for President, secretary of state in President Wilson's first term and past president of the National Dry Federation*

Water—the daily need of every living thing. It ascends from the earth, obedient to the summons of the sun, and descends in showers of blessing. It gives of its sparkling beauty to the fragrant flowers; it is the alchemy that transmutes base clay into golden grain; it is the canvas on which the finger of the Infinite traces the radiant bow of promise. It is the drink that cheers and adds no sorrow with it. Jehovah looked upon it at creation's dawn and said: "It is good."

—*Bryan's post-speech toast to his beverage of choice*

1919

NOVEMBER 15 Of 1,000 cases of delinquent girls [I have] investigated, only 19 girls blamed low wages for their downfall.... Czar-like discipline in the homes of immigrants and a lack of discipline in American homes are two causes for girls going wrong. Other reasons are: a desire to see the sights; lack of proper amusement facilities; the gap in families when children become Americanized while parents do not; broken homes; unrestrained taxicabs [dance halls]; dark corners in theaters; and feeblemindedness.

   —**Maude Miner,** *secretary of the New York Probation and Protective Association and chairwoman of the National Probation Association*

DECEMBER 6 The Korean peninsula has been the victim of oppression, plunder, murder and an acute espionage system at the hands of [Japanese] troops. There are now more than 300,000 Japanese [civilians] in Korea, in addition to the 150,000 troops..., and they are as welcome as were the Germans in Belgium.

   ...Japan is a growing menace to the world's peace.

   —**Syngman Rhee,** *recently elected president of the Korean Provisional Government in exile, describing conditions that resulted from Japan's 1910 formal annexation of his country, to which he will not be allowed to return for nearly 30 years*

DECEMBER 13 "America for Americans" sounds well at first, but it is deceptive in the extreme.... "Tribal Americans" lament that we are not of one kind as are other nations. Please God, we always shall be different.

   —**Abba Hillel Silver,** *spiritual leader of The Temple, Cleveland's largest Reform Jewish congregation*

1920

Hundreds of arrests and deportations of "anarchists" fuel the Red Scare, and even the long-dormant Ku Klux Klan begins to grow again in the South. The subject of "Americanizing" immigrants is keenly discussed across the country, and women's suffrage becomes the law of the land, just in time for a national election in which two Ohioans vie for the Presidency. At the City Club, politicians, pundits and polemicists are making news, but throughout the summer and fall many Clevelanders find themselves paying more attention to the sports page than the front page.

JANUARY 1   Attorney General A. Mitchell Palmer orders raids on suspected Reds in 33 cities, including Cleveland. More than 6,000 are arrested and detained without trial, with some 200—among them revolutionary anarchist Emma Goldman—eventually deported.

JANUARY 2 Frank Harris, editor of *Pearson's Magazine,* ridiculed [the excesses of wartime censorship by] Postmaster

General Burleson...and described American patriotism in the recent war as a "dragging to the center, a new herd instinct that trampled all the old individual liberties."

...Harris, who had been in difficulties with the United States Postal Department because of material printed in his magazine during the war, said, "Am I to talk about America and Americans with Burleson [still] in power? I know the man too well. Nowadays, if a man doesn't bow down and say 'Great is Diana of the Ephesians and greater still is Burleson and Company,' there's no hope for him."

His remarks were interrupted...by someone shouting "Hurrah for the American flag!"

"And so say I," Harris retorted quickly. "When I, born in Ireland, foreswore allegiance to the British king and swore allegiance to this country, I took oath to support the Constitution. That's where I stand now; I am fighting for the liberty guaranteed by that Constitution, not for your damned interpretation of it. It is time that we Americans awaken and fight for a return of our constitutional guarantees of free speech."

Former Cleveland Safety Director M.B. Excell then moved that a vote of thanks be tendered Mr. Harris "for saying what we would like to say if we had the ability to say them and were not too cowardly." The audience passed the motion with a loud "aye" and there were no votes in opposition. Mr. Harris termed the response of the club "the first note of that Americanism I knew 45 years ago."

—Plain Dealer

JANUARY 3

NEITHER DEAD, NOR DYING

Some people actually have more liberties than they are willing to admit. Take the matter of free speech, for instance.

The editor of a New York magazine told an audience of Cleveland business and professional men on Saturday that free speech in America is practically dead.... [Yet nearly] every point made in the address was a refutation of its major contention, that free speech is no longer tolerated in America. If it were dead, if free speech were attended with as much peril as the New York man declares it to be, the New York man would not be at large addressing city clubs....

—Plain Dealer *editorial*

JANUARY 4 *Poppycock*

—City Club secretary Francis "Pat" Hayes's handwritten comment on a scrapbook clipping of the above editorial

FEBRUARY 28 Japan is the one great power that does not intend to grab anything. Japanese militarism is misunderstood....
—J.W. Robertson-Scott, *British journalist in Tokyo*

FEBRUARY 28 It is to the shame of America that we have

1920

intelligent people assisting in this "Red" propaganda with the statement that "free speech is endangered." We are not deporting mere aliens—we are deporting enemies of this republic. And despite the Jane Addamses and the other foolish dreamers who are trying to confuse this issue with free speech, we shall continue to send away the red-flag advocates. Thank God, the Chicago state's attorney has succeeded in indicting some of them—not the ragged and poor, but some wealthy—and has asked me to help prosecute them. If we have good luck we shall send a fine bunch of piazza Reds to Joliet penitentiary.

> **—Frank Comerford,** *Chicago public prosecutor assisting the state's attorney in the Chicago "Red" trials of 1919-1920*

MARCH 2   *The ouija board provided for [City Club] members several weeks ago has mysteriously disappeared. Secretary Pat Hayes may buy another one. Says Hayes: "We'll try to have the new board tell where the other board is."*
—Press

APRIL 3   The chief objection to the Japanese [in the United States] is not racial antipathy, but the knowledge that their economic advantages make it hopeless for the white race to compete with them. The Japanese work longer hours for smaller pay than Americans, their women toil in the fields, they concentrate in close communities, they have wonderful business cooperation, and they control the produce trade in many sections. Because of these factors they gradually drive Americans out of every business they enter.

Continuation of Japanese immigration into America under present or any other suggested condition means the inevitable subjugation of this country by economic control and sheer force of numbers. The only remedy is absolute exclusion by law, in the same manner we removed the Chinese peril.

> **—Valentine Stuart McClatchey,** *publisher of the Sacramento* Bee, *who in 1923 will become executive secretary of the California Joint Immigration Committee*

MAY 1   The speed and tension of modern city and factory life are so great that we cannot be sure yet whether the race is capable of withstanding it. [And] the world is today paying for its neglect of the human element in industry. Higher wages and shorter hours alone won't settle the industrial question. There's a new element today. That's the desire on the part of the employee to participate in the management of industry....

> **—Cornelia Stratton Parker,** *nationally known economist and social worker*

MAY 29   **Pate:** Since the war started, telephone traffic has increased in Cleveland until it has become almost unbearable, with an average of 700,000 calls a day.... [With the new] automatic system, service on calls will become virtually instantaneous.

Hiram W. Johnson

Townes: Cleveland is getting a miserably atrocious telephone service.... It now takes an average of 36 seconds to get a call, where the company boasted in 1910 that the average time was...under four seconds. The automatic system that [the company] is now trying to foist on Cleveland will pass the buck to the public and slow up service by forcing the caller to get his own number.

—Debate between Robert G. Pate, assistant to the president of the Cleveland Telephone Company, and Clayton C. Townes, Cleveland city councilman

JUNE 1

*BASEBALL SCORES BY INNINGS
NOW RECEIVED DAILY AT THE CITY CLUB*
All American and National League games are reported by innings on score board in club lounge. Western Union ticker service!

ONLY SERVICE OF KIND IN CITY!
—Announcement sent to all City Club members

JUNE 2   I'm going to the Chicago convention to see that the Republican Party neither skulks nor pussyfoots on the question of the League of Nations. And I shall do all I can to see a plank in opposition to the League of Nations is written into the Republican platform. Every man in this campaign will be forced to take an issue on it—to stand either under the polyglot banner of internationalism or under our own old Stars and Stripes.

—Hiram W. Johnson, *senator from California and candidate for the Republican presidential nomination*

JUNE 12   There seem to be four types of radicals: those who believe in evolution and in peaceful means of attaining their ends; those who may be classified under a "radicalism of despair"; the dogmatic type; and the truly revolutionary type.

Unquestionably the most frequent cause of radicalism is industrial lack of adjustment. A skilled worker comes to America. He finds no market for his trade. He is compelled to take an unskilled job. He no longer respects his work—the joy of creative craftsmanship is gone. He broods over his fall in the social order.

The question arises as to the effect of various efforts to remedy radicalism by direct suppression—such as sedition laws, deportation proceedings, raids and all other manifestations of the use of force. The effect of the wholesale raids of last winter threw into the hearts of these immigrants a cold, blasting...fear. ...Several were actually converted to radicalism by repressive measures. None was won back to a love of America by them.

The way to combat radicalism is not through the instrumentalities of repression. Repression is the friend of only the agitator.

—Raymond Moley, *director of The Cleveland Foundation (first community foundation in the country), presenting the results of the foundation's survey of the attitudes of 400 foreign-born Clevelanders*

1920

JULY 3   *The northwest corner of Public Square will come into its own once more when the City Club opens its [second year of public] forum meetings there today noon. The corner, long the meeting place for soapbox orators, has heard few speeches since the war began....*
—Plain Dealer

AUGUST 26   **Ratification of the 19th Amendment gives women the vote.**

OCTOBER 12   **Players' share of the receipts of the 1920 World Series, in which the Cleveland Indians defeated the Brooklyn Superbas five games to two:**
    Brooklyn—27 men, $3,951 each
    Cleveland—22 men and Mrs. Ray Chapman, $4,204 each

OCTOBER 20   Of course, what happened was that [Republican presidential candidate Senator Warren G.] Harding [of Ohio] once more said something that he did not mean. It is simply another glaring example either of looseness of tongue or of vacillation of mind.... Thinking voters are disgusted with the campaign conducted by Senator Harding, with his vagueness and shifting of ground. They are disgusted, too, at his obvious alignment with the reactionary element in the Republican party. ...That is why they will vote for Cox.
    —Franklin D. Roosevelt, *former assistant secretary of the navy, speaking as the vice presidential candidate on the Democratic ticket headed by Ohio Governor James M. Cox*

NOVEMBER 2   **Harding defeats Cox in a landslide. The nation's first commercial radio broadcast (consisting of election returns) is carried over station KDKA in East Pittsburgh, Pennsylvania.**

NOVEMBER 6   [United States Steel chairman Elbert H.] Gary is a man of abundant good will. I am certain he does not know intimately all about the institution of which he is the head. ...The source upon which Mr. Gary relies for his information is the steel corporation espionage system, and it is thoroughly unreliable. ...It is composed of men who know exactly what their employer will be pleased to hear. They are undesirable and ignorant, so ignorant that few of them can express themselves in intelligible and grammatical English.
    Mr. Gary pictured the [1919 steelworkers'] strike as a revolt against the government. He gave no facts to substantiate that charge. No other officials of the United States Steel Corporation ever gave any facts to bear out such charges, although our commission repeatedly importuned them for facts. Nowhere did we find any evidence of Bolshevism or syndicalism in the strike.
    The steelworker is not a Bolshevist. He is simply empty-headed. He doesn't know anything, except that he has to go to

Franklin D. Roosevelt

work in the morning before his babies are up, that he gets home after his babies are in bed, takes a drink of whiskey without eating and goes to bed, to arise and repeat the same process day after day.

—**Nicholas Van Der Pyl,** *member of the Interchurch World Movement commission which had investigated the 1919 steel strike and whose 1920 report turned public opinion in favor of the strikers, eventually forcing the steel industry to eliminate its standard 12-hour day*

DECEMBER 9   **Daly:** It is apparent the day of unrestricted sales of all natural gas a consumer may wish to burn has passed. The future contains a promise of a continued supply only through cooperation of gas companies, consumers and public officials in efforts to restrict the use and to conserve what remains in nature's storehouse.

Marshall: It is very hard for me personally to believe that the present campaign of the gas interests [to raise the price of natural gas as a way to limit its consumption] is inspired wholly by a fear that the supply is almost gone. On the contrary, I am more of the opinion that the element of price has been a predominating influence.

—*Debate between Martin B. Daly, president of the East Ohio Gas Company, and John D. Marshall, commissioner of franchises (and later mayor) of Cleveland*

1921

The Republican administration raises the import tariff and imposes immigration quotas to limit the number of undesirable aliens (that is, non-Western Europeans) allowed into the country. The "high cost of living" becomes a popular phrase, and Protestant churches that subscribe to a literal interpretation of the Bible begin to refer to themselves as "Fundamentalists." Among City Club members, a topic of endless discussion is the proposal for a city manager for Cleveland; in November, voters finally approve the city-manager charter, which will go into effect three years hence.

JANUARY 27   *Pat Hayes's mob of chess beagles went down in gory defeat before the single-handed onslaught of Sammy Rzeszewski, the eight-year-old Jewish marvel Thursday night at the Hollenden ballroom. The game was called in the 12th inning to permit the visitor to catch a train for New York. At that juncture 17 Cleveland addicts had been knocked higher than the Tanguay temperament, and three others were in a state of coma. Twenty was all Sammy agreed to digest at one sitting....*

There must have been seven tons of gray matter gathered around the abbatoir when Pat's husky mob trotted out on the field and ran through a brisk signal drill.... The appearance of Rzeszewski...was a signal for much convulsive emotion.... Sammy looked like any other eight-year-old boy who was up

1921

long after his bedtime. You were for him strong as soon as he smiled at you, and you knew by the twinkle in his eye that he'd much rather be out playing run-sheep-run with the gang down at the corner than playing chess with a bunch of birds that ought to know better.
—Press

FEBRUARY 12   While the closed shop may seem arbitrary and harsh, it is the only weapon the employee has to protect himself. The open shop simply means an open back door through which the union man is driven out.
—Clarence Darrow, *nationally known attorney and defender of numerous labor leaders and liberal causes*

MARCH 12   Prior to the war, Americans were not of an internationalized mind. They lived a life of isolation and did not realize that in large part this country was the center of politics, finance and civilization.... However much we prefer to live this isolated life, we must realize that the course of events has entirely wiped out the possibility of continuing such an existence.
—Newton D. Baker

MARCH 19   I was told by British military authorities that each day they make up a list of Irishmen whose homes they will raid that night. The raid which I witnessed was in Cork. The man in question was supposed to have Irish literature in his home.

Shortly after midnight a motor bus carrying 14 soldiers and a lieutenant drove up to his home. The man, instead of coming to the door, stuck his head out of an upstairs window and began to argue with the lieutenant. Soldiers smashed in the door with rifle butts.

The Irishman was seized and hurried away to the barracks. His wife and children were taken into a room and guarded by two soldiers with fixed bayonets. The entire house was searched and everything turned topsy-turvy.

Nothing was found, and the man was released the next morning at five o'clock. But I don't think he felt much like giving three cheers for King George as he made his way home.
—C.C. Lyon, *foreign correspondent for the Scripps-McRae League, precursor of the Scripps-Howard newspaper chain*

OCTOBER 22   **Hatton:** We will have efficiency and economy in the administration of city affairs under the manager plan of government. An executive will be chosen with real ability. Not one of the mayors of this city in the last 14 years would have received a salary from any large corporation...equivalent to the salary we pay a mayor.

Harris: A city manager never can be a leader such as a mayor should be. He is selected by the council and will never be anything more than an office boy to do the bidding of the group that selects him.
—*Debate between A.R. Hatton, chairman of the City*

Manager Campaign Committee, and George B. Harris, Cleveland attorney and Republican state central committeeman

***DECEMBER 25** Eugene V. Debs is released from federal prison two days after President Harding commutes his sentence.*

1922

Fascist dictator Benito Mussolini assumes the premiership of Italy, while the League of Nations—minus American participation—formally approves its mandate giving Britain authority over Palestine. Palestinian Arabs, already embittered over the slow but steady growth of Jewish immigration, are enraged by the mandate's preamble, which includes Britain's promise of support for the establishment of a national home in Palestine for the Jewish people. On the domestic front, fear of the foreign-born continues to fester throughout the United States, and the City Club makes a point of presenting speakers of various races and nationalities. Meanwhile, Prohibition is already proving a miserable failure as bootleg whiskey floods the country. Mah Jong becomes a national craze, and a place called Teapot Dome is about to become famous.

FEBRUARY 18 Five would have been released by the police;
   Eight turned loose thru [nolle prosequis];
   Eight discharged, dismissed or found guilty of a lesser offense;
   Six turned loose because no bills were found by the grand jury;
   One would jump his bail;
   Two would be found not guilty by the court;
   Two would be declared guilty;
   Of the 10 pleading or found guilty, three would have their sentences suspended;
   The other seven would have their sentences at least partially executed.
      —Leonard P. Ayres, *nationally known economist and statistician, statistical analyst for the Cleveland Trust Company and secretary of The Cleveland Foundation, describing what would have happened to Ali Baba's 40 thieves had they been arrested in Cleveland, based on the results of the foundation's 1921-1922 criminal justice survey (which will inspire sweeping reforms in the police department and local court system)*

FEBRUARY 25 We, of all nations, are almost alone in trying to sort out the people who come [to this country] in order that their ideas may be standardized.... Now that we've reached a stage where we are trying to stop all immigration, two things are made clear: We are going to be an Anglo-Saxon nation, with the Anglo-Saxons' tendency to exploit other peoples; and we are beginning to make America an unproductive nation.
      —Frederic C. Howe, *former commissioner of immigration at Ellis Island (and former Cleveland city councilman)*

1922

APRIL 7 *Secretary of the Interior Albert B. Fall leases the Naval Oil Reserve at Teapot Dome, Wyoming, to Harry Sinclair's Mammoth Oil Company. Fall receives a "loan" of $260,000 in Liberty Bonds from Sinclair. Later in the year Fall leases the Naval Oil Reserve at Elk Hills, California, to Edward F. Doheny's Pan-American Company. Fall receives a "loan" of $100,000 cash from Doheny. Harry Sinclair also "loans" $185,000 in Liberty Bonds to Republican National Committee chairman Will Hays, to help retire the committee's campaign debts.*

APRIL 8 The phrase "Back to Normalcy" was coined by Mr. Warren G. Harding of this state, now President of the United States. There is much controversy over its meaning. Possibly it doesn't mean anything. Having read a great many Harding speeches, I am inclined to believe that if it had meant anything, he wouldn't have said it.
    —**Jack Raper**

APRIL 22 Any inclination among modern colleges to subsidize college athletics is extremely dangerous and if tolerated to excess will kill the present college spirit and make our great American games mere money-making ventures.... We must not forget that the primary purpose of colleges and universities is knowledge; sports are a part of the course and not an endowment fund.
    —**J. Duncan Spaeth,** *professor of English and varsity crew coach, Princeton University*

APRIL 29 Do we want it possible for any people on this globe to live in the highest approved form of decency, morals and customs? If we should allow Hindus, Chinese and wild African tribesmen to enter this country at will, we should say goodbye to that expectation. If there were no immigration barriers in America you would see migration of two million and three million of such races to this country every year. The more they would bring here, the lower would our standard of living fall.
    —**E.A. Ross,** *professor of sociology, University of Wisconsin*

MAY 13 The white man must arrange to live on terms of mutual respect with the colored races, because the declining white birth rate and the rise of self-respect among the "backward" races will bring them to the front. ...Most leaders of all the colored races believe the very self-interest of the white man will bring about an arrangement for living in partnership.

The Negro nowhere must be exploited, but I believe the white man, from pure self-interest, will soon come to see that everywhere the Negro must be permitted to live, be taught how to work and how to save and build himself up.
    —**W.E.B. Du Bois,** *author, editor and co-founder of the National Association for the Advancement of Colored People (NAACP)*

Jack Raper

W.E.B. Du Bois

MAY 27   Gandhi is the leader of [Hindus], Mohammedans and Christians. He preaches physical non-resistance but spiritual resistance.... He preaches for each person to stand for what he believes right, but to be ready to give his life or his liberty for it.

In short, Gandhi's whole teaching is how to live according to the precepts of Buddha, Jesus and the rest of the long line of the wise who have come out of the East. Gandhi is not a politician, not a diplomat. He is the leader of 315 million people, who are unarmed even to a knife.

—**J.N. Sahni,** *Indian journalist and scholar*

JUNE 3   We have a state board of health to protect us against physical disease and infection; why should we not have protection by the state against films that are indecent, immoral and degrading? In love stories, the movies should be limited to expressing the spiritual aspects of romantic love. Subjects that must be censored include scenes depicting murder, theft, bedroom situations, nakedness and illicit love. There is too much prominence given to debauchery; it seems to me that in the picture colony, the Ten Commandments have been forgotten.

—**Mrs. W.H. Sharp,** *member of the Advisory Committee on Movie Censorship in Ohio*

JUNE 10   I had a little difficulty in getting here to the City Club. I took a taxicab over and asked the driver to hurry. En route I believed that a policeman was following us, but we drove into a [chuckhole] and the policeman went right by without seeing us. We emerged shortly with other automobiles also concealed [there]....

I won't take any cracks at Cleveland. I never take a crack at anything that's down. You folks used to have a pretty good town.... When I was here about four years ago they were working on that bull ring called [Public Auditorium]. There was a man and a boy working on it. The boy has grown up now and I guess he's quite a help.

—**Will Rogers,** *cowboy humorist*

JULY 15   A state-wide survey made two years ago showed that a weekly wage of from $15 to $20 was necessary to provide the bare essentials for living for the average working girl in Ohio, but 51 percent of them receive less than $15 a week. No community can see its women underpaid without suffering for it.

—**Marie Wing,** *executive secretary of Cleveland's Young Women's Christian Association (YWCA) and Cleveland city councilwoman (from 1924 to 1928), appearing as the first woman speaker at a City Club Public Square Forum*

AUGUST 19   In the last five years there have been 4,672 lynchings in this country.... It is time that a federal law is passed to enforce respect for law and justice and the right of a man to fair trial, no matter what the offense.

—**Walter F. White,** *assistant secretary, NAACP*

1922

OCTOBER 19 In target practice off Hampton Roads [Virginia], I proposed to sink a captured German warship in a very short time with an aerial attack. [Then Secretary of the Navy Josephus Daniels] said it couldn't be done. So certain was he that he offered to stand on the deck of the target ship, under fire. He didn't, however, and the boat was sunk by two bombs, dropped from overhead. That is all I have to say about that.

—**William S. Sims,** *commander of U.S. naval forces in the Atlantic during the World War*

OCTOBER 21 I want to go on record as advocating making January 1st the date for inaugurating future Presidents, rather than March 4th. It is not right to leave in power for that additional two months a party defeated at the polls the previous November....

—**Theodore E. Burton,** *former senator and now congressman from Ohio, proposing a change which, in modified form, will be instituted in 1933*

OCTOBER 28 **Durand:** Prohibition has produced a staggering increase in alcoholic insanity caused from drinking improperly made liquors with an unrestricted percent of alcohol. No other doctrine or governmental policy has done more to corrupt the functions of government and multiply the possibilities of graft than this pseudo-reform. If every man voted as he lived today, the nation would be wet by approximately 10-1.

Wheeler: To vote for [a proposed Ohio constitutional amendment allowing beverages containing 2.75 percent or less of alcohol] in conflict with the federal law is disloyalty to the federal government.... By her vote of ratification of the 18th Amendment Ohio helped to fix Prohibition upon her sister states. Should she now, in effect, secede from the union by denying her obligation to support the Constitution?

—*Debate between C. Homer Durand, unsuccessful "wet" candidate in the 1920 Ohio gubernatorial election, and Wayne B. Wheeler, superintendent of the Ohio branch of the Anti-Saloon League*

OCTOBER 30 It was inevitable that a Republican Congress which...had reformed the control of expenditures should also reform the revenue system of the country. ...As every taxpayer knows, the new [tax] act abolished a host of vexatious perplexities, resulted in the abandonment of infinite red tape and established a system much simpler than that which existed before.

—**Medill McCormick,** *Republican senator from Illinois, older brother of Chicago* Tribune *publisher Robert R. McCormick and husband of former Clevelander Ruth H. McCormick, daughter of the late Senator Marcus Alonzo Hanna*

NOVEMBER 4 I am in favor of better highways and more highways and not so many highwaymen. I am in favor of a

smoother road between Cleveland and Pittsburgh. The bootleggers complain bitterly of the breakage in trucking bottled goods.
—**Jack Raper**

DECEMBER 6   The Irish Free State is established.

DECEMBER 16 Those who favor censorship [of motion pictures] would change our historic Bill of Rights to a "Bill of Don'ts...." Censorship begins with an utterly false basis. Namely, that a person is immediately going to leave a movie theater and begin acting like the characters on the screen had just acted. Shakespeare could not be enacted [on film] in New York State because no murder can be depicted on the screen in New York....
—**James J. Walker,** *state senator from (and later mayor of) New York*

James J. Walker

Q: If there were no censorship, how could the South, for instance, prevent showing of the [Jack] Johnson-[Jim] Jeffries [1910 heavyweight championship title fight] pictures?
Walker: By the police power, on the ground that [films of a boxing match in which a black man defeated a white man] would incite a riot.

1923

In August, President Harding dies suddenly, and Calvin Coolidge assumes the Presidency. Two months after Harding's death, the scandals of his administration come to light as a Senate subcommittee begins to unravel the Teapot Dome affair.

As French "doctor" Emil Coue's prescription for personal improvement—"Day by day in every way I am getting better and better"—becomes an enormous national craze early in the year, the City Club hears a dismissal of such "auto-suggestion" therapy, as well as of Freudian theory. The most divisive drama of the club's second decade is played out in February, when an invitation to Socialist Eugene V. Debs results in a bitter test of the open-forum policy. And after the November municipal election, councilmen choose Cleveland's first city manager—with a little help from the town's most powerful back-room politico.

FEBRUARY 2 In the future it will be found that good social policy is good business policy. ...If we arc going to raise [a] crop of good customers, it becomes clear that a girl earning only $7 a week will be unable to buy anything that will be profitable to anybody. If you change that and compel me to pay a girl $14 a week, then she can buy something that is of profit to herself and to the producer. [But] I have got to see that the girl drawing $14 a week is intelligent enough, efficient and well-educated enough to be able to earn $14. So that increases my interest in city government, in the schools, in housing conditions.
—**Edward A. Filene,** *president, William Filene & Sons*

1923   *department store, Boston*

FEBRUARY 8   *Eugene V. Debs, in Cleveland Tuesday, an-nounced his intention of actively reentering politics. He also will take the platform in a fight for his doctrines....*

Debs recently was invited to speak before the City Club by a vote of the board of directors after [club] president [and mayor of suburban Cleveland Heights] Frank C. Cain had opposed the invitation. "I feel a deep sense of obligation to the members of the City Club," [said Debs], "who, although not all in accord with my views, are still fair enough to me and true enough to the fundamental principles of free speech and free assemblage to accord to me the same right to a hearing that they claim for themselves."

—Press

FEBRUARY 10   The danger in auto-suggestion as taught by Coue is that it oversimplifies life. It creates the impression that there are methods of securing ends without effort.... I have little sympathy with the modern philosophy that the thing to do is to keep on smiling whether there is anything to smile about or not. The word most often associated with "cheerful" is "idiot."

If you read many of the books written about Freud and his theory of complexes—such as the mother and son complex and the father and daughter complex—you'd get the idea that the very worst thing that could happen to a child would be to have any parents at all, and that the salvation of all children depended upon putting them in orphan asylums as soon as they are born.

—Joseph Jastrow, *professor of psychology, University of Wisconsin*

Frank C. Cain...last night characterized as exaggerated reports that the membership of the City Club is split on the matter of asking Eugene V. Debs...to speak at the club.

"So far," said Mr. Cain, "the matter has not been presented to the present officers and directors of the club in any formal way, and until then it is going too far to say that there is anything like a division on the matter.... If anybody wants to know how I feel personally about this, I must say frankly that I would be opposed to having Debs on our platform, or any other man convicted of having stood in the way of the American people in the war."

Peter Witt, one of the leaders of the members who would like to hear Debs address the club, declared yesterday that the principles in the club's "creed" were at stake in the matter. "I'd like to find out if the creed means anything or if it's bunk," said Witt.

—Plain Dealer

FEBRUARY 13   *Since advising you of my acceptance of [your] invitation to address the City Club of Cleveland..., I have had occasion to learn of the disagreement of opinion among the*

Frank C. Cain

members as to the propriety of sponsoring me as a guest..., and of the dissension incident to the discussion of the question, resulting in the protest and resignation of a number of members.... Feeling disinclined...to aggravate such variance of opinion among the membership, or to obtrude where there is any question of my being welcome, or as to the right of being heard in a forum avowedly open to free speech, I beg to withdraw my acceptance and to respectfully decline the invitation of the club....

Please convey to the club and to each of its members, without regard to his opinion or attitude, my thanks for the kind invitation.... With all cordial regards and good wishes, I remain,

Yours faithfully,
Eugene V. Debs
—Letter from Debs to City Club secretary Pat Hayes

FEBRUARY 14 *Members of the club generally now regard the Debs affair as closed history. A number of members who had threatened to resign if he appeared and some who have resigned are expected to restore their memberships.*
—Plain Dealer

MARCH 17 The history of the...fight is not a new one, and today the [Cleveland city] council and thc [East Ohio Gas] company are hopelessly deadlocked.... The gas company will not recede, neither will the council. We feel we have offered them a fair return in our proposal and they say their rate is final, to be followed by the shutoff [of gas to Cleveland on] May 1st. They maintain the natural gas is theirs to sell, and if we don't take it they can sell it elsewhere, and they will be firm in adhering to their proposed rates. [But] the council will not budge an inch unless the people demand it.
—Clayton C. Townes, *president, Cleveland city council*

Q: I wonder if the East Ohio Gas Company ever heard of the Boston Tea Party?

Townes: No, but I think there will be a riot [on] May 1st if they shut off the gas.

MARCH 23 There can be no compromise in the gas rate controversy, because the company has submitted positively its final proposition. We are sorry to leave you, but your board of directors—the city council—has left nothing else for us to do. It is their responsibility and not ours, and if the gas is shut off the fault should be laid at their doorstep.
—Martin B. Daly, *president, East Ohio Gas Company*

APRIL 19 *A compromise agreement ends Cleveland's gas-rate war.*

AUGUST 11 Negroes are coming north in great numbers.

1923

They are coming to Cleveland in great numbers. They are Americans in tradition and training. How are you going to deal with them?

...Men have advised that the Negroes be segregated. This is the worst thing that could happen. The more you separate people the less they know one another, and the more they hate one another.

—**Robert W. Bagnall,** *New York area branch director, NAACP*

Q: Why don't the Negroes organize and collectively demand recognition from a government which has praised them so highly in time of war?

Bagnall: They have a larger amount of faith and patience than the white man, for one reason. For another, they know they'd be licked.

DECEMBER 8 It's the fashion to be shallow, and that's why, when the word "highbrow" is mentioned, the tired businessman has visions of Ibsen matinees and silken handkerchiefs protruding from the artist's sleeve.... The tired businessman gets what he wants. He has been seeing third-rate shows and movies, hearing bad music and reading poor books because he is too mentally languid to exert himself to appreciate anything better. *Abie's Irish Rose* ran a year in New York and is in its 13th week in Cleveland because it plays down to his intellectual languor.

—**Fannie Hurst,** *best-selling author of* Back Street

DECEMBER 15 I believe that when the people voted for councilmen this year they had in mind that those elected would stand on their own feet, would proceed to the selection of a city manager by open discussion of all candidates suggested.

As you know, no such thing happened. It is incorrect to say that the new council decided on [former subway company president William R. Hopkins] for manager. It is nearer the truth to say that a majority in the council registered a decision made for them by Maurice Maschke.

—**Augustus R. Hatton,** *recently elected Cleveland city councilman, accusing Republican National Committeeman and local party boss Maschke, for nearly a decade the city's premier political power broker, of personally controlling the selection of the new city manager*

1924

Indictments are about to spring from the Teapot Dome scandal as the Republican Party's national convention —held in Cleveland this year—chooses incumbent President Coolidge to head its ticket. Progressives, also meeting in Cleveland, nominate Wisconsin Senator Robert La Follette as their standard-bearer, and Democrats—on the 103rd ballot—pick West Virginia Senator John W. Davis. But America as a whole seems to find politics less fascinating than tales of airborne adventures,

William R. Hopkins

the schism between Fundamentalist and Modernist religion and treasures from an Egyptian pharaoh's tomb.

Hailed as a municipal administrator above the political fray, William R. Hopkins, Cleveland's new city manager, makes his first public speech at the City Club. (In ensuing months and years, the club will also be the platform for disclosures about the deal between Maurice Maschke and Democratic boss W. Burr Gongwer that resulted in Hopkins's selection as manager.) Club members also hear strong debates between organized labor and opponents of the closed shop, get details on the Fall investigation and play host to the most famous aviator of the day.

JANUARY 12   The city has reached a point where lack of facilities may seriously hamper its growth.... In fact, the city has a bad case of hardened arteries....

I shall be disappointed in the people of our suburbs if, when they see what is involved for the city of Cleveland in such projects as waterworks, highways and transportation which primarily are for the benefit of the suburbs, they aren't willing to get away from provincial and local notions and become ashamed to stay out [of a metropolitan government]. We must get the big metropolitan point of view....
　　—William R. Hopkins

JANUARY 19   It was a dramatic moment when Howard Carter, the excavator, began tapping the wall of the inner tomb with a hammer. The seals of the old priests were unbroken, and we knew the old king was inside, waiting for his awakening....
　　—Arthur Weigall, *former Inspector General of Antiquities of Egypt, describing the 1922 unearthing of the tomb of Tutankhamen, Egyptian king of the 14th century B.C.*

FEBRUARY 16   If the so-called union or closed shop is a detriment to the workers and your so-called open shop a benefit, why don't those who run open shops take the leadership in paying such wages and introducing such remedial legislation that will make it possible for every industrial worker to own his own home?
　　—Max S. Hayes, *editor,* Cleveland Citizen *labor newspaper*

FEBRUARY 23   There is no essential conflict between science and the Bible over the order of creation as told in Genesis. Science is more detailed than the Bible, which uses broad terms. To say that the Earth was created in a day might mean merely an infinite period of time.
　　—W.W. Bustard, *spiritual leader of Cleveland's Euclid Avenue Baptist Church, attempting to reconcile differences between Modernist and Fundamentalist beliefs*

MARCH 15   There are hundreds of young men and women in

1924

this country who need development to become actors and actresses, but their talent is hidden away in various corners of the cities and towns. Baseball clubs send scouts everywhere; southpaw pitchers are found in the most unlikely places. Why not adopt this system in the theater? When a worthy young actor is discovered, let him be developed—the stage needs him today more than ever.

—**Heywood Broun,** *drama critic for the New York* World *and member of the famous Algonquin Round Table*

APRIL 25 I am demanding as a Republican of Republicans that the Republican house be cleaned...[of] this unholy alliance between big business and crooked politicians. I cannot allow [former Secretary of the Treasury Leslie M. Shaw's] speeches, authorized by the President, to go unchallenged further. The callousness of it all! He calls the passing of $100,000 from Doheny to Fall a "mere friendly act...."

—**Hiram W. Johnson,** *senator from California and candidate for the Republican presidential nomination*

SEPTEMBER 27 Dr. Reeve declared the cost to the state of supporting a man in the penitentiary is $6 a week, while the cost in one of the state hospitals is much less.... "Of course, if you want the very cheapest way out, the thing to do is to electrocute them all. You can get a man electrocuted for $50."

—Press *account of speech by Dr. George H. Reeve, chief of the psychiatric clinic of Cuyahoga County's common pleas court, urging more humane treatment of the criminally insane*

Hugo Eckener

OCTOBER 28 [Zeppelin Airship Company president Dr. Hugo Eckener is] now the foremost figure in aeronautics in the world by virtue of [his] record-breaking [transatlantic] flight of the ZR-3 from Friedrichshafen, Germany, to Lakehurst, New Jersey, new home of that dirigible.... [Eckener] speaks some English but preferred to talk in German, interpreted by Captain Ernst Lehmann, chief of the executive staff of the ZR-3 and vice president of [Akron's] Goodyear-Zeppelin Company.

"The general opinion seems to be," Dr. Eckener began, "that airships exposed to heavy storms are in danger, and that such storms eventually lead to the destruction of such ships...."

—Plain Dealer

1925

The high times of "Coolidge Prosperity" and a national trend toward loosening social strictures are tempered by America's obsessive fear of immigrants, which produces "scholarly" treatises on the subject of inferior races by self-proclaimed authorities who achieve phenomenal celebrity. A new Immigration Act that has fixed restrictive quotas and virtually excluded Orientals generates strong ill will in India and Japan. The Scopes "Monkey Trial" is a showcase for the battle against the teaching of evolution, but the country

can still find time to marvel at the prodigious feats of baseball's Sultan of Swat, who gives City Clubbers his personal assessment of the national pastime.

JANUARY 10 Just a few months ago the people of Massachusetts ingloriously defeated the [proposed national child-labor] amendment. They did not vote against the amendment but against what they thought the amendment was. Farmers believed that after its passage their 17-year-old daughters could no longer wash the family dishes and make beds. Every farmer boy of 17 who went out in the barn and cranked the family flivver would probably be caught by the ever-present federal agent waiting to swoop down, confiscate the farm and send the father to the penitentiary....
    —Owen Lovejoy

JANUARY 17 Lothrop Stoddard, whose books *The Rising Tide of Color* and *The Revolt Against Civilization* first startled the country and then plunged it into controversy, defended the thesis of Nordic supremacy yesterday before the City Club. Mr. Stoddard, a Harvard...Ph.D., [said] the new immigration law rests upon a scientific basis in discriminating against the southern Europeans. The "Alpine" and "Mediterranean" types cannot be assimilated beyond a point which already has been reached. To admit further masses of these two types is to create discord.
    "It isn't that the Nordics are superior. They are simply different, and if we want to keep this country homogeneous we will exclude the unlike. We will play one racial, social and political melody. You can't expect the others to play this melody in the same key.
    "If we want America to have a basic and continuous unity, we must have a predominance of like-thinking people. The immigration law is not an instrument of fear; it simply recognizes scientific facts.... Only in the last 25 years have the older stocks realized the full implication of immigration.... One of the best informed American statesmen told me that, if the immigration law had failed to pass, an emotional reaction would have swept the country that would have made the Ku Klux Klan look like 30 cents."
    —Plain Dealer

MARCH 28 Reverend Reinhold Niebuhr, [renowned Protestant theologian and pastor of the Bethel Evangelical Church in] Detroit, deplored what he termed the "developing tribalism" in this country in "the closing of our gates and the growth of our Nordic superiority complex." The United States, he said, by lack of world thinking in dealing with Europe and by its race superiority attitude toward Japan, is unconsciously stirring that sort of hatred that has caused wars....
    —Plain Dealer

APRIL 1 The audience sat tense in their seats when Harding

1925

told about the flight through a snowstorm and fog shortly after leaving Seattle.... The trip to Japan was made across the northern rim of the world.... From Japan the flyers traveled to China.... Crowds in India were so thick that the flyers were almost unable to leave their planes.... A brief stop was made at Constantinople. The route from there was to Bucharest...and Paris, which was made in record time.... In England they were received by King George and Queen Mary.... From England the flight led to Iceland over the Atlantic.... From Iceland the journey to Boston was made.... The next step was across the continent to Los Angeles and then up to Seattle, the starting point....

—Times *account of noted aviator "Smiling Jack" Harding's description of his recent round-the-world flight*

APRIL 29   The reason for our phenomenal growth has been the vision and foresight of our present assistant sales manager, who as far back as 1875 saw the immense commercial possibilities of the Atlantic Ocean as an avenue of transportation between America and Europe, at a time when others saw only its value as a fishing and bathing utility.

—Robert Benchley, Life *magazine drama critic, quoting from the monologue he presented on the Keith vaudeville circuit*

MAY 1   **Brown:** Every automobile in Ohio is helping to wear out...every...road in the state, and it's only fair that every automobile driver should help to repair it. It's a strange quirk of human nature that doesn't murmer when the price of gas goes up from 15 to 20 cents in just a few months, as it did in Ohio, and when every cent of that increase goes into the coffers of the oil companies, and then wails when [a proposed two-cent state gasoline tax] is added, all of which comes back to the motorist.

Bender: A million flivvers can run out [Cleveland's] Carnegie Avenue every day and never harm the pavement in the least. It's the heavy trucks that tear up the roads, and if there is to be a tax on gas those fellows should pay it. This tax is going to be fought up to the Supreme Court and then in referendum, if I have to do it myself. And I am not an aspirant for the governorship, either, and I won't be two years hence.

—*Debate between John T. Brown, Democratic state representative, and George H. Bender, Republican state senator*

JULY 10   Dayton, Tennessee, teacher John T. Scopes is put on trial for violating the state's new law prohibiting the teaching of evolution. In less than two weeks he is found guilty and fined $100.

JULY 17   The ball is all right. Nothing the matter with it. It's the same as it was 10 years ago. Only reason for the increased hitting, especially of home runs, is that where seven of every 10 batters used to choke their bats, nine out of every 10 now swing from the hip.

—*Babe Ruth, New York Yankees home-run king, denying*

Henry R. Luce

the rumor of a juiced-up "rabbit" ball to club members during a midweek luncheon

SEPTEMBER 3   The dirigible Shenandoah is destroyed in a storm near Ava, Ohio, killing 14.

OCTOBER 3   The issue at Dayton was not Fundamentalism against Modernism, it was not faith against agnosticism, it was not science against religion. The issue was and is this: Shall the constitutional guaranty of religious freedom and complete separation of church and state, inspired by Jefferson, fought for by Madison and written into our fundamental law, be violated or narrowed by any creed thinking to write its scheme of salvation into law...?
      —Dudley Field Malone, *famed New York attorney and co-defense counsel (with Clarence Darrow) in the Scopes case, whose oratory during the trial earned him cheers from even those Fundamentalists in attendance*

DECEMBER 19   I have said in the past that I hoped to find the bones there. ...Now I am positive that we will find them.
      —Roy Chapman Andrews, *leader of the American Museum of Natural History's third fossil-hunting expedition to the Gobi desert, one of a series of ultimately unsuccessful attempts to prove that the first human beings were ancestors of the superior Aryan stock and had not spring up in Africa*

1926

U. S. Marines are sent to Nicaragua to impose order on a country torn by civil war. In Europe, fascism has taken root in Italy, but America continues to see Bolshevism at home as a more frightening potential threat to security. Controlling the birth rate of inferior races remains a topic of widespread interest nationally, and the City Club hears the theories of another leading exponent of Nordic superiority, as well as firsthand accounts of an assault on Everest and one of the most daring pre-Lindbergh feats of aviation. The club also plays host to two would-be publishing moguls whose weekly national news magazine is produced in offices just a few blocks away.

JANUARY 30   Happiness is not a matter of the thermometer. Life offers a man as much in Labrador as anywhere.
      —Wilfred T. Grenfell, *British humanitarian doctor who will be knighted the following year for his life's work with the people of Labrador and Newfoundland*

FEBRUARY 10   *Which is smarter—the City Club or the Big Ten University Club? Both clubs took a "skull test" arranged by Briton Hadden and Henry R. Luce, editors of* Time, *news weekly published here, and the Big Ten group won the referee's decision....*

1926   A list of 25 questions based on news of the week were asked,
and members of the two clubs wrote answers on score cards....

Examples of questions and answers: Q. To what church is
President Coolidge attached?

A. Congregationalist

Q. Liberia is in what part of what continent?

A. Western Africa

Q. Of what country is [Olympic distance runner] Paavo
Nurmi a native?

A. Finland

—Press

FEBRUARY 21   We must find out how disease and psychosis
are inherited, and a lot of money ought to be spent on this kind
of research. A man in New York recently left $45 million for the
care of inferiors, but you can't get a cent for people of superior
intelligence....

The American college graduate is a dying race, a vanishing
species. One thousand Harvard graduates in six generations will
have only 150 descendants, hardly enough to make a glee club,
while 1,000 unskilled laborers in six generations will have
100,000 descendants. Why, it takes three college-trained women
to produce one offspring while at the same time the unskilled
laboring woman is producing three.

...If the human race is to progress, man must learn to live
biologically, which means he must apply lessons learned in the
jungle, to see that the intelligent multiply faster than the stupid.

—**Albert E. Wiggam,** *self-proclaimed authority on biol-
ogy and author of* The New Decalog of Science *and* The Fruit
of the Family Tree

FEBRUARY 22   *Said Mr. Albert Wiggam to Mr. Lothrop
Stoddard,*

When they had finished dining, quite thoroughly befoddered:
"Now let us fill our glasses and drink to Racial Purity,
And may the Nordic rule supreme today and in futurity!"
"Religiously we raise our cups, and heartily we swig 'em!"
Said Mr. Lothrop Stoddard to Mr. Albert Wiggam.

Said Mr. Albert Wiggam to Mr. Lothrop Stoddard:
*"In coddling swarthy Foreigners, not only Man but God
erred.*
I've proved by science that we must breed faster or be stung—
The future of the Nordic race depends on lots of young."
*"Here's to the Young—especially that Young whose name
was Brigham!"*
Said Mr. Lothrop Stoddard to Mr. Albert Wiggam.

Said Mr. Albert Wiggam to Mr. Lothrop Stoddard:
"Of Freedom and Equality too long the books have doddered;
My Science shows Democracy to be unscientific,
Your Figures show that Black Folks are too terribly prolific."

Clarence Darrow

"Statistics are our one best bet, if we can only rig 'em,"
Said Mr. Lothrop Stoddard to Mr. Albert Wiggam.
    —*"At the Nordic Native American Society,"* poem by City
Club member and Plain Dealer *columnist Ted Robinson
published in* The New Yorker *magazine*

MARCH 19   Lieutenant John A. MacReady, army aviator, who
believes that his recent flight from McCook Field at Dayton will
break the world's altitude record, told the members of the City
Club that "the American public must be educated to travel in airplanes. They have proven their value as carriers of mail and [car-
go] and would be equally useful for carrying passengers..."
    Because of poor weather conditions in Dayton last night,
Lieutenant MacReady came to Cleveland by train....
    —News

MARCH 20   Even a highly superior Nordic Englishman cannot
admit that Chicago is cursed with crime because of the presence
of a large number of Italians and Greeks. The fallacy is
demolished by the simple inquiry why Italians and Greeks
commit in Chicago several times the homicides they do in Rome
or Athens. Manifestly, the answer is to alter Chicago.
    —**John Langdon-Davies,** *Member of Parliament, ridicul-
ing the heredity theories of Stoddard and Wiggam*

MARCH 29   It ought to be perfectly evident...that poverty,
ignorance and low mentality have some bearing on crime.... The
people won't believe it, though. They like to punish too well.
One reason why we go on hanging people is because we enjoy it.
    —**Clarence Darrow**

MARCH 31   Only 600 feet stood between our expedition and
success. Two of our men, Mallory and Irvine, were seen through
the telescope toiling up the slope at an altitude of 28,400 feet.
Then we lost trace of them, and never found so much as a piece
of clothing to tell the story of their fate....
    Our expedition showed that man can acclimatize himself to
an altitude of 29,000 feet. The next expedition, like our own,
must be made at the expense of human life, but I am convinced
there are no insurmountable obstacles.
    —**J.B. Noel,** *expedition photographer for the ill-fated
1924 British assault on Mt. Everest which resulted in the deaths
of climbers Andrew Irvine and George Leigh Mallory (the latter
being the man who, when asked why he wanted to scale Everest,
had replied, "Because it is there")*

APRIL 24   In colleges, too many specialize before they have
acquired sufficient broad general culture.
    —**George Sarton,** *lecturer on the history of science,
Harvard University*

MAY 6   *My presence in Cleveland was timed to permit me to*

1926

see another unique manifestation of the city's public spirit—the annual [Anvil Revue] of the City Club, an impromptu and amateur revue satirizing local and national politics in an audacious spirit that requires a trip back to ancient Athens at the time of Aristophanes to find a parallel.

What I like particularly in Cleveland's City Club show...is the broadmindedness of the civic and community spirit...which permits the most merciless lampooning.... In any other American city I am sure that the proceedings would have resulted in a score of suits for slander and libel. On the contrary, [in Cleveland] the slandered and the libeled...sat out front....

—Oliver M. Sayler, theater and arts critic, broadcasting over New York City radio station WGBS

AUGUST 18 *Louise Glaum, movie actress, who is appearing in person at Loew's State Theater this week, gave an after-luncheon talk at the City Club.... She said that...she doesn't like to be called a vampire, although she plays vampire roles on the screen; that she really isn't a vampire off the screen; that, in fact, she doesn't approve of breaking up homes; that the members of the City Club could assure their wives and sweethearts that it was perfectly safe to take lunch in the same dining room with Louise Glaum.*

—Press

OCTOBER 9 The Federal Reserve Act [of 1913] is the Magna Charta of American banking which has ended for all time financial panics.

—Atlee Pomerene, *former Democratic senator from Ohio*

OCTOBER 13 A modest, unobtrusive young man...told City Club members yesterday that the world-thrilling North Pole flight, under Commander Richard E. Byrd, was "no different than any other 15-hour flight."

Floyd Bennett...piloted his way to the Cleveland airport...in the very plane he had guided over the top of the world last May....

Charles F. Kunkel, representing the Guggenheim Fund which is financing the coast-to-coast tour [of Byrd's pilot], praised Cleveland's airport as the country's best. He asked factory owners to put illuminated signs on their roofs at night, with arrows pointing in the direction of the airport....

—Plain Dealer

1927

Perhaps the most wide-eyed year in a decade of excess, 1927 sees Lindbergh's solo crossing of the Atlantic; the release of The Jazz Singer, the first talking picture; production of the 15 millionth Model "T"; and Babe Ruth's record 60-home-run season.

At the City Club, the air of frivolity is tempered by serious discussions of such topics as American military

intervention in Nicaragua, growing Fundamentalist opposition to evolutionary theory, Prohibition and crime.
Cleveland's city manager plan is both derided and
praised, and Peter Witt, already the club's most voluble
orator, launches a marathon denunciation of the state of
Cleveland, with special emphasis on city manager Hopkins's performance to date.

JANUARY 29 The trouble with the dry fanatics is that they all
go to bed at nine o'clock, just when the men of tomorrow are
shining their shoes and getting ready to go out and see the sights.
The fanatics are too naive.... They don't even know that if you
keep up with the procession you have to go to five or six parties
in one night, with a drink at each stop.
   —**John G. Murphy,** *City Club member denouncing
Prohibition during an experimental forum in which any
member is allowed to make a three-minute speech*

FEBRUARY 8 A British ship, crossing the Pacific, ran short of
food while still two days out from Vancouver. The Chinese cook
reported to the captain.
   "That's all right, John," the captain said. "Just take whatever
the passengers have left on their plates, put it in a big kettle,
chop it up fine and add any sprigs of celery you can find."
   Thus chop suey came into the world, according to Juo Fung,
Chinese tenor, appearing this week at Keith's Palace theater, who
spoke at the City Club yesterday....
   —Plain Dealer

FEBRUARY 12 [Former *Plain Dealer* staffer] Fred C. Kelly,
magazine writer and nationally known humorist, believes
prosperity is dependent upon a good steady supply of stupidity
[and] is optimistic about the future....
   "Stupidity is especially valuable in the moving picture
industry. One of the big producers has carefully selected 300
boys and girls, all attested as to lack of intelligence, and every
new picture is shown to them first. If there is anything in the
picture that they don't understand...it is cut out. The pictures I
have seen recently convince me that the system is still in
successful operation."

   Q: To what extent are we indebted to the stupid for the
attitude of [our] government toward Nicaragua?
   Kelly: Entirely.
   —Times *and* Plain Dealer *accounts*

FEBRUARY 19 The United States would have no more
staunch supporters in case of war in the East than inhabitants of
the [Philippine] archipelago. [The Japanese] might take the
islands before we could get over there in sufficient force. But
with 7,000 islands stretching 2,000 miles it would require all of
Japan's naval and military strength to hold the Philippines,

1927

leaving their own land to our mercy.

—**Carmi A. Thompson,** *former Ohio state representative, secretary to President William Howard Taft and U.S. treasurer, recently returned from conducting an economic and political survey of the Philippines for President Coolidge*

MARCH 5 Mussolini has done much for Italy. In less than five years he has balanced the budget, put gold in the treasury, cut taxes, funded the U.S. [war] debt, restored Italian credit and prestige, made public service efficient and put Italians to work.... But he is a foe of democracy..., and I think that someday Italy will have to undo all of his work and start in all over again.

—**Tom Skeyhill,** *writer and lecturer on international affairs, recently returned from a European tour*

MARCH 12 Talk that morality is degenerating is nonsense. The average man today is more humane and considerate than ever before.... Woman is the civilizing agent. It was woman who taught man agriculture and domesticated the animals. Some day she will civilize man.... Women will lift us up in refinement of character, and the higher their eyes go the higher will our civilization go.

—**Will Durant,** *professor of philosophy at Columbia University and author of the best-selling* Story of Philosophy

APRIL 23 I am opposed to censorship in the guise of legislation.... Decency can't be legislated into people....

In a democracy, people have a right to go to hell if they want to. If they persist in going to hell in spite of our advice, then all we can say is, "Go along, then, and God bless you."

—**Barnett R. Brickner,** *spiritual leader of Cleveland's Euclid Avenue Temple*

APRIL 30 If we set our best minds to devise something to increase degradation, they could find nothing better than the conventional prison of today. Some day we shall awaken to the fact that criminals need treatment, just as we have changed our attitude to the insane.... We have made practically no progress in crime treatment from Moses to Clarence Darrow.

—**Harry Elmer Barnes,** *professor of sociology, Smith College*

MAY 9 Trade leads to an exchange of ideas, to a better understanding and to a better feeling.... It also, strange as it may seem, is often a guarantee of good relations between people, and I would, therefore, establish...friendly relations with all governments and all peoples.... [That] applies just as thoroughly to Russia as it does to Japan.

—**William E. Borah,** *Republican senator from Idaho and chairman of the Senate foreign relations committee*

William E. Borah

MAY 21 *Charles A. Lindbergh lands at Le Bourget*

Field in Paris, completing the world's first solo trans-atlantic flight.

NOVEMBER 5 Peter Witt, classic denouncer and [currently Cleveland city] councilman, broke all records for marathon condemnation yesterday by speaking [for more than] three hours without a pause...before the City Club. Previous records, both in length of time and number of subjects covered, all held by Witt, are shattered. Hardly anything political that has happened locally or nationally for 25 years was overlooked....

At 3 p.m. he took off his coat, hitched up his trousers and announced he was only half through. At this time he had been going two hours flat.

At that hour he had declared in favor of only five things:

Proportional representation, in theory

The city manager plan, in theory

Tom L. Johnson as a municipal executive

A stadium on the lake front

A .7-mill levy for police and fire pay increase

By that time he had denounced several hundred persons and things, in such profusion that tabulators lost count. In the final hour and 15 minutes he increased his list of denunciations by several hundreds, but found nothing else he could be for.

Only a small and incomplete list of persons, things and customs pounced upon by Witt could be compiled. It follows:

The wets; the drys

Maurice Maschke, Burr Gongwer, Carmi Thompson, Newton D. Baker

The Board of Elections; the City Council in toto

The theory of checks and balances in the federal government

Warren G. Harding and Albert B. Fall

Congressmen

Negative voting in America

The caliber of elective mayors generally

The Interstate Commerce Commission

The New York Central Railroad

Gerrymandering of congressional districts

[City Manager] W.R. Hopkins's financial policies

The World War

The protective tariff

The attendant evils upon political landslides

The dictators of Italy, Poland and Spain

The "blah" and nonsense of the present charter campaign

The [proposed] superhighway along the lake front....

When he had been speaking for nearly two hours, Witt proceeded to concentrate all his attack on City Manager Hopkins and his administration.... "According to...Hopkins, the only thing he hasn't built is Niagara Falls; the only thing he hasn't invented is gunpowder. I suspect lateness of birth is responsible for these two omissions. After an intimate acquaintance with [him] during the last few years I've become convinced that he's another Mussolini. His is the spirit of egotism. He admits that he

1927

himself is the only one who can get things done. As a matter of fact, *I* should be given credit for most of the good things that have been accomplished since Hopkins became city manager...."

—Plain Dealer

NOVEMBER 6 *Witt's action in making an election-eve attack is in keeping with his performances in city council. After sitting silent in the council when measures are up for passage, Mr. Witt waits for months or years and then proceeds to denounce them. He habitually remains silent when he should speak and then speaks when by every rule of fair play he should be silent. He never allows the facts to influence his oratory....*

—*William R. Hopkins, quoted in the* Plain Dealer

NOVEMBER 12 There seems to be a boycott of office-holding on the part of the more intelligent people. You men who would spill your last drop of blood in the war are unwilling to try to save your city in time of peace by becoming candidates for the [city] council.

—Augustus R. Hatton, *making his farewell address to the City Club before leaving to become professor of political science at Northwestern University, Evanston, Illinois*

DECEMBER 3 The concept of the city and the countryside is now fundamentally the same as it was in the Middle Ages. But today, with rapid transportation and intercommunication, the rural districts are becoming urbanized, and one cannot tell where the city ends and the country begins. The whole district belongs to Cleveland; the real Cleveland does not stop at the boundary lines.

...I'll bet 10 cents that if George Washington were alive today he would favor a central metropolitan government that would make Cleveland the efficient metropolis it ought to be.

—Thomas Harrison Reed, *professor of political science at the University of Michigan, advocating consideration of a borough plan of metropolitan government for Cleveland and her growing suburbs*

DECEMBER 10 What a relief when the scaffolding was torn away! ...A glance sufficed to show that the best traditions of 1893 and the Chicago World's Fair had been adhered to.

It formed no jarring contrast, but rather harmonized in all essential details with its little neighbor, the Soldiers and Sailors Monument. The eye is led gently from one to the other, and the feelings inspired by the monument are intensified by the tower.

The stranger looks at the monument and smiles—he glances at the tower and bursts out laughing. There at the top stand the glorified cruet, with the salt, pepper, mustard and vinegar at the four corners—a sublimation of the happy memories of his boyhood. Nothing is lacking but a red tablecloth and a glass of toothpicks.

—Ted Robinson, *offering his first impressions of the*

Augustus R. Hatton

nearly completed Terminal Tower above Public Square's Union Station

1928

Republican Herbert Hoover defeats the "Happy Warrior"—New York's Democratic Governor Al Smith—in the presidential race, primarily because much of small-town America is suspicious of Smith, a Catholic and a "wet." Meanwhile, Russia implements its first five-year plan, and many in the West fear that the Bolsheviks are trying to export revolution. A revolution of a different sort is discussed in an open debate sponsored by the City Club: A shocking and controversial new idea called "companionate" marriage—marriage for a reason other than producing children—which has engendered violent protests across the country, draws thousands to the Masonic Auditorium to hear arguments pro and con.

JANUARY 21   During the war the youngsters were fed a lot of propaganda in editorials by Liberty Loan celebrities and by authors. They were told that the war was an idealistic upheaval. When the war was over the youngsters found out it was no such thing. [H.L.] Mencken was the only one who had continuously talked against war—who had said it was a commercial matter, not an idealistic one. So now they worship Mencken. He may not be a great thinker but he is one to be trusted. He believes in nothing—and neither does the younger generation.
  —**Floyd Dell,** *author of such realist novels as* Moon Calf *and* An Unmarried Father

FEBRUARY 4   I am a teetotaler, and in local elections I always voted dry. But...Prohibition...has proved as unwise as would be the attempt to control Mississippi floods with a dam at the headwaters.
  How many in this audience, knowing that a murder had been committed, would report it to the police? [Many hands raised] Most of you. Now, how many of you who ever had knowledge that the Volstead law had been violated, reported it to the police? [Four hands raised] There you are.
  —**W.H. Stayton,** *national chairman, Association Against the Prohibition Amendment*

  Q: The 19th Amendment took care of the woman proposition, and the 18th took care of the wine. How soon may we expect an amendment to take care of song?
  Stayton: Since woman was taken out of the home, and booze along with her, there hasn't been any song.

FEBRUARY 11   Even as [President] Coolidge was dispensing pious platitudes [in January at the Pan-American Congress in] Havana and paying lip service to the memories of George Washington, newsboys on the streets of Havana were selling

1928

extras telling about American bombing planes scattering death and terror over defenseless Nicaraguan villages, and American Marines in overwhelming numbers were remorseless in hunting down a pitiful handful of Nicaraguan liberals under [rebel leader General Augusto] Sandino who are fighting for the principles of liberty that our revolutionary forefathers fought for in 1776.

—**Burton K. Wheeler,** *Democratic senator from Montana*

Lindsey: The companionate marriage is legal marriage with legalized birth control and legalized divorce by mutual consent for childless couples, usually without alimony. Companionate marriage..., I contend, is modern marriage.....

I say we must legalize what is already being practiced as a custom, as a habit, in modern marriage.... Why legalize it? Because it is illegal [under the federal Comstock law of 1873] and [the laws] of every state, [which] have forbidden the sale of contraceptives [and the dissemination of] information...concerning contraceptives....

[Today] we are bootlegging booze, we are bootlegging in love, we bootleg in sex information, we bootleg in marriage and in divorce. We are the greatest nation of bootleggers the world ever saw, and I am doing the best I can for honesty and decency against the bootlegging of our time.

Hayden: [Couples] are waiting too long for economic security before [having] children.... I would like to have men and women, before we move too lightly into this whole realm of the companionate, realize its contrast to what we call the permanent family relationship.... I would say in the last analysis [marriage] is a psychological relationship in which team work...is the very essence of the whole procedure, playing the game right straight through, taking the bitter with the sweet and not for a single minute regarding the satisfaction or dissatisfaction of momentary sex impulses or economic handicaps...to shake down or away for a single minute that great drive that holds two people together who have made up their minds to play the game clear through....

—*Debate between Denver Juvenile Court Judge Ben B. Lindsey, originator of and leading spokesman for the concept of companionate marriage, and Joel B. Hayden, spiritual leader of Cleveland's Fairmount Presbyterian Church*

MARCH 24 James Gordon Bennett, the elder, who founded the New York *Herald* back in the 1830s, set the pattern for the betrayal of the reader that has been crystallized in journalistic conventions. Bennett sent eight men to cover a horse race and printed three extra editions. We can't improve on that even today.

Bennett frankly appealed to the emotions of his readers, with the emphasis on sex, crime and mystery.... We have never tried publishing a newspaper that would be intellectual instead of emotional.

—**Silas Bent,** *nationally known free-lance journalist and*

author of a 1927 critical examination of American newspapers,
Ballyhoo: The Voice of the Press

Q: What methods can readers employ to bring about an improvement [in the quality of newspapers]?
Bent: I don't see why anybody should read a daily paper. You can get all you want from three or four weekly journals.

MARCH 31   Russia has not given up the idea of a world revolution. It expects it to occur first of all in Asia. Because of the unspeakable poverty of the people, China offers ideal germinating soil to the idea of revolution. And the revolution, if it comes, will not pause at the national frontiers. It will engulf all of Asia.
   —Maurice G. Hindus, *nationally known authority on world affairs, recently returned from the Far East*

APRIL 28   Fall knew, for he took the bribe. Hays knew, for he took Sinclair's bonds for the Republican National Committee and purposely deceived the Senate committee. Mellon knew, for he took some bonds to dispose of and concealed the information from the Senate.
   Harding knew, for he ordered the transformation of the oil reserves from the Navy to the Interior Department. [Secretary of the Navy Edwin] Denby knew, for he signed the order.
   The Republican National Committee must have known where its money was coming from. The stand-pat senators, who tried to form a cordon around the culprits, knew or they wouldn't have tried so hard to defend them.
   Did the cabinet of Harding and Coolidge know? There came a time when they did, and they said nothing....
   Where the meat hangs, there the wolves will gather.
   —James A. Reed, *senator from Missouri and candidate for the Democratic presidential nomination, giving his version of the Teapot Dome scandal before a standing-room-only City Club crowd*

OCTOBER 20   Governor Smith is one of the most dignified men in public life today. He can address a bar association like a lawyer appearing before the Supreme Court. Nobody ever saw Al Smith drunk anyplace. He's the master of his appetites, the master of his soul, the master of his conscience.
   It has often been said that if everyone knew Alfred E. Smith as we know him in New York, his election would be unanimous.
   —Frank P. Walsh, *New York attorney and chairman of the Progressive League for Alfred E. Smith*

OCTOBER 27   Senator Charles Curtis [of Kansas, Republican nominee for vice president on the ticket headed by Hoover], delivered the most smashing, fighting speech of his Ohio campaign.... The senator had declared he could not talk here, due to the condition of his voice, but...he tore into Democratic

1928

doctrines and Democratic candidates with a speech that lasted 30 minutes.

He took his injured hand from the sling in which he has been carrying it, grabbed a huge wooden gavel, swung it in circles around his head, pounded the speaker's table, shook his fist and shouted his defiance of Democratic government.... He spoke until his voice virtually became a whisper.

"[Republicans] have removed 2.5 million taxpayers from the tax rolls of the nation. In 1919 a married man who had an income of $3,000 a year had to pay a tax of $60. Today he does not pay a cent of tax upon an income of $3,500. The man with a $4,000 income in 1919 paid a tax of $120. Today he pays only $5.63.

"Not alone did we reduce taxes for the small salaried man, but we reduced them likewise on the higher tax brackets, so that money which had been in hiding could be brought out and invested in the industries of the nation...."

By this time the senator's necktie was askew, his collar was unbuttoned at his throat and he was swinging his gavel with savage vigor. "Governor Smith will be the worst-defeated candidate in the history of the Democratic Party...."

An aide handed the senator a cough drop. "I don't want any cough drop," he said defiantly....

—Plain Dealer

NOVEMBER 10   Race pride is not an instinct. Children show it not at all. I knew a Mississippian who admitted, "I was nearly 14 years old before I knew I was better than a Negro."

—William Pickens, *executive secretary, NAACP*

DECEMBER 8   I see you encourage professors as members of your club. That's nice, but maybe it accounts somewhat for your club's deficit. Our experience in Montreal is that we can take only so many professors before reaching a saturation point—but, of course, you don't have saturation points down here any more.

—Stephen Leacock, *Canadian humorist and head of the department of political economy at Montreal's McGill University*

1929

The City Club at last moves into a permanent home of its own, at 712 Vincent Avenue. In their comfortable new surroundings members hear strong cries for the end of the city-manager plan and for boss Maurice Maschke's head on a platter. Bertrand Russell announces the death of romantic love and a report from Nicaragua bodes ill for the future, while activist Margaret Sanger advocates birth control for all—but especially for the poor. And little more than a month after the nation's worst stock-market crash, club members—in a reaction that typifies America's continuing blind faith in Wall Street—play out an ironic culmination to the decade of prosperity.

Ida Tarbell

FEBRUARY 9   "[Standard Oil of Indiana chairman] Robert W. Stewart belongs to the old swashbuckling, buccaneering days.... I don't know when we have had anything more outrageous than this Continental Trading Company deal."

Stewart was the leading figure in the Continental Trading Company, out of whose profits Albert Fall was paid $230,000 for his part in the now famous [Teapot Dome] oil-lease scandal.

"Stewart has justified himself by saying the Standard Oil of Indiana made a lot of money. If I were a stockholder—which I am not—I would say I don't want that kind of money.' Why, why—it is a pure piece of theft."

Miss Tarbell shook her head, grayed by years of relentless crusading for right with the pen—"muck-raking," some people have called it....

—Press *account of an address by Ida Tarbell, author of* History of the Standard Oil Company, Life of Abraham Lincoln *and numerous other books*

FEBRUARY 16

> OUST MASCHKE, TURNER URGES
> LASHES G.O.P. CHIEF
> IN VOTE FRAUD EXPOSE
> *Ex-Attorney General's Speech*
> *Greeted With Wild Applause at City Club*
> —Press *headline*

The removal of the old Board of Elections and its clerks [after a state investigation] was the biggest step that could possibly be taken toward clean elections. ...The governor [had] ordered [me] to make a grand jury investigation.... [I] came to Cleveland and was enthusiastically welcomed and supported by your newspapers. Your editors advised everybody to come forward and help. But no one came forward....

Going right to headquarters, I invited both [Republican party boss Maurice] Maschke and [Democratic party boss W. Burr] Gongwer to come in. Mr. Gongwer came, told his story, but gave nothing specific. Mr. Maschke said he would answer any specific questions, but he declined to come and make any recital of what he knew. He said that he was no purist.

When Mr. Maschke told me that he was no purist, I began to feel that things were not right....

—Edward C. Turner, *one month after leaving office as Ohio attorney general*

FEBRUARY 17   *If I am such an undesirable person, why was it that Mr. Turner always sought my support whenever he ran for state office in Ohio?*
    —*Maurice Maschke, quoted in the* News

MARCH 9   The United States is building up a degree of hostility in Latin America with which we will have to deal later, [free-lance

1929

foreign correspondent] Carlton Beals...told the City Club yesterday. Beals achieved...a bewildering amount of publicity when he trekked through the fastnesses of Nicaragua to be the first American to interview [rebel leader] General [Augusto] Sandino....

In his interview with Sandino, Beals said he was told that the general was merely emulating the example of [George] Washington, himself a rebel until he had thrown off foreign yoke....

—News

APRIL 13   Within five years the American people will have become convinced that the 18th Amendment has failed, that it cannot be enforced, and they will thereupon remove it from the Constitution in the same manner in which it was placed there.

For my part, I'll laugh Prohibition to scorn!

—Fiorello H. La Guardia, *Democratic congressman from New York, speaking four years before becoming mayor of New York City*

OCTOBER 29   *Panic selling of securities on the New York Stock Exchange wipes out thousands of investors and begins the country's worst economic collapse.*

NOVEMBER 16   *Somewhat with the feeling of rushing in where angels fear to tread, a number of women accepted the invitation of the City Club to view its new quarters.... Every one of them seemed to voice the same opinion, to wit: "I certainly wouldn't miss coming for I'll probably never get in here again...."*

—Plain Dealer *society-column note by "Tatler"*

NOVEMBER 16   You can take it from me that the 18th Amendment will be repealed only after human slavery has been put back in the Constitution.

—Josephus Daniels, *former secretary of the navy and lifelong advocate of prohibition*

NOVEMBER 23   Romantic love cannot persist toward one person forever, and marriage has outgrown its primitive uses and now faces transition. Man's instincts call for a loosening of the [marriage] bonds.

...For the future I see the possibility of a change which I do not welcome—particularly in Europe. The state will more and more take over the duties of the father, and marriage and the family will disappear. Children will be reared in a kind of universal asylum, and that won't be pleasant.

—Bertrand Russell, *renowned British philosopher and mathematician*

DECEMBER 14   Mrs. Sanger...said that, according to available statistics, 85 million of the 105 million people in the United States have the mentality of a 15-year-old child. There are 45 million

Margaret Sanger

feebleminded persons in the country, she said, and the upper group capable of raising and properly caring for intelligent children numbers only 20 million.

"...Population must be controlled—that is a necessity recognized by all students.... Why should the 20 million who are physically and mentally capable and who compose the upper group assume the burden of supporting the oftentimes mentally deficient offspring of the lower group?

"If a mother is not physically fit to bear a child and the father is economically unable to support it, why should such a couple be permitted to have eight or 10 children? Many of these children are death-doomed anyway. We spend billions yearly to care for the poor families in the lower group. Why not get at the heart of things and spend a good deal less money wisely?

"Federal law...prohibits use of the mails to disseminate information on birth control, but federal law does not interfere with the practices of animal breeding, in which only the wholesome stock is permitted to increase. On the other hand, federal law limits the number of aliens into the country. They must be physically and morally sound and must have a certain amount of capital so that they will not become public charges.

"Why shouldn't the same principles apply in the rearing of families?"

—**Margaret Sanger,** *America's leading advocate for the universal availability of birth control*

DECEMBER 21 [Former University of Michigan professor of economics] David Friday...predicted that in 1930, despite the present business depression, corporations would be able to pay dividends as high as those in 1929.... The year 1930 will bring an industrial-production output greater than that of any year with the possible exception of 1929..., and the business depression now apparent will extend only a month or two into 1930.

...Friday so impressed [City Club members] that following his talk he was besieged by questioners who asked advice on the buying of the "proper stocks."

—Plain Dealer

1930-1938

Help
Wanted

Even the sturdy oak door of the club's new home could not keep the Depression from being felt inside.

1930

Although the impact of the Wall Street debacle is beginning to be felt nationwide, its full force has not yet hit, as evidenced by the large proportion of City Club guests who address topics other than the economy. Psychoanalysis and self-help medicine are derided, while such international matters as fascism and the rising tide of violence in the Middle East are becoming subjects of increasing concern. Toward the end of the year, a last vestige of the carefree, adventurous tenor of the Twenties affects thousands of Clevelanders as they forget their troubles for a day and flock to hear a club-sponsored speaker's enthralling tales of Polar exploration.

JANUARY 4 A dozen years ago everybody was interested in Freudianism. The novelists introduced it into their plots, the essayists were taking a shot at it, the historians were using it to explain historical mysteries and above all the biographers were finding new explanations for the puzzles and problems of the careers of great men. Have you noticed how it has all died down? Psychoanalysis is going out so fast that in another 10 years people who read the literature of 20 years before will wonder what happened.
        —Dr. James J. Walsh, *medical director, Fordham University School of Sociology*

JANUARY 18 The situation today in Europe is no less dangerous than it was in 1914 as far as a war is concerned. Fascism is the danger through which war may come.... Unless fascism is abolished, peace cannot endure in Europe.
        —Count Michael Karolyi, *exiled former president of the short-lived Hungarian Republic*

FEBRUARY 15 If the *Mauretania* sailed at full speed up the Amazon it would take six days to make the trip. That's longer than it takes the Mauretania to cross the Atlantic; one day longer. The Amazon is the longest river in the world. Incidentally, Africa isn't the Dark Continent; South America is. Everybody knows all about Africa, but two thirds of South America has never been seen by a white man.
        —Robert L. Ripley, *creator of the syndicated newspaper cartoon "Believe It or Not," impressing club members with a few hard-to-believe facts*

MARCH 1 My personal objection to capital punishment is simply explained. It is a terrible waste of good guinea pigs. We don't know much about the manner of man that kills. Until we do, we are not going to get far in reducing the homicide rate so long as we kill off our perfectly good laboratory material.
        —Dr. Karl A. Menninger, *nationally known psychiatrist and president of the Menninger Foundation for Psychiatric Education and Research*

1930

MARCH 8 The coming of the Zionists to Palestine has resulted in land values increasing 20-fold, and, as a result, many Arab land holders have grown enormously wealthy. But wealth can never compensate for the presence of the Jews in their midst.

The sight of the Jewish flag beneath the windows of the Mosque of Omar is still enough to enrage any Arab. That is what [caused the bloody anti-Jewish riots of the Twenties] and what will undoubtedly happen again, with this difference, however: The surrounding tribes will probably join in the next outbreak, and the Bedouins will come from Transjordan. When they do, I hope that I am not in Palestine.

 —Vincent Sheean, *journalist, world traveler and author of* An American Among the Riffi

APRIL 5 The man who contributes money to finance a lobby at Washington is just as guilty of corruption as Albert Fall. If you give as little as $1 to an association seeking legislative revisions, then you believe that government is corrupt and you are demonstrating that government can be bought.... People who maintain and contribute to these lobbies lose all sense of honor, and the people are beginning to believe that you can buy anything you want, if you have money enough.

 —Thaddeus H. Caraway, *Democratic senator from Arkansas*

AUGUST 12 There must be a new deal on distribution of the national income....

 —Benjamin C. Marsh, *executive secretary of the People's Lobby, coining a phrase that three years later will gain national currency*

OCTOBER 4 Much concern has been expressed...because of the fact that certain American manufacturers have established factories in foreign countries, and they profess to fear that these manufacturers will transfer business to their foreign plants and import the products thereof to the detriment of American labor....

 —Robert J. Bulkley, *Democratic candidate for the Senate from Ohio, who will win election in November*

NOVEMBER 5 *Rear Admiral Richard Evelyn Byrd [American explorer who flew to the North Pole in 1926, across the Atlantic in 1927 and to the South Pole in 1929]...today gave his endorsement to Cleveland's proposed lake-front airport.... Gazing over the long stretch of land, recently recovered from the lake, and the misty shoreline, the admiral declared, "You have here an ideal landing field for land and sea craft. The trouble with most airports is that they're too far from the center of the city.... I sincerely hope [you] make the most of it."*

 —News

NOVEMBER 6 *[Byrd's City Club-sponsored] visit in Cleve-*

Richard E. Byrd

land...touched the wells of spontaneous and sublime admiration for bravery that springs alike in the six-year-old and the octogenarian. He...packed Public Hall with 12,000 children yesterday afternoon and 10,000 adults last night. Police had to be called at the afternoon session to maintain order among the 5,000 that were turned away....

"Antarctica is 75 degrees colder than the Arctic," he said. "It is covered with eternal snow, is the center of a plateau 10,000 feet high and 500 miles north and south. We never found the eastern limit...."

Lights went out and his [motion pictures] illustrated the rest of his talk.

"To connect the house at Little America, which we established on the Bay of Whales, we made tunnels of snow blocks and food cases. It grew so cold that our Arctic dogs couldn't stand the outside life as they did at the North Pole, and we built kennels along the tunnels.... Our breath rattled, our eyelashes stuck together, and while we worked we had to watch each other's faces to prevent them from freezing...."

His audience held [its] breath at the flight over the high mountain pass to the South Pole plateau and shouted when the camera showed the dropping at the Pole of the American flag....

—News and Plain Dealer accounts

NOVEMBER 17 The [current national self-help] health fad will last no longer than other fads, I believe. People will come to their senses.... They will learn that...a few minutes' reading in the popular magazines and newspapers is no substitute for what it takes a doctor seven years to learn.

—Dr. George E. Follansbee, Cleveland surgeon and member of a national committee performing a survey of the cost of medical care in the United States

NOVEMBER 29 J.S. Newman introduced David Dietz, science editor of the Cleveland Press, as "Admiral Chickie," Arctic explorer.... Dietz, dressed in the uniform of a Swiss admiral, declared that his expedition endorsed three more brands of cigarettes, two more brands of beans and one more make of ginger ale than any other Arctic expedition. He exhibited a photograph of the "cyclone center of the universe," which turned out to be a picture of Pete Witt making a speech to some pelicans.

—Plain Dealer account of the annual City Club Candidates' Field Day

DECEMBER 20 Is Russia a good risk? I find they are good traders and, like everyone else, want to drive as good a bargain as possible. We have found them honorable in their dealings and they have paid according to contract.

...Whatever doubts we may have of Russia's [five-year] plan, it is the best plan for industrialization ever conceived. It is one of the wonderful conceptions of history. Just imagine what

1930

would happen if all American industries were operated under the Russian plan....

—**W.J. Austin,** *president of the Austin Company, a Cleveland engineering firm hired by Russia to construct a $60-million automobile factory and industrial city popularly known as "Austingrad"*

1931

The country's population is now 122 million, of which nearly five million are unemployed. Yet as the nation and the world descend into the abyss of depression, much of the City Club's year is devoted to the discussion of local issues. Peter Witt hammers away at questions of public transportation, the seemingly endless feud between the municipal light plant and the Illuminating Company erupts into open war and another new initiative to toss out the city manager plan is introduced. By far the most arresting sessions occur in October, when City Manager Hopkins lashes out publicly at his quondam mentor, Maurice Maschke. The following week, Maschke makes headlines when he breaks with his own longstanding policy and goes public with a vitriolic denunciation of Hopkins.

FEBRUARY 7   Repeal of the Prohibition statutes would help prosperity by increasing the demand for white aprons, cuspidors, brass knuckles, corn, hops and limburger cheese. But it would shrink the market for shotguns, home-bottling and -capping apparatus, wash boilers, wood alcohol, corn sugar and tombstones, and cut the purchasing power of policemen, judges and politicians.
   —**Jack Raper**

FEBRUARY 21   A period of prosperity is an unhealthy situation, but Americans cannot see it. The things we do in prosperity, but which we can do without, should be postponed until business begins to decline. Public works should be planned so that they can be started when an industrial slump begins, and industry should make similar preparations for its own protection.
   All that is required is a few brains, but they are scarce....
   —**C.C. Arbuthnot,** *professor of economics, Western Reserve University*

MARCH 7   The net result of our helping to build up the [Soviet] government will be that we will lose a billion dollars worth of American exports...during the next four years. ...Our manufacturers have furnished the tractors, cotton gins, saw mills and other equipment which has made the Russian five-year plan successful.
   ...Lenin, who was a great man, was right when he said that capitalists will commit suicide for a temporary profit.
   —**Hamilton Fish, Jr.,** *Republican congressman from New York*

MARCH 14 The bootlegger insists on knowing who his patrons are because he is wary of stool pigeons, knowing that they mean trouble for him. In the same way, the saloonkeeper or the wholesaler would be cautious in his sales if he knew he would be held to account under laws of civil liability for wrongs done by a customer....

—**Robert C. Binkley,** *professor of history at Western Reserve University, advocating repeal of Prohibition and creation of a system by which a liquor dealer would be held liable for damage done by patrons under the influence of alcohol he had sold them*

MARCH 21 The Cleveland Electric Illuminating Company has shown the way in giving six rate reductions..., the natural result of the installation of modern equipment, low generating costs, new transmission and distribution methods, interconnection, quantity production and enormous load increases. ...The influence of the [Municipal Electric Light Plant] on rates is nil, and will, in my opinion, remain so.

—**Howell Wright,** *former public utilities director of Cleveland*

Q: Do you mean to stand there and say that a private corporation reduces its rates out of charity just because it bought new equipment?

Wright: I thought I answered that.

OCTOBER 10 What is there in this manager plan that will give us better government by taking the power of picking the chief executive away from the people...? If a mayor must play politics, isn't it reasonable to suppose that a manager must play politics with 13 councilmen, all of whom are politicians, in order to get his job and keep it?

The records will show that the first manager was chosen by the council, but I strongly suspect a meeting in a little green room in [the Hotel Hollenden] had something to do with it. Mr. Maschke and Mr. Gongwer, the [political] bosses who were to be driven out of power, were at that meeting. ...No, politics has not been eliminated by the manager plan.

—**Saul S. Danaceau,** *Cleveland attorney, City Club member and author of a charter proposal to return Cleveland to the mayor-council form of city government*

OCTOBER 17 During the last 20 years the people of Cleveland have allowed [Maurice Maschke] to build up under every form of administration a power which is at last complete. He has *become* the Republican organization. His word determines the choice of Republican candidates for local office. He has grown strong enough, through the use of public money and patronage and power, to choose openly a political chief executive....

No Tammany chief ever was more contemptuous of law or the public will. None ever pursued with more singleness of

1931

purpose the business of extracting private profit from government. How far has this sort of thing gone? Ask any contractor...any officer in the police department...any representative of any company which sells city equipment...[or] any city employee.

...Cleveland has the dubious distinction of being possessed by the last of the personal bosses and he will leave no personal successor. But, as in other cities, Cleveland must expect an effort to prolong the power of the boss through a corrupt oligarchy composed of former subordinates such as those which still curse New York and Philadelphia and Pittsburgh.

The profits of gang rule are never willingly surrendered....

—William R. Hopkins, *candidate for Cleveland city council on an "Overthrow Maschke" platform, attacking his erstwhile ally*

OCTOBER 24 I cannot but believe that a mind capable of directing public charges...against other persons without a single syllable of proof and based solely upon the irresponsible imputations heard on street corners is shown to be reckless to the point of depravity....

...It is evident upon the undeniable facts that there are two Mr. Hopkinses—one the bland, plausible pseudo-idealist, carrying the torch of civic uplift and parading, as his own original pretended credo, the rhetoric of magazine authors and writers of books; the other Hopkins, the real Hopkins, at once the product and apostle of political opportunism who, in his franchise-seeking, in his office-seeking or in his quest for power and personal gain, knew neither right nor left, trafficking indiscriminately with both Democrats and Republicans....

Such a man is unsafe in public office, unsound as a leader in a public cause. No government, national, state or local, has ever made progress with a liar and a hypocrite at the head of it.

The true Hopkins is false, spurious, hypocritical, treacherous; [a] poseur and phrasemaker; a man whose inherent propensity for deception has put him back on the sidewalk, where Gongwer and I picked him up in 1923.

—Maurice Maschke, *replying to Hopkins's attack*

OCTOBER 26 *Maurice Maschke abandoned a lifetime rule last Saturday against making speeches except at Republican organization meetings....*
—Press *editorial*

Maurice Maschke

OCTOBER 28 We've reached the philosophy where we'll have to accept a criminal government or a revolution.... We can't control crime until we control the economic forces, such as the power trust. We must repeal privileges and franchises. But the Russians say we can't do that step by step. We must do it all at once, and that would be revolution. The depressions will go on until they force us. I had hoped the present one would do it, but I'm afraid not. It won't last long enough.

—Lincoln Steffens, *author of* Shame of the Cities *and other muck-raking exposes*

NOVEMBER 21 If we are to have a situation where the perverted patriotism of the [Daughters of the American Revolution], the stupidity of the Ku Klux Klan or the special interests of political parties are allowed to interfere with universities, these institutions might well perish.
—**Herbert A. Miller,** *former professor of sociology at Ohio State University, who was fired for espousing liberal views on race and opposing compulsory military training at the university*

DECEMBER 5 President Hoover, after faltering himself for the past two years, will now try to hurry Congress into doing something [about creating national unemployment insurance]. The President appears to have been very slow to recognize the existence of the Depression.
—**Robert J. Bulkley**

1932

The unemployed number some 13 million as incumbent Herbert Hoover and New York Governor Franklin D. Roosevelt vie for the Presidency. The City Club hears partisans of both candidates as well as stirring mayoral-campaign speeches, after the voters renounce the city-manager charter and return Cleveland to a mayor-council form of government. Huey Long makes a pitch to share the nation's wealth, and late in the year the City Club becomes the first public forum in the country to hear a detailed explanation of Technocracy, a theory propounded by a group of scientists and engineers who foresee a revolution of the unemployed unless the social and economic systems are changed radically under the control of technologically minded thinkers. Indicative of the deepening desperation of the American people for some way out of the Depression, Technocracy's hold on the public's imagination is immediate and formidable. Within two months of its debut, however, it will be almost completely forgotten.

JANUARY 10 *There they were, those fat gentlemen who never missed a meal in their lives, shaking hands with me. Those gentlemen—the same crowd who beat me up at a council meeting at City Hall a year ago—were so friendly I thought they were going to kiss me.*

We sat down to lunch first. There was I, a Bolshevik, eating chicken at The Hollenden. I know I ate $2 worth. It was the best meal I ever had in my life. On three meals like that I could live a month. If I'm elected mayor, comrades, I'm going to try to get you just one meal like it.

Well, when the eating was over they invited me to speak

1932

first.... Think of that, comrades: They gave me $150 worth of capitalistic radio [time] to broadcast the gospel of Karl Marx....
—I.O. Ford, *Communist Party candidate for mayor of Cleveland, describing his previous day's appearance at the City Club's mayoral candidates' debate to 1,300 supporters in Public Auditorium*

JANUARY 22   On the recommendation of President Hoover, Congress creates the Reconstruction Finance Corporation, a federally funded effort to restore confidence in the monetary system by providing loans to banks, insurance companies and railroads.

JANUARY 23   The Reconstruction Finance Corporation is a federal dole to the corporations. Why not one to the jobless and starving people? We are told that it would demoralize their characters. It is only government cash that demoralizes, they pretend. Cash from private relief funds and local organizations does not demoralize.

Bunk! The government will have to come to the dole. And that, sooner than it expects.
—Oswald Garrison Villard, *nationally known liberal thinker and editor of* The Nation

MARCH 19   I'll utter a prophecy: If you keep this atrocious [mayor-council] system, you'll have not Tom L. Johnsons and Newton D. Bakers, but a succession of [incompetents]. Count on it, you'll be in trouble.
—Augustus R. Hatton

APRIL 2   [Former Secretary of the Treasury Andrew] Mellon advocated and, through political control over Congress, brought about tremendous reductions in the tax rates on upper-bracket incomes. He cut the millionaires' surtax to less than one third its former figure. To do it he backed a campaign of learned propaganda to the effect that great wealth must be released from taxation for purposes of production, even though a greater portion of the burden would then be carried by the poorer man.

When this pretty-sounding theory resulted in increased production far beyond the country's power to consume, the economic crash occurred....
—Gifford Pinchot, *liberal Republican governor of Pennsylvania and himself a multimillionaire*

APRIL 9   Individuals and corporations are finding it impossible to meet federal taxation extorted with all the ruthlessness of the Germans in Belgium. ...The course which our rulers have laid out for us...will bring upon us a fall like the fall of the Dutch Republic and the Roman Empire. No serious thought of retrenchment [from continually raising taxes] appears to have entered the heads of our office-holding tyrants.

If you are to exist, you must tear these weasels from the throat

Huey P. Long

of the nation.

—Robert Rutherford McCormick, *editor and publisher, Chicago* Tribune

APRIL 23 We ought to quit whittlin' away at the tariff and at Prohibition—although I'd like to have a good drink myself, right now—and...abolish hunger, the real enemy of mankind in this land of plenty. ...[And] there ought to be a limit to the amount of money any man can accumulate to the destruction of anyone else.

In 1928, when the country was supposed to be prosperous, 435 independent retail businesses were failing every day. Take six retail stores, whose employees formerly would be in a position to buy six Packards, six Buicks, six Dodges and six Fords. One chain store has taken their place, with a manager getting $18 a week. He couldn't buy a foghorn on a steamboat.

...Any man who says he doesn't know how the country can be rescued from its predicament either has his head in a half bushel or is looking through the wrong end of a telescope. One thing is sure: We're facing an evolution or a revolution in the United States in 10 years.

—Huey P. Long, *Democratic senator from Louisiana, advocating redistribution of the nation's wealth*

MAY 29 ***The first of some 17,000 World War veterans arrive in Washington to demand immediate payment of their "soldiers' bonus." Federal troops under General Douglas MacArthur drive them out on July 28th.***

OCTOBER 15 Time and again Governor Roosevelt has pointed out that the way to restore prosperity is to spread the buying power of the American public; to restore agriculture in order that through the prosperity of agriculture industry and commerce may be restored.

The policy of the other side is to stimulate production from the top....

—Raymond Moley, *Columbia University professor, adviser to Democratic presidential candidate Franklin D. Roosevelt and soon to be unofficial chief of Roosevelt's "Brain Trust"*

OCTOBER 28 We don't know who should go to college. We don't actually know that education is any good. It requires faith; we cannot prove it.

At Chicago we changed the system. We removed the restrictions. A student is not required to attend classes. We feel that if he comes for the purpose of obtaining an education he will attend. And results have been very satisfactory.

—Robert Maynard Hutchins, *33-year-old president of the University of Chicago*

NOVEMBER 5 Monday, piffle; Tuesday, bushwa; Wednesday, buncombe; Thursday, hooey; Friday, baloney; Saturday, bull;

1932

Sunday, applesauce.

—**Jack Raper,** *classifying the content of political speeches in the last days of the 1932 presidential campaign*

Howard Scott

DECEMBER 3 [Technocracy project director Howard] Scott envisages a continent in which there is technical control—a technocracy—where there is no price system, no business, no foreign trade, no insurance, no philanthropy, no borrowing, no lending and no wages, yet in which each person has security, each person must work or starve, and the standard of living is 10 times as high as in 1929.

This could be done with no one working before the age of 25 or after 45, and with persons between those ages working only...four days a week and four hours a day.

"At the present rate of technological advance," [said Scott], "three years will see 20 million to 25 million unemployed in this country. The question, then, is whether the [current] system can carry them without this crowd overthrowing the system....

"The increase of the energy output of industry is irreversible. We are compelled to go forward continually with the substitution of mechanical energy for the hand work of men.... Despite the fact that we have increased our output-per-man enormously, 76 percent of all the wealth we produce by machine is turned back into industry for the creation of further debt.

"In the face of these figures, the philosophies of government all the way from Plato to Karl Marx are intellectual approaches to dementia praecox. [Social change] can be brought about only by the extension of technology with the aid of those driven by social extremity.... Social change is proportional as the rate of approach from the front of the stomach to the spine. As that distance becomes less, through necessity there will be more action."

—Press *and* Plain Dealer *accounts*

1933

As the Depression worsens, President Roosevelt begins to institute such New Deal programs as the National Recovery Administration (NRA), which are welcomed by an American people who have come close to losing all hope for recovery. But by the middle of the year, after the "New Deal Honeymoon" ends, many people—especially businessmen—question the wisdom of deficit spending, government intervention in commerce and large-scale federal relief programs. Although opposition to Roosevelt's policies grows (and many wonder if the President is not, in fact, a "dictator"), the pattern for a new relationship between the public and private sectors has been set.

The City Club hears speakers from both sides of the FDR question, as well as an early, ominous warning about the true nature of Adolf Hitler's regime.

JANUARY 28 If I get hit by a taxi on my way to the City Club today, I fail to see why the government should take care of me. And yet hospitalization of this very character for war veterans costs the government $2 million a year.

—**Ernest Angell,** *former Cleveland attorney, husband of* New Yorker *magazine fiction editor Katharine Angell, World War veteran and nationally known opponent of increased veterans' benefits*

MARCH 4   Modern cities today are planned in the interests of downtown land owners, and government "of, by and for the people" has become [merely] a nice phrase. Bus interests in the future, I warn you, will be the...private dictators of city policies, just as electric railway companies were two or three decades ago.

—**Paul Blanshard,** *director of the City Affairs Committee of New York City and a leader in the fight against Tammany Hall corruption which resulted in the resignation of Mayor James J. Walker*

APRIL 15   First, federal relief adequate to meet the minimum needs of hungry, distressed people suffering from long unemployment. We have recommended appropriation of not less than $1 billion....

Second, a huge public works program to involve expenditure of $5 billion [for] construction of public buildings, highways, eliminations of grade crossings, reforestation, flood and soil-erosion control, reclamation and other governmental projects designed to supply work at decent wages for those who are now idle.

—**William Green,** *former head of the United Mine Workers and current successor to Samuel Gompers as president of the American Federation of Labor, proposing the A.F. of L.'s program for national recovery*

OCTOBER 14   Germany could not start a war for another 10 years, and I don't know of any other nation that could....

In my opinion, much is owed to Germany—her saving of the world from Bolshevism was one of the greatest feats of modern times. [And] we must remember that the Hitler government *does* stand for capitalism.

—**Karl F. Geiser,** *head of the political science department of Oberlin College, Oberlin, Ohio*

NOVEMBER 18   [President Roosevelt's] whole life is defiance of tradition.... One grouch once told me, "Hoover could never learn anything new, and Roosevelt could never learn anything old."

—**Paul Mallon,** *Washington correspondent, North American Newspaper Alliance*

NOVEMBER 25   The thing we most need to get back on our feet is confidence in banks, which some bankers undermined. I can imagine nothing that will so give confidence as insurance of

1933

deposits. But bankers fought it bitterly, just as they did the Federal Reserve Act....

I [could] make a jury of monkeys understand the soundness of insurance which will mean that the deposit slip will be treated like a government bond.

 —Henry B. Steagall, *Democratic congressman from Alabama and coauthor of the Glass-Steagall Banking Act of June 1933, which created the Federal Deposit Insurance Corporation (FDIC)*

DECEMBER 5 *Prohibition is repealed.*

Dorothy Thompson

DECEMBER 9 No matter what may be asserted, we foreign correspondents in Berlin—only two are Jews—pooled all our information and concluded that hundreds if not thousands had been murdered; that hundreds, maybe thousands, had been tortured and thousands of others sent to concentration camps....

More than 60,000 Jews have been dispersed over the face of the earth by Hitler's Jewish persecutions. Even that Jesus was an Aryan is to be taught now. ...His basis of attack was that the Germans didn't lose the war at the front, but were stabbed in the back by communists, Jews and capitalists at home.

Hitler withdrew from the League of Nations for the express purpose of keeping foreign investigators out of industrial plants where armaments are being made on a gigantic scale.... In the next two years we shall see in Germany the rise of the greatest military power in the world.

 —Dorothy Thompson, *longtime foreign correspondent, syndicated columnist and wife of novelist Sinclair Lewis, who will be expelled from Germany in 1934 for her anti-Nazi writings*

1934

The New Deal seems to be making some headway toward recovery, but its more radical provisions —not to mention a widespread and deepening concern over the 20 percent increase in the national debt—are stoking the fires of anti-Roosevelt feeling in many parts of the country. In addition to its domestic worries, America begins to pay more attention to world affairs, as evidenced by City Club speakers who offer sharper warnings about the militaristic attitudes of Germany, Italy and Japan. The club also hears John Dewey's explanation of the origins of the Depression and—a full 30 years before the publication of Marshall McLuhan's famous treatise—critic Gilbert Seldes's theory that the medium is the message.

FEBRUARY 3 The Japanese militarists...may make some sort of spectacular move outside of Japan to distract attention from the bad economic situation at home. This move may take the form of war against Russia, or possibly the United States....

 —Grover Clark, *writer and editor in the Far East*

FEBRUARY 10   Any time you try to control the New York Stock Exchange you've got your hands full. But we've got the goods on them this time. If [the Fletcher-Rayburn stock-exchange bill, to be introduced in Congress the following day] passes, you'll be able to speculate, of course, but you'll do it with your own money and not with other people's.

[The bill] will take away the weapons which the trader uses—the tools of options, secrecy, credit, fictitious activity, short selling and alliance with either specialists or floor traders. It will put a powerful check on the gambling operations of officers and directors and insiders of corporations....

   —John T. Flynn, *economist, writer and co-drafter of the Fletcher-Rayburn bill*

FEBRUARY 24   With the...power that existed in concentrated wealth, it was inevitable that government would eventually become a mere reflex and shadow of economic power. Jefferson saw it coming [and] feared industrialism as a menace to democracy; Lincoln saw it [and] warned against it; Cleveland, Roosevelt, Wilson—all saw the danger.

But the war boom came on and the idea began to prevail that these few had given us prosperity and therefore were the proper guardians of our destiny. Government of the people for the people by the people became, actually, government of corporate interests for corporate interests, and we condoned it in the hope that the resulting benefits would indirectly come on down to us.

Centralized control of industry and finance in a few hands has now outlived its usefulness. ...The time has come when the government must go into partnership, not with business alone but with all the people, including the consumer and laborer.

   —John Dewey, *noted education theorist and pragmatist philosopher, Columbia University*

MARCH 3   Every new form of an art draws off the worth from the thing it supplants. For instance, [talking] motion pictures drew off the melodrama of the silent film. The phonograph drew off comic recitation from vaudeville. Radio is [...now] the universal sewer of the arts. It has taken over the vaudeville sketch and the stage comedian and turned them into comic strips like *Amos and Andy*. Each time there is a change in an art it is necessary to simplify and vulgarize it.

   —Gilbert Seldes, *playwright, critic, editor and writer for the* New Republic *and* Saturday Evening Post

MARCH 10   Russian prisons are like colleges, only with a lot more fun. There are no walls or even fences. Prisoners work and attend academic and trade schools in the prison or nearby. They are permitted to have their families, on the theory that they are being reformed. For good conduct they get two weeks' vacation.

   —Fred C. Kelly, *offering impressions garnered from a recent trip to the Soviet Union*

1934

APRIL 14 I venture that if we went to war with Japan, our men would be mowed down by munitions sold to the Japanese by American makers. As to [military] preparedness as peace insurance, you have but to note the American-Canadian border, entirely unarmed, to give that idea the lie.
—**Gerald P. Nye,** *Republican senator from North Dakota*

OCTOBER 13 This project has been opposed, I think shortsightedly, by the railroads. Careful studies show it will not hurt the railroads; on the contrary, its effect will be to create many thousand tons of additional tonnage just as did the Panama Canal, which railroad men also opposed.
—**Frank P. Walsh,** *chairman of the Power Authority of New York, arguing in favor of the proposed St. Lawrence Seaway to connect the Great Lakes and the Atlantic Ocean*

OCTOBER 17 While the Tennessee Valley [rural electrification] experiment may do much present good, it will create nothing of permanent value, because all its improvements come from the creation of new debts...

I believe Mr. Roosevelt is sincere in his desire to bring about recovery, but he lacks knowledge of the underlying economics. To orthodox capitalism, his financing of consumption is... lunacy.
—**Fred Henderson,** *British engineer, economist and author of* Economic Consequences of Power Production

OCTOBER 27 However dull the [1890s] appear to us today, there were many items to which we held fast. We all knew what it meant to be an American, we all believed only an act of God would stop what we regarded as the certain, inevitable future of America. We had confidence—much of it unjustified, of course...—that if we did certain things well we should have the privilege of living satisfactory lives.

The really important books [of recent years] have tended to destroy confidence..., and now we are ready and anxious for a new confidence and waiting for someone to lead us to it.
—**Henry Seidel Canby,** *editor,* Saturday Review of Literature

NOVEMBER 10 Perhaps, when you worry about business, about the currency and the future at Washington, you may say to yourself, "If only a man on horseback should come." You perhaps think then there would be no strikes, but compulsory arbitration; perhaps no Congress to do strange things; trains on time and everything smoothly running. But try it for three years and you will see.
—**Giuseppe A. Borgese,** *Italian exile and professor of international relations at Smith College, discussing the dangerous allure of fascism*

NOVEMBER 14 *Their chief function in the community seems*

to be to arouse suspicion, stir up opposition to reforms which do not originate with them and to vent their personal spleen in unbridled and totally unwarranted attacks on individuals and organizations which are sincerely trying to bring about constructive improvements in government and administration.
—Mayo Fesler, director of Cleveland's Citizens League, denouncing the members of the club's Soviet Table in the league's monthly bulletin

NOVEMBER 15   *That sounds like a pretty good description of the table.*
—Edward W. Doty, charter member of the Soviet Table

Mayo Fesler

NOVEMBER 16   *Masters of negation today were hailing as brethren members of the City Club Soviet Table for their creation of the post of "honorary non-life member" for Mayo Fesler.... The appointment...was announced today by [Cleveland attorney] Edward S. Crudele, secretary-treasurer of the table group.*

"Because of Mr. Fesler's publicity in our behalf," explained Mr. Crudele, "the membership fee of the table has gone up from $2.25 to $5.10 overnight. Also, the fee for anyone to have his name taken off the table is now $100."

Exact definition of Mr. Fesler's non-life membership was not forthcoming.
—Press

NOVEMBER 17   If a President is a boob, [newspapermen] are the first to turn away from him. If he has personality and nothing else, as Harding had, they may be kinder to him than they should.
—Drew Pearson, *coauthor (with Robert S. Allen) of the syndicated newspaper column "Washington Merry-Go-Round," explaining the dearth of early reporting on the Teapot Dome scandals*

DECEMBER 22   Many women have passed part of their work to other women, such as laundry workers, but that is no gain for women in general. A comparatively few capable women have succeeded in making notable careers outside the home, but the great majority...are essentially homemakers.
—Dr. Ralph Borsodi, *originator of the subsistence homestead plan, which recommends that families leave cities and live on small, self-sustaining farms*

1935

Little more than a decade after its introduction, commercial radio has become ubiquitous, and both Roosevelt and his detractors—most notably Michigan's anti-communist, pro-fascist Father Charles E. Coughlin—use the medium to spread their gospels nationwide. Dr. Francis Townsend prefers a more personal approach as he crisscrosses the country drumming up support for his idea of a national old-age pension, even after the Social Security Act is signed into law in August.

1935

While conservatives curse "the dole" and insist that the unemployed simply do not want to work, welfare agencies struggle to feed and clothe millions in poverty. In Cleveland, local relief administrator Marc J. Grossman uses the City Club Forum to make a stirring defense of relief efforts, in one of the most impassioned speeches of the club's early years. And in December, newly elected reform mayor Harold Burton (who in 1945 will become the second City Club member to be named a justice of the U.S. Supreme Court) chooses as Cleveland's new safety director a former Chicagoan of untouchable character by the name of Eliot Ness.

JANUARY 19   So far as the race is concerned, we see inferiority more and more placed at a premium. One of our rules is to make every provision to shelter the physical and mental defectives so they may propagate their kind. Millions are spent annually to maintain institutions for the feebleminded, correction homes, epileptic colonies, reformatories and penitentiaries. Every year some new philanthropy is established, endowed with millions to save human life in some way. Of course, this is only human; no one would advocate abandoning these poor unfortunates.

But how long shall we disregard Mother Nature's ace in the hole...?

—**Dr. Roy W. Scott,** *physician in chief, City Hospital of Cleveland*

MARCH 14   If Hitler is overthrown, anti-Semitism will soon disappear. That is not a common attitude of the German people. But the Nazis will never give up their persecution of the Jews.

—**Gerhart Seger,** *German Social Democratic leader who fled to the United States after escaping from the Oranienburg concentration camp, where he had been imprisoned for his political views*

MARCH 30   There are 75 books whose titles can be obtained from the American Library Association which contain the whole of our social progress, but even among [university] students I find only six of them read.

—**Mortimer J. Adler,** *professor of the philosophy of law at the University of Chicago, decrying a general lack of attention to the classics, which 10 years later he will attempt to remedy as associate editor of the* Great Books of the Western World

APRIL 3   Cancer is curable. The most important thing to remember is the necessity of early recognition and treatment. If all cases of cancer could be diagnosed early and treated promptly [with X-rays, radium or surgery] in their incipient stages, the death rate from this disease could be reduced by many thousands.

—**Dr. Malcolm T. MacEachern,** *associate director, American College of Surgeons*

Marc J. Grossman

APRIL 6 The Soviet Union was the initiator and chief promoter of nonaggression pacts, and we are ready to sign [them] with all countries in the world. ...Anything in the nature of a donation to the cause of peace will find in our country the most ardent supporter and partisan.

—**Alexander A. Troyanovsky,** *first Soviet ambassador to the United States, speaking to one of the City Club's largest crowds*

The stocky ambassador, who himself served as an artillery officer with distinction through two wars, said war preparations [in Europe] today were on a greater scale than before the World War. He pictured the next conflict as far deadlier than any seen before.

"Physics and chemistry," he said, "will produce new weapons for annihilation...."

—Press

APRIL 29 *When they leave you out of a City Club show, you must be getting old. Well, I've been beaten before and I've come back.... I'll be in next year's show if I have to turn political handsprings down Euclid Avenue. Yes, sir, I'll do something ridiculous and they'll have to acknowledge it.*

—*Maurice Maschke, former Republican Party boss of Cleveland who was a "character" in 21 of the City Club's 22 Anvil Revues, vowing to win back the spotlight in the 1936 edition of the show*

OCTOBER 19 This growing bureaucracy, this centralizing of power in Washington and in the hands of the executive, will, if continued, snuff out all signs of state rights and state responsibilities. A study of this philosophy can lead to but one conclusion —a dictatorship by our executive....

—**Chester C. Bolton,** *Republican congressman from Ohio*

DECEMBER 8 I have invested some money in the Irish Sweepstakes each year [and] I see no reason why I shouldn't invest in a state lottery to help pay public expenses.

—**Howard Kahn,** *anti-crime crusading editor of the St. Paul (Minnesota)* Daily News, *advocating state-run lotteries*

DECEMBER 14 And so they come to us; men like yourselves, many of them, who after steeling themselves for days against the ordeal of asking for help, turn back at the door of the relief office, overcome with shame. Or, having entered, cannot bring themselves to ask for bread, but beg for work instead. Pinched faces at home ultimately bring the surrender, and at last they are among that army of the condemned—strangely silent and isolated in our...city.

...You hear it said that relief is made too attractive—that industry has difficulty prying the relief client loose of relief.

1935

Well, let's see. Yes, we try to maintain food on the basis of the average minimum subsistence allowance of the United States Children's Bureau. About 20 cents, on the average, per person per day. That's the best we can do.... Clothing we give on an emergency basis.... Shelter and rent? Well, you landlords...know all about that. Fine men, women and little children evicted as many as eight or 10 times a year....

These people on [direct] relief [as opposed to WPA-type work relief] are among those everyday Americans so often called the bone and sinew of the nation. But what kind of men and women will they be after long years of enforced idleness, after years of daily spiritual, mental and economic stress—and what kind of children will they raise?

—**Marc J. Grossman,** *chairman of the Cuyahoga County Relief Committee, making one of the nation's first public defenses of relief clients*

DECEMBER 16 *Marc J. Grossman, in his stirring speech at the City Club Saturday, gave effective answer to the wishful-thinking school of relief criticism, as well as to that small but voiceful group of Bourbons who "believe they can keep themselves safely on the roof by driving the masses further into the pits." ...Cleveland is fortunate that Grossman...has the courage and force to jolt us out of [our] apathy....*
—Plain Dealer *editorial*

1936

C ivil War breaks out in Spain as Italy continues to crush opposition in Ethiopia, which it invaded the year before. In the American West, the Dust Bowl sends thousands to California seeking a new life, while President Roosevelt—opposed in editorials by most of the country's newspapers—carries all but two states in defeating Kansas Governor Alf Landon to win his second term. The Great Lakes Exposition begins its two-year run in Cleveland, providing a boost for the morale of an economically beleaguered region and an indication of the commercial potential of the city's long-neglected lake front.

Nazi Germany's potential threat to peace in Europe is more widely acknowledged in America, and fears grow that the country may again become "entangled" in a foreign war. Yet a clear understanding of Naziism's ultimate aims is not universal, as evidenced by the ease with which the City Club finds a spirited defender of Hitler for a Forum debate.

JANUARY 4 I know how wars are got up—I helped do the work. We make 'em believe the cause is holy, as we did when we went over to Europe and told the boys they were defending their homes against pillage and their womenfolk against worse.

We ask them, "Are you worms or men?" We whip them up with music and drilling and uniforms. We invent the term "slacker," the preachers help by declaring it's God's own cause—and a little group sits about a table and gloats, "They're so dumb, we can feed 'em anything."

My God! Are you going to let them use you as suckers again?

—Smedley D. Butler, *retired U.S. Marine Corps major general, arguing for an isolationist America protected by purely defensive military forces*

FEBRUARY 1 **Auhagen:** Suppression of the Jews was made necessary because Germany had thousands of young men who, in looking for employment, found the Jews had a stronghold on the legal and medical professions in particular.... The entire directorate of the Supreme Court, for example, was made up of Jews. Fifty percent of doctors in Berlin hospitals were Jews. ...I don't deny they were good lawyers and doctors, but the fact remains there were thousands of Germans who found these professions practically closed to them....

The news of the violence against the Jews and others [that was] printed in American newspapers was grossly exaggerated by correspondents who were none too friendly to Germany —many of them having been kicked out and others on the verge of being kicked out of the country. Go to Germany and see for yourselves that there no longer is any of the violence or terrorism....

Seger: If Hitler has 90 percent of the nation behind him, why does he have a secret police force of 62,000 men, 53 concentration camps and numerous revived jails and penitentiaries? Why did the Nazis fail to give the people the free election they promised for 1935 if they were so sure of the backing of the nation?

...Anything [positive] that Hitler and the Nazis have accomplished was at too high a price. ...If one has lived in a concentration camp as I have, and borne the traces on his back, and if one has a gray-haired wife at 30, you will pardon [my making] the distinction between "Nazis" and "gentlemen."

—Debate between Frederick E. Auhagen, professor of engineering at Columbia University, and Gerhart Seger

FEBRUARY 15 After freeing Manchuria from Czarist rule in the war with Russia, Japan could not very well leave it to the threat of communism. She has set up a government incomparably better than anywhere in China.... The territory now is much safer....

With an orderly China there will be nothing more for Japan to desire....

—Seijiro Yoshizawa, *counselor of the Japanese Embassy, Washington, D.C.*

FEBRUARY 22 When a patient has a severe pain, the physician administers a narcotic. Then if future doses are demanded, the physician knows the great danger of making a drug fiend. Our great danger in this relief matter is doing just that—making

1936

permanent relief patients.

—Laurens Hamilton, *Republican state assemblyman of New York and great-great-grandson of Alexander Hamilton*

MARCH 14   Childbirth is a relatively minor cause of death among women of the United States, exceeded twice over by automobile accidents and surpassed to a greater degree by 10 other causes, Dr. Scott C. Runnels [chief obstetrician of Cleveland's Huron Road Hospital] told a City Club audience.

...The belief that home delivery is safer than hospitalization is highly erroneous, he said, [and] there is not the slightest evidence that babies are marked by mothers becoming frightened by elephants....

—News *and* Plain Dealer *accounts*

APRIL 18   In Japan, alone among the advanced countries of the world, specific provision is made by the constitution, supplemented by Imperial ordinance, that the heads of the military and naval establishments shall not be subjected to the control of the civil heads, including the foreign office....

It does not need to be pointed out that so long as Japan possesses a government of this sort, she is necessarily a danger to the entire international community.

—Tswen Ling Tsui, *second secretary of the Chinese Embassy, Washington, D.C.*

OCTOBER 17   Q: Is Roosevelt mortgaging future generations?

Johnson: Any long-term debt has got to be paid by future generations. Whether it's an unbearable burden, I don't know. I lived in a sod house on the prairie once, and [compared to that] the way the younger generation lives now is duck soup.

Q: How close to the Constitution should the government stay in times of economic stress?

Johnson: During the [World] War we suppressed the press, we put in Prohibition, we took over the railroads and telegraph lines, and there wasn't much authority in the Constitution for the draft law. We did what we thought we had to do to win the war. I don't know what the limits are.

Q: You're speaking of war times. I asked about times of economic stress.

Johnson: I wouldn't care whether I was starving to death or being shot to death—the problem would be the same to me.

—Question-and-answer period following the address of General Hugh S. Johnson, former administrator of the National Recovery Administration

DECEMBER 5   *Elected or not, I shall jolly well marry whom I please.*

—Howell Leuck, Cleveland attorney, campaigning for a City Club director's seat at the annual Candidates' Field Day, five days before England's Edward VIII abdicates his throne to marry Wallis Warfield Simpson

Hugh S. Johnson

DECEMBER 12 Unless they move fast to catch up with public opinion, Republicans may find themselves playing the same role in the next few decades that the Democrats have played since the Civil War—the role of the minority party. ...Political parties, if they want to be successful, must scrap their 100-year-old tactics and adjust themselves to the "streamlined" age....

These were some of the views expressed yesterday by Dr. George Gallup, director of the American Institute of Public Opinion....

—Plain Dealer *account of a speech by Gallup, whose pre-election poll was the only one in the nation to correctly predict a Roosevelt landslide*

1937

Tensions build in Europe as the Spanish Civil War drags on and Germany and Italy grow more bold in their support of the rebels under General Francisco Franco. After a decade of bitter rivalry, Chinese nationalists under Chiang Kai-shek and communists under Mao Tse-tung form a united front against Japanese forces attempting to overrun their country. At home, charges of "dictator" become more frequent as Roosevelt attempts to "pack" the Supreme Court with his own appointees. Much New Deal legislation is tied up by the judiciary, and the general lack of action on the domestic front, a precipitous slide in stock prices and growing fears about the European situation produce a widespread national malaise.

FEBRUARY 20 All across the American continent, at the heart of every county seat, the tower of a county courts building stands as a symbol of justice to all. And in the popular mind, the Supreme Court stands at the pinnacle of all these.

...I am not charging that Roosevelt wants to be a dictator [based on his proposal to increase the number of U.S. Supreme Court justices from nine to 15]. What I am afraid of is that there may be an opening in the line for someone who may not be so high-purposed. A high purpose is always the beginning of tyranny, and then it becomes not so high, and finally it becomes malevolent.

—Gilbert Bettman, *former attorney general of Ohio*

MARCH 20 Dr. Edward Spease, dean of the School of Pharmacy of Western Reserve University, [said] Congress should pass a new pure food and drug act with teeth in it.

"...I do believe that the names and quantities of the ingredients should be printed on the label, so that the consumer may know what he is getting."

—Plain Dealer

Peter Witt asked [Dr. Spease] how old whiskey should be before it is fit to drink.

"It should be aged a minimum of four years in wood," Dr.

1937

Spease replied. "Another year or two would help it, but I'm not worried much about it after that."
—Plain Dealer

MAY 6 *The dirigible* **Hindenburg** *explodes and crashes while landing at Lakehurst, New Jersey. Among the 36 killed: former Goodyear-Zeppelin Company executive Ernst Lehmann.*

OCTOBER 16 For two years the evils of your administration have been covered up by the newspapers. Today you stand alone before this large audience and before 100,000 listeners on the radio. There is no newspaper to protect and defend you....

...When I said [publicly] last week that the streets were full of crime, the papers said in effect, "Oh, dear, no—with Harold Burton mayor and Eliot Ness safety director? Why, that couldn't be!"

How do you like this one? Sunday afternoon, the Cleveland *Plain Dealer* was held up by gunmen and robbed of $2,000 in broad daylight.
   —John O. McWilliams, *county engineer and Democratic opponent of incumbent Harold H. Burton in the Cleveland mayoralty race*

NOVEMBER 27 While the situation is acute only in Spain, the rest of the continent is resigned to the Italo-German philosophy that to the strong shall go the spoils, and innocence and virtue have nothing to do with the matter.... Europe is a mad house.
   —Jacob Meyer, *associate professor of history at Western Reserve University, recently returned from a tour of Europe*

DECEMBER 4 An open forum such as the City Club stands for is not accepted today as a matter of course. It is something to be safeguarded jealously, and it is worth all the sacrifices we may be called on to make in order to preserve it.
   —Daniel E. Morgan, *making the keynote speech of the club's 25th anniversary celebration*

Daniel E. Morgan

1938

Hitler makes his demand for the Sudetenland territory of Czechoslovakia, and British Prime Minister Neville Chamberlain acceeds by signing the Munich Pact, ensuring, he believes, "peace in our time." Despite the obvious threat posed by Germany, American isolationists become even more vocal in urging that the United States stay out of European affairs. The City Club hears these and other timely subjects discussed, as well as a lively debate on a topic of interest to municipalities around the country that will come up more and more in future years—the responsibility of the suburb to its parent city.

JANUARY 8 [Holding companies] are the machine guns of

corporate racketeers. You may as well pin a gardenia on Al Capone and call him a useful citizen as try to reform holding companies.
      —Harry Elmer Barnes

FEBRUARY 10 **Fesler:** I have no hesitation in saying that Cleveland does not have the civic consciousness which she had in those days when Lincoln Steffens was led to declare that Cleveland was the best-governed city in America. And the prime reason for that decline, in my opinion, is the fact that 300,000 of the cream of her population...have separated themselves politically from the parent city and transferred their civic allegiance and interest to the suburbs, where they partly avoid their obligations to the greater community.
      Fahrenbach: [The suburbs] pay for transportation. We pay for our light and gas. But Cleveland gets the thousands of dollars for taxes these companies pay on their Cleveland property. We get none, except our share of the county taxes.
      Many of Cleveland's officials, municipal judges, law directors, police prosecutors and so forth get part of their salaries from the county, and we pay our proportionate share of that.... Really, are we such parasites after all?
      —Debate between Mayo Fesler (himself a resident of suburban Shaker Heights) and William F. Fahrenbach, president of the city council of suburban Lakewood

FEBRUARY 19 In the dictator-ruled countries, a constant flow of laudation for the ruling powers and incessant attacks on other forms of government...are pouring out floods of news colored to suit the governments in power and covering [them] with a steel coat of prejudice and bias through which truth is powerless to penetrate. ...This kind of violently partisan doctrine is broadcast to all parts of the world and in a great variety of languages.
      Men have never before faced such a situation. And radio, with all its benefits, must be charged with some of these consequences. It must be recalled that even the illiterate can be reached by radio....
      —James Rowland Angell, *former president of Yale University and current educational counselor for the National Broadcasting Company, warning of the dangers of the unbridled use of radio for the dissemination of propaganda*

MARCH 3 Our first concern should be for those at the bottom, and instead of the old way of letting prosperity trickle down from the top, we must somehow cause it to trickle up to the top from the bottom.
      —Marvin C. Harrison, *Cleveland attorney, defending the economic policies of the New Deal*

MARCH 16 I was behind boulder. I was jump up to see what was going on. My mother always pull me back. The soldiers

1938

were coming down on a ridge. On either side was deep ravine. The white man was coming down the ridge, blowing bugles.

Our [war-party leader] say, "Go after them." The Indian boys get on their horses with bows and arrows and war clubs.

At one place on the ridge the white cavalry went into whirlpool. The Indian boys closed in, knocking them off horses, using their tomahawks. It was like polo game.

—Chief Buffalo Bear, *Sioux council leader, describing to a City Club luncheon gathering Custer's Last Stand as he had witnessed it 62 years before, at the age of 10*

MARCH 19 It is impossible to point to one important constructive step taken in the United States in the last eight years which represents either the inventiveness, the initiative or the supporting activity of the American press.... The greatest shock ever experienced by the newspaper publishers of America was to wake up on the morning of November 4th, 1936, and discover that they had no influence in a presidential election.

—Irving Brant, *editorial writer, St. Louis* Star-Times

APRIL 6 The United States has recognized in these islands the pivot upon which world events seem destined to swing and therefore has fortified them more formidably than any other place in her history.

—Lawrence M. Judd, *lifelong resident and former governor of the Territory of Hawaii*

APRIL 23 Communism is three times more dangerous than Naziism....

—Homer L. Chaillaux, *national director, Americanism Commission of the American Legion*

SEPTEMBER 26 *There is probably no other period in the history of the City Club of Cleveland in which so many strong personalities kept quiet for so long a time.*

They were crowded around the radio, leaning back in leather chairs, serious faced, completely silent....

[Then] Reichsfuehrer Adolf Hitler spoke—and the world listened. Intently, as if the listeners expected to hear siege guns start grunting....

—Plain Dealer account of City Club members listening to Hitler's demand for annexation of the Sudetenland

OCTOBER 22 Generally speaking...legalized gambling does not work out.... The police chief in a city with legal gambling told me, "If you can prevent legalized gambling, do it! Your crime problem will increase beyond your belief."

—Eliot Ness, *Cleveland safety director*

OCTOBER 29 *The largest luncheon Forum meeting in the City Club's 26-year history was gathering this noon in Hotel Statler for the...debate between [Democratic incumbent] Senator*

Robert J. Bulkley

Robert J. Bulkley and Robert A. Taft, his Republican opponent.

More than 2,000 people were expected to jam the Statler's main dining room, its balcony, the Euclid ballroom and the corridors.... Among the audience will be women for the first time....

—News

Taft: Mr. Bulkley thinks that unless we suspend the Constitution we can't relieve unemployment. I don't believe it. We can do it by encouraging industry and balancing the budget. Fifty percent can be cut off the operating cost of every governmental agency in Washington....

Senator Bulkley is apparently 100 percent in favor of granting unlimited power to the administration.... His policy is to grant unlimited power to the chief executive, permit domination of Congress and the Supreme Court and allow complete regulation of the people. This policy is inconsistent with the Constitution [and] with local self-government and is bound to bring about termination of individual rights.

Bulkley: The truth of the matter, I believe, is that we and other nations of the world are facing a new day. Acute and disinterested thinkers believe that the disturbances of our time are more than an ordinary crisis and that we are passing from one stage of civilization to the next.

The true significance of the New Deal must be found in the extent to which it has caught the spirit and sensed the needs of this new day...and the determination and eagerness with which it has revitalized the hopes and spirits of our people....

The egg of the old order has been broken, and all the king's horses and all the king's men—all the Landons and the Tafts and the Hoovers—can never put it together again.

NOVEMBER 2 *Sir: I want to express my thanks to the City Club for admitting women to the Saturday luncheon of October 29..., and am looking forward to the time when women will be admitted regularly to hear the prominent speakers there.*

Mrs. Perl Griffin
1547 St. Clair Avenue

—Letter to the editor of the News

NOVEMBER 10 The plea of the medical profession is that it be left in the hands of medical men.... I think that when the people know they can get medical care for nothing..., the volume would be so great as to militate against private practice.

—Dr. Harry G. Sloan, *past president of the Cleveland Academy of Medicine, arguing against federally funded medical care for the indigent*

NOVEMBER 12 The blowoff is coming soon. We are going to have to shake up our entire national defense system.... What we need is a separate setup to handle the airplanes...[with] another cabinet member in charge of it—a third complete arm

1938

of national defense. [Even] then it will take 10 or 15 years to really develop it.

—**Al Williams,** *former New York Giants pitcher who became a combat flyer in the World War, the inventor of vertical divebombing, holder of the world's air-speed record as a Navy test pilot and eventually a syndicated columnist for the Scripps-Howard newspapers, urging creation of an air force separate from the other military services*

NOVEMBER 19   The theory that fascism is the last stand of the capitalist system is only as true as the theory that the grave is the last stand of all of us. If the [American] business interests leaning toward fascism would notice what fascism has done to private property in Germany, they wouldn't lean that way.

—**Herbert Agar,** *associate editor of the Louisville* Courier-Journal *and Pulitzer Prize-winning author of* The People's Choice, Land of the Free *and* Who Owns America?

NOVEMBER 26   I am one of those who agree almost entirely with the New Deal objectives but revolt at its bungling, highhanded methods. ...I believe there has been such a reversal in [President Roosevelt's] personal popularity that any Democrat carrying the President's blessing will be automatically defeated.

—**Phil S. Hanna,** *editor,* Chicago Journal of Commerce

Q: What would you suggest instead of the New Deal measures to attain the social objectives that are agreed as desirable?

Hanna: That is the hell of it. I haven't any suggestions.

DECEMBER 3   In a world where we elect a candidate for high office because he has a pleasing voice, or where we buy our soap because we have been told that brand will help us get a husband or wife, it is easy to control the public by propaganda. Hitler merely looked at American achievements in...political campaigns and advertising and applied the same methods to achieve his own ends.

—**Harry D. Gideonse,** *professor of economics, Barnard College*

1939-
1945

A Glow
on the
Horizon

With hard times behind them, City Club members prepared to greet a new year—and a new age.

1939

Early in the year the City Club hears a remarkably accurate prediction of the tragedy awaiting Europe. Although few believe that war is inevitable, the August signing of a German-Russian nonagression pact is an unmistakable sign that the Continent is about to explode, as it does less than a month later. Roosevelt assures the country of American neutrality but sets the stage for the 1941 Lend-Lease program by urging Congress to au-thorize the "cash and carry" sale of arms to belligerents. Coincidentally, Ernest Lawrence wins the 1939 Nobel Prize in physics for developing the cyclotron, an instrument that will be fundamental to the creation of the weapon that strikes the final blow in what proves to be a six-year struggle.

JANUARY 11   Mechanically, television is here. We can televise acceptable pictures for a radius of about 30 miles. One of the main troubles is the cost of preparing programs. All of the writing that was done for the entire American motion-picture industry in 1938 would not supply commercial television for 30 days.

    —Vernon Pribble, *manager, Cleveland radio station WTAM*

JANUARY 14   The Munich Pact was not a sellout, but one of the greatest events in recent history.... War was threatened at the time. Would you have had war as the solution? How much better that statesmen, in the spirit of international cooperation, should work out the problem in this manner.

    ...We haven't given Germany a chance. We have presupposed it to be wrong in everything.... When and where has Hitler been an aggressor?

    —Karl F. Geiser

    Q: What are Germany's ambitions?

    Geiser: For the first time in its history all Germans are under one roof, and that's all Hitler wants—at least, that's what he said.

FEBRUARY 4   I do not share the view that there will be war [in Europe] next spring or early next summer, because it would not suit Germany to fight in the spring or summer.

    Germany, situated as she is, must make the most of whatever she can grow. She needs all available men for the fields in the spring and summer. ...[Her] armies do not get really tuned up until the crops are harvested.

    After mid-October war would be difficult because of the climate in northern Europe.... Depending on [air power] as Germany would, it is unlikely that she would deliberately plan to begin a fight between late October and March.

    And so the greatest threat of war would come in late August or early fall.

    —Sir Arthur Willert, *British diplomat and former journalist*

Bertrand Russell

MARCH 11 *Dear Sir,*

I write on behalf of the Prime Minister to acknowledge the receipt of your letter of the 14th February, in which you invite him to be present at the City Club of Cleveland, Ohio, for the Anvil Revue on Saturday, the 18th March.

I am afraid that there is no likelihood that Mr. Chamberlain will be in America at that time, and in the circumstances he can only decline this invitation.

—Letter to the City Club from the secretary of British Prime Minister Neville Chamberlain offering his regrets at being unable to attend the 26th annual Anvil Revue, "Sauce for the Goose-Step, or Debt Takes a Holiday"

APRIL 8 You'll say the trouble in Europe doesn't concern you, that you're neutral, but you can't follow that line. There will be atrocities aplenty in this war, and first your radicals and then your public opinion will bring you into it.

—Bertrand Russell, *predicting a second world war that he expected would break out were Germany to invade Poland*

APRIL 29 I, for one, am not so guileless as to believe that, with all the thinking people working for peace, a few cockeyed, power-crazed men, strutting with brief authority, will be permitted to butcher and beggar us all.... A man would have to be a lot crazier than Hitler to start a war now.

—Walter M. Harrison, *managing editor,* Daily Oklahoman

SEPTEMBER 1 *Hitler invades Poland, and two days later Britain and France declare war on Germany.*

NOVEMBER 18 Russia's army is too weak to fight, and military authorities who know it consider it strictly second-class.

—Eugene Lyons, *editor, the* American Mercury *magazine*

NOVEMBER 25 I do not favor the passage of any new laws to combat [American communist, fascist and Nazi organizations] or any infringement on civil liberties. We do not want to fight these groups with force, for that is exactly what they want us to use.

—John C. Metcalfe, *chief investigator for the newly formed congressional committee on un-American activities (chaired by Congressman Martin L. Dies) and former Chicago newspaperman whose articles exposing the German-American Bund led to the creation of the Dies committee*

DECEMBER 16 The administration of [New Deal policies] is confused, illogical and ineffective. It is almost impossible to realize how badly reorganization is needed....

—Robert A. Taft, *senator from Ohio and candidate for the Republican presidential nomination*

1939

Q: Have you a plan for operation of the country's economic machinery and for balancing the budget?

Taft: Yes, but it is too long to give here.

1940

The Republicans nominate Wendell L. Willkie, a non-politician from Elwood, Indiana, as their standard-bearer in the presidential race. Perceived as a plain-spoken Everyman of the Midwest (although in fact he is a power-company executive, called by the Democrats the "barefoot boy from Wall Street"), Willkie travels the nation challenging the Democrats' administration of New Deal policies. Despite his strong appeal—and the endorsement of 81 percent of the country's major newspapers—Willkie is defeated as Roosevelt wins an unprecedented third term, in part because the country does not want to change leaders in the middle of the European crisis. Domestic concerns about relief and the national debt are voiced at the City Club as elsewhere, but more and more attention is being given to reports from the front and speculation on whether—and when—America will enter the fray.

JANUARY 13 A national defense hysteria seems to be sweeping the country. More than 30 percent of a budget in excess of $8 billion is devoted to the national defense. I cannot approve the diversion of millions and millions from constructive government activities for giant battleships of doubtful defense value. ...We have nothing to fear from a mad dictator in Europe, but we do have much to fear from continued unemployment and an unsolved agricultural problem....

—**Burton K. Wheeler,** *isolationist senator from Wyoming and soon-to-be candidate for the Democratic presidential nomination*

JANUARY 20 A banker is a fellow who lends you an umbrella when the sun is shining and asks for it back when it rains.

—**Philip La Follette,** *former governor of Wisconsin and son of the late Robert La Follette*

JANUARY 27 We must rearrange our budget for public services and consider relief not as a temporary emergency to be met by loans but as a regular expenditure supported from taxes. ...I believe relief is here to stay—not for a few years, but permanently.

—**Rowland Haynes,** *president, University of Omaha*

Philip La Follette

FEBRUARY 3 President Roosevelt will probably run for a third term and be reelected, although his major blunder in not using his influence to stop the Dies committee's work will make it difficult for any liberal candidate. ...The bitterness of the [1940] campaign will be supplied by the third-term issue and the dangerous pattern of opinion which has inspired anti-Semitism, the Red scare, the anti-alien drive and the growing hostility towards labor. This same pattern of ideas led to the rise of Hitler in Germany....

—**Max Lerner,** *former editor of* The Nation *and current professor of political economy at Williams College, Williamstown, Massachusetts*

FEBRUARY 17 [British foreign correspondent] Robert Dell maintained [that] failure of the French and British governments to take the risk of war earlier encouraged Hitler to run amuck until the present impasse leading to war came about. Dell...made several sallies and pointed observations in his discussion...: Neither Hitler nor Stalin will keep his agreement any longer than is convenient to either...; the European war is a fight to the finish, since the British have finally realized Hitler aims at world domination rather than being just the biggest European power...; if Germany attacks on the western front, it probably will be through Holland; the Allies will win after a long, bitter struggle, and the only equitable peace [will] see Germany broken up....

—Plain Dealer *and* News *accounts*

FEBRUARY 24 [Senator Martin] Dies is not out to get subversive forces but liberal forces, and to smear them with the communist label.... The Dies committee has called...witnesses to smear better men than they without those who were smeared having an opportunity to reply....

—**John A. Lapp,** *chairman, Chicago Civil Liberties Committee*

MARCH 2 Legal pussyfooters have made a mess of [Cleveland's] lake front for a hundred years.... Forget the parks and the posies, the yacht basins, the docks and the housing, and concentrate first on a road along the shore from one end of the county to the other.... Once you get the highway, which benefits everybody—navigation, commerce, industry, housing, recreation and everything else—then you can go as far as you like with development.

—**Hugh L. Beavis,** *planning assistant, Ohio State Highway Department*

MARCH 9 Mr. Watterson at one time used no [editorial] cartoon, because he said his subscribers could read. I don't, however, agree with that view. The cartoon is very valuable. But it must be drawn by a man who is permitted to express himself, and there are and always have been too few publishers who will permit that.

—**Tom Wallace,** *editor of the Louisville* Times *and former associate of "Marse" Henry Watterson, legendary editor of the Louisville* Courier-Journal

MARCH 23 You and I cannot possibly pay all of this [national] debt. We cannot avoid passing it on to our children and our

1940

children's children. We have forgotten not only the taxpayers of today, but those of tomorrow....

    —Styles Bridges, *senator from New Hampshire and candidate for the Republican presidential nomination*

APRIL 13   I do not see how a man who is supported by the government can at the same time control that government.

    —S. Wells Utley, *president of the Detroit Steel Castings Corporation and a vocal anti-New Dealer, explaining why relief clients, WPA workers, farmers and others receiving federal aid should not be allowed to vote in national elections*

JUNE 22   **Following the fall of Denmark, Norway, Holland, Belgium and Luxembourg, France surrenders to Germany.**

OCTOBER 12   After seeing this German military machine in action, I don't think we can afford to waste a single day in bringing our own armed strength to its peak. If we don't do this quickly and give up some of our comforts, we will lose the comforts and much else besides.

    —Kenneth T. Downs, *war correspondent, International News Service*

OCTOBER 24   [American movies] must stop looking at the cheery side all the time. I do not advocate nothing but realism, but the theaters today have found some part of their audiences asking for the elimination of war scenes from newsreels, and some theaters have advertised that no scenes from abroad are shown.

    —Walter Wanger, *independent producer of such motion pictures as* Stagecoach, Foreign Correspondent *and* The Long Voyage Home

OCTOBER 26   He's a real Wall Streeter, as slick as they come.

    —Luther Patrick, *Democratic congressman from Alabama, describing Republican presidential candidate Wendell Willkie*

NOVEMBER 9   Japan is a terrific nuisance but not a threat to anybody. Japan suffers from rationing of nearly all essentials —rice, water, electricity, matches, sugar, leather, cotton, wheat, medical supplies, wool and gasoline. How could a nation that can't meet its own requirements threaten one that has all the goods it lacks?

Even the Chinese are better off than the Japs....

    —James R. Young, *Tokyo bureau chief, International News Service*

DECEMBER 14   If the Germans grow weaker Hitler will undoubtedly attack Russia while he is still able.

    —Otto D. Tolischus, *Pulitzer Prize-winning* New York

Walter Wanger

Times *correspondent in Berlin and former managing editor of the* Press

1941

Lend-Lease is instituted to provide arms to the democracies at war and is extended to include Russia after Germany attacks its erstwhile ally in June. German submarines are menacing all shipping in the Atlantic, including U.S. merchantmen and military craft, but the America First Committee, with such widely known members as Charles Lindbergh and Henry Ford, continues to urge isolationism. Much of the country does indeed choose to ignore the hostilities overseas; at the City Club, for example, the annual shenanigans of the Candidates' Field Day take place as scheduled—four days before the Japanese attack on American ships and military installations at Pearl Harbor shocks the country out of its lethargy and unites the democracies in a true world war.

JANUARY 4 Invasion of a free people with a fine morale is not so easy as some people think. For further information apply to one Adolf Hitler, somewhere in Germany and overdue in England since September 1 last.
—**Edward Blythin,** *mayor of Cleveland*

FEBRUARY 15 **Busch:** [The] Lend-Lease bill provides the effective means of giving the Allies prompt and adequate assistance. It affirms our belief that those who are resisting fascist aggression are buying time for us....

Does Mr. Taft think...we should have [Charles A.] Lindbergh's naive and childlike faith in the pledged word of fascist powers not to attack us? We know through the blood and tears of Czechoslovakia, Poland, Norway, Holland and Belgium that a dictator's pledge means nothing....

Taft: We can only finance Britain by borrowing money from our own citizens.... [Lend-Lease] would make Uncle Sam the best and biggest Santa Claus the world has ever seen....

I have no question but that a long war—and this would be a long war—would end the American way of life as we have known it. There is only one policy which can keep this country [at peace]. That is to recognize the Atlantic and Pacific oceans as our boundaries and to defend our coasts.
—*Debate between Henry M. Busch, local chairman of the Committee to Defend America by Aiding the Allies, and Robert A. Taft*

MARCH 1 Learning to work is a good thing for the boy and girl. Parents have made a fatal mistake in saying they don't want their children to work as hard as they had to. I think also we've made a mistake in letting every pupil believe he can be President.
—**T. Luther Purdom,** *director of the Bureau of Vocational Information, University of Michigan*

1941

MARCH 29   There seems to be an impression in this country that the incredible collaboration which went on between the democratic states and the fascist powers up to the beginning of the war will suddenly be dropped altogether through the influence of war hatreds. As a matter of fact, the probability is that at the end of the conflict a resumption of business between the belligerents on something like the old basis will be a virtual necessity.

—**Devere Allen,** *pacifist Quaker, former associate editor of* The Nation *and head of the Nofrontier News Service, whose 150 "correspondents" smuggle suppressed news out of occupied Europe*

MAY 28   If we're going to win this war without a great American Expeditionary Force, we'll have to have a great American Expeditionary Idea—and that idea is freedom for all men equally through Union Now. Unless we join the English-speaking democracies now and organize them into a union we will be right back at Versailles again at the end of [this] war.

—**Clarence K. Streit,** *former* New York Times *correspondent to the League of Nations and author of* Union Now, *a proposal for a federation of the United States, United Kingdom, Canada, Australia, New Zealand, Ireland and the Union of South Africa that would ensure lasting world peace*

OCTOBER 11   If Goebbels himself came to America to run his propaganda, he would not say "Heil Hitler" but "America First."

—**Jan Valtin,** *German communist revolutionary whose book* Out of the Night *detailed his four-year imprisonment in and eventual escape from Nazi concentration camps*

NOVEMBER 8   Responsible quarters in Washington believe that Hitler...has decided that the time has come to take a gamble and force the United States into the war [by attacking U.S. Navy ships in the North Atlantic].... His trump card in this gamble is the Axis pact with Japan, under which Japan is pledged to go to war with the United States in the event we become involved in a war with the Axis.

[But] the United States, if it has to, can clean up Japan in six months....

—**Robert S. Allen,** *coauthor of "Washington Merry-Go-Round"*

DECEMBER 3   What this club needs is wisdom and maturity, tempered with boogie-woogie.

—**Nathan Loeser,** *Cleveland attorney, campaigning for himself at the City Club's annual Candidates' Field Day*

DECEMBER 7   *Japanese planes launch an unprovoked attack on American ships and military installations at Pearl Harbor, Hawaii. President Roosevelt asks Congress to declare war on Japan the following day;*

Jan Valtin

three days later, Germany and Italy declare war on the United States.

1942

The war in the Pacific consists of a series of Allied setbacks until the victories in the Corral Sea and at Midway Island. The bombing of Tokyo in April is a psychological blow to the Japanese and a proof of the viability of high-level, long-distance aerial warfare. In November American forces land in North Africa, while at home rationing is the order of the day, and the witholding of income tax from weekly paychecks—rather than paying a lump sum at the end of the year—is proposed as a way to help finance the war.

In a nationally broadcast speech from the City Club, Secretary of the Treasury Henry Morgenthau proposes a number of tax-law changes to close loopholes and increase revenues. Unwilling to go further than read the White House-approved policy statement, Morgenthau surprises everyone by refusing to answer club members' questions after his talk.

JANUARY 3   **Silver:** The first World War was fought for the same objectives against the same enemy, yet the world entered one of its most disastrous periods in 1919.... It is difficult to assume an era of peace and good will is ahead.... We must prevent a recurrence of the great tides of bigotry which spread through the United States after World War I.

Love: We shall have following the war what many will mistake for cyclical depression. It will set in motion a new wave of public projects which will collide with the revival of individual spending, and the two together will produce an extreme prosperity, a land boom and a building boom....

Fesler: There will be...a consolidation of units of local government forced upon our urban communities by the sheer burden of taxes which this useless war will ultimately entail....

Wickenden: If goods as well as people can be transported economically by air, we may see a development of the airplane industry rivaling that of the automobile and truck following the first World War. New industries such as synthetic rubber and plastics...will help us to progress in the years to come.... There is also the future use of atomic energy, and while this is not on the horizon, we can see the glow of expectation.

—Discussion of the probable state of the postwar world by Abba Hillel Silver; John W. Love, business editor of the Press; *Mayo Fesler; and William E. Wickenden, president of Cleveland's Case School of Applied Science*

JANUARY 24   Loopholes in the federal tax laws cause an annual loss to the government of almost $1 billion a year, about one eighth of the entire receipts from income tax during the year, Secretary [of the Treasury Henry] Morgenthau said ....

1942

"We need $9 billion in additional revenue," Mr. Morgenthau said. "I should like the very first $1 billion of that amount to be obtained by closing the remaining loopholes. If this is accomplished it will be a contribution to the financing of the war, the morale of our people and the victory of our cause....

"In wartime, when we are drafting young men to fight and risk their lives for their country, any special privilege for a few becomes inexcusable."

—New York Times *account of Secretary Morgenthau's nationally broadcast speech at the City Club, in which he proposed closing tax loopholes for tax-exempt municipal securities, the community-property system, separate returns for husbands and wives and the mining- and oil-depletion allowances*

[Morgenthau] parried specific tax questions that were not covered in his prepared address, and declined to hold a question-and-answer period at the close of the program.

"Afraid someone might put you in a corner?" he was asked.

"I know very well someone would," he answered. "My talk has been carefully checked. If I'm going out on a limb, I'm not going out alone."

—News

FEBRUARY 21   And what about our homes? The atmosphere of home, the influence it wields, is the reflection of its central figure. We women have a tremendous responsibility..., for does not the home reflect our spirit, our courage, our strength, our standards? I would emphasize the deep significance of the position of the homemaker and the work that lies before her in the days to come.

—Frances P. Bolton, *Republican congresswoman from Ohio*

FEBRUARY 28   If you pay your gasoline, sales and tobacco taxes as you go, why not pay your income tax the same way?

—Harley L. Lutz, *professor of public finance at Princeton University, advocating the withholding of federal income tax from pay checks, which will in fact be instituted on June 10, 1943*

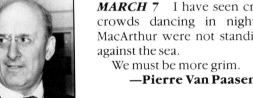

MARCH 7   I have seen crowds streaming south to the resorts, crowds dancing in nightclubs and crowds at bars—as if MacArthur were not standing [in the Philippines] with his back against the sea.

We must be more grim.

—Pierre Van Paasen, *Dutch-born journalist and author*

APRIL 4   The trend [away] from the true representative form of our constitutionalism is apparent in two phases of a prevalent evil practice. One phase is the tendency of the people to direct governmental action by pressure groups or blocs, and the other

Henry Morgenthau

is the tendency of governmental agents to substitute the counting of telegrams and letters for independent investigation and to substitute polls of public opinion for detached judgment.
—**Robert N. Wilkin,** *judge of the United States District Court of Northern Ohio*

MAY 6   American and Filipino forces surrender the Philipines to the Japanese.

OCTOBER 10 We must put a final end to this status of inferiority we have attempted to pin on the Negro. We must admit him into our every phase of activity, not as philanthropists or as "liberals," but as sensible people who realize that we can gain much from the remarkable contributions the Negro has to offer our national life.
...We have promised the Negro time and again to give him the rights to which he is entitled as a citizen, and always we have failed to live up to our promises. We shall just have to ask him to believe that this time we really mean to fight for the freedom and equality of all peoples.
—**Rockwell Kent,** *noted American artist, speaking at the dedication of the City Club's "free speech" mural—painted by black Cleveland artist Elmer Brown—on the 30th anniversary of the club's founding*

NOVEMBER 7 Warfare is moving rapidly into the third dimension, evacuating the surface of the earth. Airplanes and submarines are the leading weapons in this age.
—**Alexander P. de Seversky,** *noted aircraft designer and author of* Victory Through Air Power

1943

War news takes precedence over all other events as America invades Italy and Douglas MacArthur makes headway against the Japanese. At home, full war production means jobs are plentiful and well-paying, and it is not too soon to begin thinking about the nature of a postwar world, especially the Soviet Union's place in it. Only one manufacturer in the country refuses to renegotiate a war-procurement contract under the government's newly instituted contract-review policy, and he defends his actions—and causes no small controversy—in a speech at the City Club.

JANUARY 15 I asked [him] why he didn't simply write whatever he wished and attribute it to us, since we had no means of repudiating it. He said, "That wouldn't be honest."
That will give you an idea of how difficult the Japanese mind is for an American to comprehend.
—**Robert Bellaire,** *United Press correspondent in Tokyo, describing his seven-month ordeal as a prisoner of the Japanese, who used torture to induce him to write a favorable article about Japan.*

1943

MARCH 13   Tires made of reclaimed rubber are not capable of withstanding high driving speeds, and these new Victory tires are important factors in national planning to keep the nation on rubber for the duration. Conservation of rubber must bridge the gap until our rubber problem has been solved.

[But] I am informed there is increasing evidence of reluctance to rigidly observe the 35-mile speed law which is now a national regulation....

—**John L. Collyer,** *president, B.F. Goodrich Company*

MAY 1   There is nothing to back the fears expressed by some that Russia after the war will attempt a world revolution. In the first place, Russia already has said she will not interfere with internal policies of other nations....

—**Henry C. Cassidy,** *Moscow bureau chief, Associated Press*

OCTOBER 23   The machines on which the Allies depend for the fighting of this war are largely made here.... Why is it? It is because of the outstanding genius of the American manufacturer and nothing else.

Now, I warn you, that is the only reason why the Allies are winning the war.

—**James F. Lincoln,** *head of Cleveland's Lincoln Electric Company and the only manufacturer in the United States to refuse to accept renegotiation of the terms of a war-procurement contract under the War Production Board's contract-review policy*

DECEMBER 4   Dr. Haden said the new sulfa drugs had been of inestimable value and would be responsible for a great decrease in the number of deaths caused by wounds as compared with previous wars.

Further developments of penicillin, he added, will show that it will be one of the most effective drugs in the fight against bacterial diseases of every kind.

—Plain Dealer *account of a speech by Dr. Russell L. Haden, chief of the medical division, The Cleveland Clinic*

James F. Lincoln

DECEMBER 8   *Last evening...we got out some of our home-work and began to read the transcript of a [recent City Club of Cleveland speech by] James Lincoln.... One would hardly have known from [Lincoln's] address that the United States was engaged in a war for survival and that things were not as usual. It was his position that renegotiation was unfair and..."a raw deal."*

...We wondered how [our soldiers overseas] would react to the words of the speaker...who declared that the only reason the Allies are winning is the outstanding genius of the American manufacturer.

We wondered how the Britons, who through one long crucial summer stood up against the Nazi hordes, would react, how the

*Russians, who had died by the millions, who had seen their
territory overrun and their people murdered, would react.*

*We wondered how those who had worked long and hard in
American war plants would react.*

*We guess Jim Lincoln didn't mean what he said. If he would
like to make a public apology..., we offer him the facilities of
this column.*

    —Robert P. Vanderpoel, *financial editor of the Chicago*
Herald American, *commenting in that paper*

1944

With the Allied invasion of France and American
victories in the Pacific, the end of the war is in
sight. The Servicemen's Readjustment Act—
known as the "GI Bill of Rights"—is enacted, and Franklin
D. Roosevelt wins his fourth term in office, defeating
Republican Thomas E. Dewey. At the City Club, members
hear a firsthand account of the devastating effects of the
German V-2 rocket, and many speakers speculate on the
fate of postwar Europe. The most remarkable event of the
year is the appearance of Chicago *Tribune* editor and
publisher Colonel Robert R. McCormick, who follows a
vitriolic speech with a display of boorishness never
before equaled at the club.**

JANUARY 22 I think all European governments should be
required to liquidate their holdings in this hemisphere [at the end
of the war].... We should insist on retaining such of the islands
as we have saved from, retaken or taken from the Japanese as
will secure our future safety from attack. We should retain air
bases and radio stations wherever we have built them; and we
should secure now—by treaty—the right to fly directly wherever
we want to go. ...[After that] we may do what we can for the
general welfare of the world.

    ...Nothing could be more fatal to our country, and for the
countries which some of our citizens prefer to their own, than
some grandiose scheme of world government. ...Our soldiers are
enduring great hardships in this war, and after it is all over they
will not allow themselves to be used as Hessians to carry out the
ambitious views of people who have large foreign investments
and who are thoroughly enjoying the war at home.

    —Robert Rutherford McCormick

    Q: Do you believe we should let other countries fly anywhere
they want to go, including over our country?

    McCormick: Other countries haven't earned that right. We
have.

    Q: Do you think it wise to attack Great Britain to the extent
that you do?

    McCormick: I don't attack Great Britain.

    Q: What do you do?

    McCormick: I merely do not prefer her to my own country!

    Q (second voice): Who does?

1944

McCormick: Apparently the gentleman who asked the question does. And I think *you* do.

Q: Do you approve of the [isolationist] America First party?

McCormick: I hope everyone in this room is for America first, but apparently some of [you] are not.

Q: [You have mentioned] foreign control of certain leading [American] newspapers. Would you care to particularize?

McCormick: That would certainly include the newspapers which have bought into [British] nobility, and their hangers-on. And if you wish me to be specific, I mean the [New York] *Herald Tribune* and the Marshall Field newspapers [Chicago *Sun* and New York's *PM*].

Q: I understand the Colonel justifies the Fulbright editorial [in which the *Tribune* accused Arkansas Congressman J. William Fulbright of betraying his country by introducing a resolution that called for U.S. participation in policing the postwar world]. May I ask whether others are justified in calling the Colonel's Chicago *Tribune* and the McCormick-Patterson papers Axis papers on the same measure of justice?

McCormick: If anybody did, he would use the same [foreign-sounding] accent as the gentleman who just questioned me.

JANUARY 24   On the basis of his City Club [speech], the danger of Colonel McCormick's principles ever being adopted would appear to diminish in ratio to the frequency of his platform appearances.
    —Press *editorial*

JANUARY 31   *Colonel McCormick...doesn't want any back talk. In Cleveland a week ago, he delivered [a] speech at a City Club luncheon, then submitted to a brief question-and-answer period, during which he was booed and heckled by the audience for his arbitrary and heavy-handed treatment of his questioners.*

Disapproval reached its climax when McCormick brushed aside a query because it was asked by a man with a "foreign accent." Soft-spoken peacemakers, loath to offend a guest, managed to stop the heckling and the question period adjourned. McCormick hurried away to catch a Chicago train, apparently confident that everybody else was wrong.

"I had fun," he told a Cleveland News *reporter.... "I've been up against these crackpots before...."*
    —PM *account*

Robert Rutherford McCormick

FEBRUARY 26   The American economic system of completely free competition has about as much chance of reestablishment after the war as the old high-wheeled bicycle.... Since a free competitive society will be impossible, and because the American people are psychologically opposed to the alternatives of a completely rationed or a completely socialized economy, we will strike a compromise.
    —**Stuart Chase,** *economist and author of the 1932 book* A

New Deal, *whose title is credited with being the inspiration for Roosevelt's later use of the phrase*

MARCH 11   The Nazi effort would entail far less danger were there not in the United States a noisy minority who, day by day and month by month, strive to destroy America's confidence in her allies.

These champions of disunity seek to incite a positive hatred of the Soviet Union and Great Britain. ...Sly attempts to belittle England's heroic accomplishments belie facts which will live through history.
        —Marshall Field III, *alluding to Colonel McCormick's anti-Russian and anti-British rhetoric*

APRIL 15   Invasion is something from which Napoleon shrank and Hitler shrank, but which General Eisenhower is going to do. When he does, we hope to have a man on the third or fourth barge to report it. In fact, it is said that we have more men in England than Ike has.
        —Paul W. White, *news director of the Columbia Broadcasting System (CBS), discussing his plans to provide radio news coverage of the coming Allied invasion of Europe*

JUNE 6   Allied forces invade Europe at Normandy.

NOVEMBER 11   After a long drive through the blackout we arrived at the nightmarish scene. It was like some horror shocker suddenly flashed on a movie screen. A pleasant, peaceful tree-lined street had been transformed into a battlefield appearance.

The crater in the middle of the street—and running to both curbs—was 25 or 30 feet deep. Eight two-story houses, four on either side, had been knocked into their backyards. Other residences in the neighborhood were listing.

...Of course, there was some...half-jocular comment such as, "Well, anyway, you can't hear this one coming; if it hits you, that's that." [The British] have endured so much they are pretty well immunized to terror, or even to sudden death dropping noiselessly from 70 miles in the sky.
        —Hugh Baillie, *president of the United Press news service, describing his first encounter with the effects of a German V-2 rocket*

NOVEMBER 18   The Russian occupation of the Baltic states, parts of Rumania, Czechoslovakia, Finland, Bulgaria, Hungary and Yugoslavia are accomplished facts and there seems to be no reason to believe that Russia will give up this territory.
        —William Henry Chamberlin, *former Moscow correspondent,* New York Herald Tribune

NOVEMBER 25   Russia wants only to see the political self-determination of Europe's people; it is not attempting to

1944

foster Soviet communism throughout the Continent.
> **—Corliss Lamont,** *chairman, National Council of American-Soviet Friendship*

DECEMBER 9 If two separate spheres of influence are built up in Europe, and this obviously is the present tendency, we have simply laid the groundwork for World War III.
> **—Spencer D. Irwin,** *associate editor,* Plain Dealer

1945

I n February, Roosevelt and Churchill meet with Stalin at Yalta and consent to Russian occupation of eastern Germany and virtual control of postwar Eastern Europe. Two months later Roosevelt is dead, and Harry Truman is sworn into office. As the war nears its end, domestic labor unions begin to flex their muscles nationwide, and manufacturers plan to fill what they believe will be a huge postwar demand for goods.

Hostilities in Europe end on May 9th, leaving Germany a smoking ruin divided into zones of occupation. On September 2nd the war in the Pacific is over. But in Korea Japanese troops south of the 38th parallel surrender to the American army, while those north of the parallel surrender to the Russians. The shooting has stopped—and the cold war has begun.

JANUARY 13 I'm glad I don't have to face today any of the...soldiers with Patton's army. I'd be ashamed. I couldn't explain to those kids who work on an around-the-clock shift how war production was tied up here because one fellow didn't want to work nights.
> **—Roelif Loveland,** Plain Dealer *reporter recently returned from covering General Patton's Third Army in Europe, alluding to a recent illegal strike by workers at the Cleveland Electric Illuminating Company*

FEBRUARY 17 [Spanish fascist dictator Francisco Franco] couldn't last three months without our present help. There is but one way to deal with the Spanish question. We must...step on Dictator Franco and step on him hard.
I'm but a voice crying in the wilderness, though....
> **—John M. Coffee,** *Democratic congressman from Washington, arguing that the United States should sever diplomatic relations with Spain*

MARCH 3 Prediction that a monorail rocket train, using alcohol as fuel, will be crossing the country from New York to Los Angeles in 10 hours by 1950 was made today by [Dow Chemical Company research consultant] William J. Hale....
The alcohol industry, he said, will be the greatest of a triumvirate of great industries 25 years hence because, he said, it will supersede gasoline as fuel. ...Plastics will form the second largest industry, and light metals, such as aluminum and

Karl A. Menninger

magnesium, will form the third. He predicted the passing of steel except for ultra-heavy installations....

"Heaven speed the day," Dr. Hale said in his talk, "when every block of coal and every gallon of petroleum is gone. We don't need them. We can make everything we need from sunlight."

—News *and* Plain Dealer *accounts*

MARCH 10 The dearth of psychiatrists is a national problem. For civilian and postwar needs alone we will require 10,000 trained psychiatrists, 5,000 psychiatric clinics, 5,000 psychiatric social workers and 5,000 psychiatric nurses.
　　—Dr. Karl Menninger

MARCH 24 After the war we will start, amid much confusion, with a mongrel system in which the elements of private capitalism will run with state controls.... Private capitalism in this country—run without government interference—is finished and done for.
　　—Norman Thomas, *perennial Socialist Party candidate for President*

APRIL 21 Within two years the military operations of Russia have achieved far greater conquests in territory and prestige than the Communist International accomplished by propaganda and conspiracy in 23 years.
　　—Reverend Edmund J. Walsh, *vice president, Georgetown University*

MAY 5 There will be a civil war in China that will make Spain's civil war look like a backyard fight.
　　—Harrison Forman, *free-lance correspondent recently returned from four years in China*

AUGUST 6　***The United States drops an atomic bomb on the Japanese city of Hiroshima. Three days later a second bomb is dropped on Nagasaki, ending the war in the Pacific.***

OCTOBER 13 Let's stop this nonsense. The secret cannot be kept.... Eventually all of the nations will have the formula, and our keeping it a secret now will keep others suspicious of us. Russia and the United States already are on the road to mutual understanding. Let's join hands over atomic energy....
　　—Victor A. Yakhontoff, *former Czarist general now an American citizen*

OCTOBER 27 Let exclusive control of atomic power be invested in the Security Council of the United Nations organization, and let the council have the power to enact legislation on a world scale for production and control of atomic power. If we don't begin here we will...drift into rivalry and eventually

1945

chaos.

　　—Frederick L. Schuman, *professor of government, Williams College*

Hugh Baillie

NOVEMBER 10　The electronics industry, now bigger than the automobile industry was before the war, is about to eliminate the push buttons from the push-button age and run the world automatically, a self-styled "screwball engineer" told an appreciative City Club audience....

　　The young scientist was Gordon Volkenant, one of the "gang of hay-shakers" from the Minneapolis Honeywell Regulator Company.... Volkenant described the electron tube as the "greatest single invention of the 20th century" and predicted it would be in "hundreds of peacetime automatic contraptions that will make this a much sweller world to live in."

　　Among the "contraptions" he mentioned:

　　Giant planes, electronically controlled, carrying 400 to 700 passengers at 400 miles an hour...;

　　Electronic dust catchers to be installed in furnaces to trap all dust and germs coming into the house...;

　　[Appliances] to...broil a steak from the inside out in a few seconds....

　　—Plain Dealer *and* News *accounts*

DECEMBER 8　The atom bomb does a much cleaner job.

　　—Hugh Baillie, *recently returned from Japan, describing the difference between Japanese cities bombed with conventional high explosives and Hiroshima and Nagasaki*

1946-1952

Fear

in

Abundance

McCarthyism was denounced by only a few brave voices, including those at the club's Soviet Table, of which Peter Witt was perhaps the most outspoken member.

1946

As Cleveland celebrates its sesquicentennial, the country enters one of the most tense and bitter years in the history of American labor relations. By the end of January, more than 1.5 million workers in the steel, automobile and coal industries, among others, are on strike, protesting wages still set at prewar levels. Twice that number are rendered jobless as a result.

At the City Club, Republican presidential aspirant Harold Stassen makes an impassioned plea for an enlightened new federal labor policy, but Congress, deeply troubled by incidents of labor violence and near-anarchy, will go on to pass what unionists term a "slave labor" law the following year—the Taft-Hartley act. A subway for Cleveland gets yet another hearing, while an eyewitness to America's further testing of the atomic bomb discusses the disturbing international ramifications.

MARCH 16   With the rise of two powerful national unions of labor and numerous large independent unions, it appears clear that we need a new labor policy in America. With equal emphasis I say that it is important that the new labor policy should not be an anti-labor policy.

Government must not provide for compulsory arbitration. It must not expose labor to injunction and other legal proceedings to the extent that a ruthless employer could break a union by keeping it continuously in court.

If government turns to measures of this kind, they can only be made effective by giving government the right to force men to work. If that power is ever given, democracy is gone. The rights of capital and private enterprise will go out with it.
    —Harold E. Stassen, *former governor of Minnesota*

APRIL 6   *Ben Sapp: When we get our nuclear energy on the assembly line...people won't work eight hours a day, nor six, nor four. Four minutes maybe—just time enough to turn over in bed. There will be nothing but leisure in ever-larger lumps.*

Mrs. Sapp: It won't work. When there's nothing to do, how will labor be able to exercise its God-given right to strike?
    —Opening scene of the 33rd annual Anvil Revue, "Our Post Bellum-ache, or The Stars and Strikes Forever"

APRIL 14   Wages left to themselves in free competition will so adjust themselves that there will be the greatest possible employment and production and the best possible standard of living. When the natural processes of wage setting are interfered with through violence and governmental intervention, you have created a little group of men with a monopoly wage that hurts the working class more than anyone else.
    —Neil Carothers, *economist*

APRIL 27   **McCarter:** There is a creeping paralysis coming over the town. Downtown congestion is caused by people

Harold E. Stassen

driving automobiles to work...because public transportation is too slow....

Byers: The newspapers bleeding for the poor downtown real estate operators is a little nauseating. They say Cleveland is rotting at the core. I think so, too, but not for the same reason. The high pressuring going on today is so much like the hoopla in the papers at the time we built a baseball park for the owners of the ball club. Preposterous nonsense. You can't reconcile good transportation and special interests.

McCarter: Ed is worried about special interests. I am worried only about my customers.

Byers: If people of East Cleveland, Cleveland Heights or Lakewood want this rapid-transit system, they should pay for it.

—Debate between Walter J. McCarter, general manager of the Cleveland Transit System, and Edgar S. Byers, attorney and former director of CTS's predecessor, the Cleveland Railway Company, on the merits of a $25-million proposal to build an east-west rapid transit linked to a downtown subway

JULY 1   *The United States explodes an atomic bomb over Bikini Atoll in the Marshall Islands in the Pacific. An underwater test follows on July 25th.*

OCTOBER 12   Neither the diplomats nor the military show any signs of having learned the lesson of Bikini. The most dangerous idea now gaining currency is that when every nation has atomic bombs, no nation will use them.

—David Dietz, *who witnessed the atomic tests*

OCTOBER 26   Huffman: Communism is a red herring which my opponent is dragging across his trail to cover up his connections with certain big-business interests. He well knows that I am no more communist than he is.

Bricker: No, Jim, you are not a communist. You are just a country boy who went to the city and got into bad associations with the New Deal. But I still like you.

—Debate between Democratic incumbent Senator James W. Huffman of Ohio and John W. Bricker, his Republican challenger

NOVEMBER 2   *Proving their national campaign slogan—"Had Enough?"—prophetic, the Republicans put an end to 16 unbroken years of Democratic control of the Congress. Among the victors: John Bricker.*

NOVEMBER 23   America has performed one miracle in this generation. We have provided the necessary power to smash the armed might of the greatest aggressor nations in history. If we perform the second miracle of making democratic capitalism work to the full, then we Americans will have become the greatest people in history.

—Louis J. Alber, *lecturer and globe-trotter*

1946

NOVEMBER 29   Russia faces no present prospect of equaling us in the production of atomic bombs, because the industrial effort we put into the project could not be matched by any nation, let alone the Soviet Union, until the better part of another generation has passed, say 15, 20 or 25 years.
—**A. Allen Bates,** *former Manhattan Project engineer*

1947

Anti-communist sentiment begins to sweep the country, stirred by the revival of the House Un-American Activities Committee (HUAC), which had first been established in 1938 to investigate the activities of Nazi agents in prewar America. Now it decides to conduct hearings in Hollywood on communist infiltration of the movie industry. In March President Truman issues an executive order inaugurating loyalty checks of all federal employees and asks a joint session of Congress for $400 million in foreign aid to Greece and Turkey to prevent Soviet expansion in the Near East and Balkans. Truman's request is condemned at the City Club, but the Truman Doctrine—American's responsibility "to support free peoples who are resisting subjugation by armed minorities or by outside pressures"—will prove to be a keystone of U.S. foreign policy thereafter.

JANUARY 16   *The French Parliament names a socialist the first President of the Fourth Republic of France.*

JANUARY 18   The Jews in Palestine are fighting mad because of broken promises, ruthless tyranny and brutal acts of injustice. The country is overrun with military dictatorship, troops, tanks and armored cars. That is what has converted a peaceful folk of pioneers and builders, who came there to rebuild unhappy lives, into a bitter and restive people.
—**Abba Hillel Silver,** *president of the Zionist Organization of America, criticizing the British government for mishandling its mandate in Palestine*

MARCH 1   *Red Chinese forces begin a large-scale offensive against Chiang Kai-shek's Nationalist Chinese strongholds in Manchuria.*

MARCH 29   There is little danger that the communists of China will take over or attempt to set up any form of communism such as Russia has. They know, or should know, by this time that China is the last country in the world in which to attempt to set up a dictatorship. There are no more rugged individualists than the Chinese coolies and peasants....
—**Gunther Stein,** *former Asia correspondent of the* Christian Science Monitor, *assessing the aftermath of the collapse of Chiang Kai-shek's government, which he predicted would take place within the year*

Robert A. Taft

Eliot Ness

APRIL 5 Hitler may still be alive. Many army intelligence people believe the same. There are 28 versions of Hitler's supposed death. No insurance company would pay off on this evidence.

    —Kurt Singer, *author of* Spies and Traitors of World War II

APRIL 12 Even the most slavish supporter of the Truman policy will not deny that the present Greek government is extremist, reactionary and undemocratic. The Turkish government is even worse. In expending our resources, and possibly American lives, in the effort to combat the spread of communism, it is also vital that we do so for the preservation of genuine democratic forces and institutions.

    —Robert S. Allen, *former co-author of the syndicated column "Washington Merry-Go-Round"*

JUNE 5 *Secretary of State George C. Marshall unveils the broad outlines of his European Recovery Plan in a commencement speech at Harvard University.*

OCTOBER 25 We cannot go on indefinitely supporting another nation in a higher standard of living than they are earning.

    —Robert A. Taft, *citing his basic disagreement with the Marshall Plan*

NOVEMBER 1 The mayor spoke first because he lost a toss of the coin to [Eliot] Ness.

As he assailed the many charges leveled against him during the campaign by his Republican foe, he displayed a large black book to his audience which he said contained every word Ness had uttered to date in the campaign.

Waving the black stenographic record before Ness, Burke declared with vehemence: "You have made many charges in this campaign, and I challenge you, as an ace investigator, to produce even one scrap of evidence to substantiate these charges.

"I give you my word, gentlemen," added the mayor, "that I am not in league with the communists...."

As he opened his speech, Ness said: "There are two factions in the local CIO [Congress of Industrial Organizations]. One is headed by [William F.] Donovan and one by [A.E.] Stevenson. The faction headed by Stevenson is the 'pink' faction of the CIO. Both have endorsed Mr. Burke. And when I mentioned communist support, whether it is pink or red or whatever color you want to call it, I am referring to Stevenson's group, for I think highly of the Donovan faction."

    —News *account of the mayoral debate between Republican incumbent Thomas A. Burke and former Cleveland Safety Director Eliot Ness*

NOVEMBER 11 Western Europe can be made a going concern if it can get immediate help from the United States. But that help

1947

must be directed toward the stimulation of production of consumer goods. The cost is secondary. There is the very real possibility that the communists will win control of France and Italy and then the rest of western Europe.

—**Frederick Sterbenz,** *foreign editor of the* Press, *recently returned from a tour of England, France, Belgium and the Netherlands*

NOVEMBER 13   Britain informs the U.N. of its decision to withdraw all of its troops from Palestine by August 1, 1948.

DECEMBER 13   The big temptation in communism is that it is the only government we haven't tried yet.
—**Jacques Walch,** *French journalist*

DECEMBER 19   President Truman asks Congress to appropriate $17 billion to fund the Marshall Plan for the following four years.

1948

As America prepares for a presidential election, international tensions increase in the Middle, Near and Far East. On January 30th, Mohandas Gandhi is assassinated by a Hindu nationalist. On May 16th, armies from the Arab nations of Transjordan, Egypt, Syria, Iraq and Lebanon invade Palestine, the day after the Jewish National Council declares Israel an independent state. The same month the Russian-backed People's Committee of North Korea proclaims the entire country under its control. A few days later U.N.-sponsored elections in the American zone of Korea result in a victory for Syngman Rhee as leader of the soon-to-be-created Republic of Korea.

Through fortuitously chosen speakers the City Club is able to closely monitor these and other important international developments, but it is the Stassen-Taft non-debate that generates the year's greatest excitement.

JANUARY 15   The Arab League nations declare they will occupy all of Palestine immediately after Britain withdraws.

FEBRUARY 21   [The Arabs] will never accept partition. They are afraid that a U.N. army to enforce partition will include many communists and Palestine will become a second Korea [now under joint occupation by U.S. and Soviet troops]. More important is the fact that the ignorant, uneducated Arabs, who are having a hard enough time adjusting themselves to modern ways after jumping out of medievalism, will regard it an excuse for continued guerrilla warfare.

They won't accept a large Jewish immigration because they see that the present immigration consists mostly of young men of military age and fear that the Jews eventually will be strong enough to occupy the whole country.

They will die to hold Palestine because it is for them the heart of the Arab League, and they think of it as the people of California consider Los Angeles.

—**Bayard Dodge,** *president, American University, Beirut*

FEBRUARY 25 The communists seize control of Czechoslovakia in a bloodless coup.

FEBRUARY 28 Czechoslovakia's submission to communist power is a parallel case to that of Poland. It had all the same characteristics of police activity, arrests, even murder, the same drives against opposition leaders. What has happened in Czechoslovakia only shows again that in a country where 95 percent of the population is anti-communist the government can be taken over by a minority.

—**Stanislaw Mikolajczyk,** *former premier of Poland, who went into exile to escape a death sentence pronounced on him by his country's new communist rulers*

MARCH 20 They have reached the point of desperation. They no longer fear death. I believe they will face the Arabs and the world with a *fait accompli.*
will —**Pierre van Paasen,** *predicting that the Jews in Palestine proclaim themselves an independent state within a few weeks*

APRIL 10 *He has now reached the point where he can put his foot in his mouth without taking aim.*
—*Carl D. Friebolin, on Senator Taft, in his curtain speech at the 35th annual Anvil Revue, ''The Power of the Purse, or Divided We Stand''*

APRIL 24 I do not regard it as an infringement of the freedom of speech and constitutional rights to bar an organization that follows directions of a foreign power and has as its purpose the undermining of our liberties.

—**Harold Stassen,** *opponent of New York Governor Thomas E. Dewey and Senator Taft in the race for the Republican presidential nomination, declaring that the American Communist Party should be outlawed*

The Ohio senator declined an opportunity for a direct debate with Mr. Stassen before an audience of 1,000.... Senator Taft engaged time over local radio stations tonight for his rebuttal and sent two stenographers to the midday City Club session to transcribe his opponent's speech.

—New York Herald-Tribune *account of the Taft-Stassen battle for Ohio's 53 delegates to the 1948 Republican National Convention*

Slips of paper carrying loaded questions were prepared in

1948

advance and handed to several in the audience by Paul Walter, Taft's Cleveland manager. Forewarned, Stassen...refrained from mentioning politics—or Taft—in his radio address.
—*Minneapolis Sunday* Tribune

MAY 8   Whoever the Republican convention selects as candidate is destined to be the next President of the United States.
—**Marquis Childs,** *Washington correspondent, Scripps-Howard newspapers*

JUNE 21   The Republican National Convention opens in Philadelphia, with Dewey leading Taft in the number of committed delegates. He wins the nomination on the third ballot when Taft and Stassen are unable to agree on forming a ticket to stop him.

AUGUST 3   In testimony before HUAC, a Time *magazine editor, Whittaker Chambers, implicates Alger Hiss, former director of special political affairs for the state department, as having been a fellow communist during the Thirties.*

OCTOBER 16   England has made amazing progress in the last 15 months. London is rapidly rebuilding and will be a better-looking city a couple of years from now than it was 10 years ago. Poverty is disappearing. So are the rich. But it is most notable that there are no more of the unhappy, cringing people you used to see....

The Germans are unregenerate. They are less hard at work than any people in Europe. They are paralyzed with self-pity. Germany is saying to us, "You'd better be good to me or I'll become a communist state."
—**John W. Vandercook,** *author, journalist and radio commentator, recently returned from a trip to Europe to study firsthand the impact of the Marshall Plan*

OCTOBER 20   Peter Witt dies at the age of 79.

OCTOBER 23   *Most of all he symbolized, almost as if he were already an illuminated statue, the independent voter, the angry taxpayer, the frustrated citizen, the guy who wanted less bunk and more action and, above all, wanted plain speech and an honest answer from his public officials.*
—Plain Dealer *eulogy of Witt*

NOVEMBER 2   America, and the Chicago Tribune, go to bed believing Dewey has beaten Truman. But at 9:30 the following morning, final tabulations reveal that Ohio has gone Democratic, putting Truman over the total number of electoral votes he needs to be reelected.

Marquis Childs

NOVEMBER 6   The political impact of the Roosevelt era was infinitely greater than most people imagined. During the years of his administration Roosevelt succeeded in convincing the largest number of voters that the Democratic party was the one that nourished the people's interest.

We assumed that the [Henry] Wallace split weakened the labor vote and consequently Democratic strength. Actually, we find that once labor was purged of the ideological wing represented by Wallace [the Progressive Party candidate for President], it was a stronger political force than before. Other factors that counted heavily were the lush prosperity of the country and more than 61 million jobs at high wages.

Dewey kept his eye on January 20th, 1949, instead of November 2nd, and so did hundreds of thousands of Republican voters. It was the greatest demonstration of overconfidence since Dempsey lost to Tunney at Philadelphia.

—**James B. Reston,** *foreign and Washington correspondent of the* New York Times, *analyzing the election results*

NOVEMBER 10   *Nanking is placed under martial law as communist forces close in on the Nationalist Chinese capital.*

NOVEMBER 13   The Russian people want peace and the good life. Every contact with foreigners convinces them that their propagandists lie when they tell them their own standard of living is superior to that of the "slaves" in the Western world. So it becomes necessary for the government to create incidents showing the people that foreigners in Moscow are spies, saboteurs, black-market racketeers, degenerates, warmongers and so-called Wall Street imperialists.

—**Robert Magidoff,** *former correspondent for the Associated Press and NBC, who was expelled from Russia for "spying"*

1949

America loses two decisive battles of the cold war in September. On the 21st the largest nation in the world officially becomes the People's Republic of China under the communist rule of Mao Tse-tung. Three days later President Truman shocks the nation with the news that the Russians have exploded their first atomic bomb. The announcement of a pioneering heart operation at the City Club makes news of another kind, while a CIO spokesperson defending a steelworkers' strike vote is greeted with surprising hostility.

JANUARY 21   *Nationalist Chinese president Chiang Kai-shek resigns.*

FEBRUARY 5   China is going communist, and I know of no steps we could now take that would restore United States prestige there.

But Indonesia and French Indochina are other matters. We should let the people of those areas know we are sympathetic

1949

toward their desires for independence. At present the Dutch and French are opposing them with war materials made in America, and this leads the people to believe that we do not want to see them throw off their colonial yokes.

—**John Scott,** *foreign correspondent,* Time

MARCH 8   The French enter into an agreement with Bao Dai, the former emperor of Annam, to recognize the independence of Vietnam, but retain the right to maintain military bases there. This accord only strengthens the determination of the communist nationalists under Ho Chi Minh to fight for their own state.

MARCH 12   Dr. Beck and his associates have performed approximately 5,000 experimental operations...since 1932...to restore circulation in "dry areas" of the heart...blocked off by clotted arteries. His newest...has caused a considerable stir in the world of surgery. This method involves the establishment of a new link by grafting a section of vein between the aorta and the coronary vein and thus reestablishing a new "feeder" into the heart muscle or dry area.

—*Newspaper account of speech by Dr. Claude S. Beck, heart surgeon and professor of neurosurgery of the School of Medicine of Western Reserve University, in which he describes his invention of revascularization*

It sounds like an impossible idea. But ways will be devised to stop the heart, keep the brain alive, open the heart, close it and start it beating again. This development would make it possible to repair defects inside the heart.

—**Dr. Beck**

Q: Is it conceivable that the entire unit of the heart could be replaced in a human being?

Beck: It sounds fantastic. Yet how do we know you can't take the heart from one animal and put it into another? Why doesn't society afford doctors the facilities to work on such an idea?

APRIL 30   Since May 15th, 1948, when the State of Israel was proclaimed, a war has been fought to a successful conclusion against five nations outnumbering the people of Israel 40 times; a government has been established and is functioning; and at the same time the population of 700,000 took in and cared for some 200,000 homeless immigrants. No place in history will compare with it.

Now Israel has declared itself prepared to absorb a million or more immigrants in the next two years. If this country undertook a similar project of the same proportions, it would mean the influx of 15 million immigrants a year. It is not hard to imagine the howls and protests that would arise.

But in Israel there are no protests. The immigrant is welcomed, not only on humanitarian grounds, but on the principle that the

Carl D. Friebolin

country must be colonized and the wastelands made to bloom.

If enthusiasm and confidence will do the trick, then the plan will succeed, providing, of course, that the finances are provided by the outside. And that means, under present world conditions, by American Jewry.

—**Lawrence F. Levenberg,** *foreign affairs editor of the* News, *just returned from a month's tour of Israel*

MAY 2   The Nationalist Chinese government withdraws to the island of Taiwan.

MAY 7   *He has not, like his fellow Republicans, spent his time figuring out how the party lost the last presidential election. He is openly busy with plans on how to lose the next one.*
    —*Carl D. Friebolin, on Senator Taft, in his speech at the 36th annual Anvil Revue, "Some Punkins, or Time Marxes On"*

SEPTEMBER 14   The president of U.S. Steel, the nation's largest steel producer, refuses to accept the recommendation of a presidential commission that the steel industry establish a pension program.

OCTOBER 1   Half a million persons walk off their jobs as the United Steel Workers begin a nationwide strike over the pension question.

OCTOBER 29

*CIO SPOKESMAN RAISES
HAVOC AT CITY CLUB*
    —Press *headline*

The first query put to Carey at the opening of the question period was whether he believed management had any rights and what kind of legislation he would propose to protect the rights of both labor and management.

"I am not so sure we should run to government for rules for management and labor," Carey said....

Rumblings began in the audience that Carey was evading the question....

The cries from the floor rose in volume when Carey was asked if it were true that the men on strike had no opportunity to vote on whether they desired to take such an action.

Carey said it was a myth that labor leaders did not represent the viewpoint of the workers....

"The workers formulated their demands," Carey said, "They voted for a strike if management refused to give them their rights. Is there anyone that denies that a vote was taken?"

Former Common Pleas Judge David Ralph Hertz, labor arbitrator in matters affecting employees of the Cleveland Transit System, at this point asked Carey to tell how a strike vote was taken.

"Each organization," Carey replied, "takes a vote in the

1949

manner it prescribes. I might say that some of the methods may be different from the way you do it here in the City Club."

There was another roar of laughter and cries of "Answer the question."

"It is extremely difficult," Carey said, "for me to make a defense against every idea that runs around in your minds. I have asked you in my main talk and I ask you again to come to our [national] convention in Public Hall next week and see how the CIO is run...."

It was at this point that [City Club Vice President Ben D.] Zevin threatened to adjourn the session....

"It is the tradition of the City Club that speakers who submitted themselves to questioning be required to stick to the question in making replies. These men who have come to hear you," Zevin said, "are, I am sure, bursting with questions."

"I am not so sure," Carey retorted, "that these men are not bursting with indictments."

"It comes down to this," Zevin said. "Each speaker is given a period for his address. That time is all his own. It is expected that he will answer the questions asked.... If you do not intend to answer the questions it seems to me that this meeting should be adjourned."

Edgar S. Byers, a club member of long standing, protested Zevin's attitude as unfair. He maintained that it was up to Carey to answer the questions as he saw fit, whether the audience agreed with the replies or not.

    —Newspaper accounts of a Forum session with James B. Carey, secretary-treasurer, Congress of Industrial Organizations

NOVEMBER 2 *When [Cleveland] Safety Director Al Sutton spoke recently to the City Club Forum, he described the operation of the form of gambling known as policy, and in so doing he mentioned a certain number at random in illustrating how the game is played.*

An unexpected result, Sutton learned later, was a "run" on that number in the policy belt. If the number had "hit," which luckily for the policy operators it didn't, nearly every operator still left in the racket would have gone bankrupt.

    Plain Dealer

NOVEMBER 11 Q: Are you a communist?

Cole: The man who says he is a communist under such conditions of whipped-up hatred is free only to reap the whirlwind of a savage, hysteria-driven mob. Such a man is either foolhardy or a martyr.

And the man who, in such an atmosphere of diseased, depraved morality, under pressure of inquisition, seeks to save himself by saying he is not a communist, thus hoping to divert the violence toward others, is both a fool and a coward.

I trust I am not a fool, and I pray I'll never be a coward.

    —Question-and-answer period following the speech of

Lester Cole, former president of the Screen Writers Guild and one of 10 Hollywood writers cited by HUAC for contempt of Congress two years previously for refusing to respond to the question of whether they were members of the Communist Party

DECEMBER 10 Although there are more college graduates today than ever before in history, we are not making spectacular progress toward the solution of the world's problems. The rates of divorce, crime and delinquency remain high. Neuroses, ulcers and other evidences of undue strain are increasingly commonplace. Social conflict is intense in almost every phase of living. Economic ills persist. If education is the answer, we may reasonably question whether the education we are receiving is the right education.

—**Douglas McGregor,** *president of Antioch College (Ohio), advising the public to pressure educators to undertake bold experimentation with educational methods and programs*

1950

T he McCarthy era begins, and war breaks out in Korea. Against this backdrop of rising anti-communist sentiment in the country, the Soviet Table weighs a name change.

Arthur M.
Schlesinger, Jr.

JANUARY 7 The debate over the welfare state is largely a phony debate. The welfare state is not new in American history, and it does not conflict with American principles. Alexander Hamilton with his system of government aid to business through his tariff proposals was the first champion of welfarism. What is being proposed now is to make available for all members of the community the kind of aid which Hamilton projected for the business community.

—**Arthur M. Schlesinger, Jr.,** *professor of history at Harvard University, defending Truman's Fair Deal proposals to increase the minimum wage, extend Social Security protections to more Americans and expand fair-employment practices*

FEBRUARY 9 Addressing a local Republicans' Lincoln Day dinner in Wheeling, West Virginia, U.S. Senator Joseph R. McCarthy of Wisconsin attracts national attention with his declaration that he has a list of names of 205 communists working for the state department.

MARCH 8 A subcommittee of the Senate Committee on Foreign Relations, chaired by Maryland Democrat Millard Tydings, begins an investigation into the charges made by McCarthy.

APRIL 15 If the Kremlin ever paid Owen Lattimore anything, they got cheated.

—**Weldon James,** *former Far East correspondent and now chief editorial writer of the Louisville* Courier-Journal, *in*

1950

defense of the Far East expert denounced by McCarthy as "the top Soviet espionage agent in the state department"

JUNE 25   North Korean troops invade South Korea, and Truman immediately orders American armed forces to the combat zone.

JULY 17   The Senate subcommittee investigating McCarthy's charges against the state department labels them "a fraud and a hoax." Republicans strenuously object to the findings, and subcommittee chairman Tydings is defeated in the fall in a smear campaign by his opponent.

JULY 29   They will not change the name of the Soviet Table.

At least they will not change it just because the Soviet Socialist Republic is more unpopular than ever as a reaction to the Korean War and the key word in the table's name is anathema to many persons.

Members of the table frowned on the suggestion of a change as an evasion as crass and obvious as trying to change sauerkraut to "liberty cabbage" when we were at war with Germany....

"Anyone who knows the City Club knows what the Soviet Table stands for, and it stands for more bull than anything else," said E.S. Byers....

—News

OCTOBER 15   At a meeting on Wake Island to plot strategy, General Douglas MacArthur, supreme commander for the allied powers in Japan and commander of U.N. forces in Korea, assures President Truman that chances of Chinese intervention in the war are minimal.

NOVEMBER 11   All we seem to care about is to throw out the communists. Gentlemen, that's important. But it is not enough.

—**Barnett R. Brickner,** denouncing American support of such dictators as Syngman Rhee and arguing for a return to morality in foreign policy

NOVEMBER 15   Rabbi Barnett R. Brickner was so convincing at last Saturday's forum that the audience was overwhelmed. No questions.

—The City

Edgar S. Byers

NOVEMBER 24   MacArthur launches what he announces as a general offensive to end the war in Korea and bring the boys home by Christmas. The war is escalated two days later when waves of Red Chinese "people's volunteer" troops cross over the Yalu River into Korea to mount a counteroffensive.

DECEMBER 2 Even if this frightening moment passes —without becoming World War III—it is impossible to guarantee a balance between claims of national security and individual civil liberty. We shall have to go on trying to work out this precarious balance in the midst of global turmoil which the 18th and 19th centuries never knew.
    —Patrick Murphy Malin, *director, American Civil Liberties Union*

1951

Rookie centerfielder Willie Mays joins the New York Giants, Humphrey Bogart and Katharine Hepburn star in *The African Queen,* radio war correspondent Edward R. Murrow begins hosting the weekly TV news show *See It Now* on CBS...and the Korean war drags on. The first whispers of the urban and financial crises that will rock the nation 25 years hence are heard at the City Club.

JANUARY 13 Many well-meaning and honest persons have wanted so much to see a real revolution in China, based on reforms they thought had taken place. But we're not dealing with a new China. Instead of being an authentic or indigenous revolution, it was in reality a military conquest by a strong, well-organized Chinese group completely in accord with the aims of communist Russia.
    —Robert Aura Smith, *editorial writer and Asian specialist,* The New York Times

MARCH 3 In a world that is two-thirds colored, there is a social revolution on the march and the Russians are taking full advantage of it. Every case of lynching or cross-burning or other examples of discrimination against the American Negro are played up as a failure of democracy by the communists. America's race problem is no longer a question of what we're going to do with or for the Negro. It's a question of whether or not democracy will survive.
    —Walter White

APRIL 1 I think that MacArthur has outlived his usefulness in Japan. He is a man who plays military hunches. He had the information that the Chinese communists would intervene [in Korea], but he didn't believe it. MacArthur has a brilliant mind, but his eccentricities of character are dangerous.
    —Hanson W. Baldwin, *military analyst,* The New York Times

APRIL 10 *Truman relieves MacArthur of his command because of the general's repeated public questioning of the President's Korean strategy.*

APRIL 14 A Marine officer told me that if MacArthur wanted to become a permanent deity for the Japanese people what he

1951

should do now is commit hara-kiri. Another said MacArthur would much rather commit Harry Truman.

—**Bennett Cerf,** *president of Random House publishers, who had been touring the Pentagon when the news that Truman had fired MacArthur was announced*

MAY 12 *His distinction is that, unlike so many of his colleagues...he is not in the habit of going off half-cocked when a serious question confronts the country. He gives it the most careful thought and intelligent study—and then goes off half-cocked.*
—Carl D. Friebolin, on Senator Taft, in his curtain speech at the 38th annual Anvil Revue, "The Vice of America, or Hero Today and Gone Tomorrow"

JULY 8   Talks to negotiate a ceasefire in Korea begin at Kaesong, near the 38th parallel.

NOVEMBER 3 I've been asking the mayor when he plans to go to work on the lake-front pollution problem. Isn't it a disgrace that a city with almost 10 miles of lake front doesn't have a single beach you dare step into?
—**William J. McDermott,** *juvenile court judge and the Republican challenger of incumbent mayor Thomas A. Burke*

NOVEMBER 4   Burke is reelected to a fifth and final term.

NOVEMBER 10 During the search for a new commissioner baseball fans were given to believe that the owners of the major league clubs were a bunch of disreputable skunks and someone had to keep an eye on them. It's not true at all. They are fine men, doing business in an honest way.
—**Ford Frick,** *commissioner of major league baseball, in his first public address since being appointed*

NOVEMBER 17 We spent billions trying to prove that military aggression could not be safely undertaken today. But we only succeeded in proving that we can do something against a small aggressor, accidentally, but can't do anything about a big aggressor. The net result is that we are back where we were three years ago, except that 100,000 boys are dead or wounded, and a whole country we went to save has been leveled.
—**Robert A. Taft,** *candidate for the Republican presidential nomination, on the Korean War*

DECEMBER 1 The same self-interest that would lead the Reds to accept an armistice in Korea would keep them out of involvement in Indochina.
—**Dean Rusk,** *assistant secretary of state in charge of Far Eastern affairs (who will serve as secretary of state under Presidents Kennedy and Johnson)*

Dean Rusk

1952

The GOP unveils its vehemently anti-Democrat election-year slogan—Korea, Communism and Corruption (K1C2)—but the turning point in the presidential race seems to come at the City Club, when Harold Stassen, himself a candidate for the Republican nomination, announces "I like Ike." In the fall, California congressman Richard M. Nixon saves his place as the Republican vice-presidential nominee when he goes on television to make his famous Checkers speech denying that he has a secret slush fund. And the club celebrates its 40th anniversary.

JANUARY 19   Taft is the highest type of civil servant. But the feeling of Republicans that they must pick a winner this time or abandon the party may lead them to pick General Eisenhower on the argument that he will draw the independent vote and do better in the South than a man with the label of "Mr. Republican."

—**Merryle Stanley Rukeyser,** *economist and editorial writer,* New York Journal American

JANUARY 26   Forget them.

—**Frank W. Story,** *chief of Cleveland police, advising what to do about the 575,000 parking tickets issued since 1946 for which the city has not received payment*

FEBRUARY 2   An uprising is not only possible, it is imminent.

—**Constantin Boldyreff,** *leader of the anti-communist underground in Russia*

MARCH 1   There are some people...who would have us believe that the public schools are full of commie teachers. I don't know of a communist in the Cleveland public school system. If I did know of such a teacher, I would move in on him faster than a fast talker could say "Jack Robinson."

—**Mark C. Schinnerer,** *superintendent, Cleveland Public Schools*

MARCH 15   In the final analysis, Israel is a Western country, Western in thinking and in culture, Western in its orientation. It is a Western stronghold in the turbulent Middle East. In a showdown we in America will probably need Israel as much as Israel needs us today.

—**Lawrence F. Levenberg,** *recently returned from his second trip in three years to the four-year-old nation*

MARCH 29   Those who couldn't read voted by symbols—a pair of bullocks, a tree, a bicycle, a ladder.

—**Phillips Talbot,** *correspondent,* Chicago Daily News, *who witnessed India's first general election in which eight out of nine of the 100 million persons who voted were illiterate*

1952

APRIL 5   I would have no political objection to hot pursuit across the Yalu.
   —Estes Kefauver, *senator from Tennessee and a candidate for the Democratic presidential nomination, voicing approval of widening the war in Korea to include attacks against North Korea's supply sources in Red China*

APRIL 26   I am pleased the general has declared his Republican affiliation, even though he has greatly reduced my own chances of nomination. I think the Republican Party would have a poor chance of winning if it was tainted with isolationism in November.
   —Harold Stassen, *in a surprise announcement of his support of Eisenhower's candidacy over Taft's*

MAY 2   *Recent events in Washington have tended to show that mere courage without intelligence is dangerous. And Bob Taft, to a remarkable degree, has intelligence—that rare quality of mind which tells him in 1952 exactly what should have been done in 1948.*
   —Carl D. Friebolin, on Senator Taft, in his curtain speech at the 39th annual Anvil Revue, "The Mink Dynasty, or Operation Eyewash"

OCTOBER 6

SPOT FURTHEST FROM MOSCOW
   —Headline of a Plain Dealer *feature on the City Club on the occasion of its 40th anniversary*

OCTOBER 10   *May the City Club savor many more slugfests....*
   —News *editorial congratulating the City Club on its anniversary*

OCTOBER 11   Perhaps we shouldn't have lasted; maybe we did expire and didn't know enough to lie down. Surely it would have been difficult to choose a more fabulous time for our institutional birth than 1912 turned out, in retrospect, to be. Mr. [William H.] Taft was President and normalcy was in effect. How were we to know that we were having one last siesta before a spate of Armageddons....
   When our colonial forefathers heard of national and world affairs, as circuit riders or stagecoaches or occasional periodicals brought the news, they could consider these reports at leisure, discuss them at length and ultimately perhaps have the occasion to register their settled convictions through political action. Now, with radio and video piled on top of telegraph and telephone, and with polls and quizzes demanding instant answers on every issue, the volume, velocity and impact of the in-rushing raw materials of communication can be a bewildering, indeed a terrifying, thing.... We might therefore look on this enterprise

that we are fostering here as a sort of strengthening of the lines of communication...that are so essential if our nation is creditably to effectuate its role in the affairs of a world becoming smaller by the hour.

...This forum didn't invent free speech, nor can we beguile ourselves that we can even say anything about its virtues that others have left unsaid. But we have done this much for it: We've exercised it till the cows come home!

—**Ralph Hayes,** *author of the City Club creed and keynote speaker at its 40th anniversary celebration*

NOVEMBER 16   The United States completes tests of the hydrogen bomb at Eniwetok Atoll in the Marshall Islands.

1953-1963

Back

to

Normalcy

Fifties prosperity allowed the club to deliberate on world issues in peace and calm, a tranquility broken only by the annual antics of the Anvil Revue.

1953

Eisenhower takes office as the 34th President of the United States. Stalin dies and the Korean War officially ends in July, but U.S.-Soviet relations remain tense, especially after the Russians announce the development of their own H-bomb. Nonetheless, a brave voice is raised against McCarthyism at the City Club, which also hears a prediction of the coming of cable TV. Anthony J. Celebrezze begins the first of four terms as Cleveland mayor, and, after many years of debate, Cuyahoga County voters approve a $35-million bond issue to build a subway in downtown Cleveland.

JANUARY 17   America is the most hated nation in the world.
   —Adam Clayton Powell, Jr., *Democratic congressman from Harlem, reporting his findings on foreign opinion about segregation after official trips to Europe, the Near East and the Caribbean*

JANUARY 24   Use of subscription television, still in the planning stage, was offered today as the answer to university financing, falling movie receipts, the declining Broadway theater, dropping sports attendance and parents' problems on what to let their children see on TV.
   ...The new system could be put into effect on all sets now in use by the addition of a scrambling and unscrambling gadget which would control the viewing of the special programs. ...The bill for viewing would come at the end of each month. Charge for each program would be nominal.
   —News *account of a speech by Millard C. Faught, president of the Faught Company, a New York City management firm*

FEBRUARY 7   The most distinguishing characteristic of this new administration is going to be its moderation. It will be a moderation not likely to satisfy the extremists of either side, but a moderation likely to please the great middle majority of voters.
   —Roscoe Drummond, *chief Washington correspondent,* Christian Science Monitor

MARCH 26   In talks with the French premier, President Eisenhower makes a commitment to aid France's war in Indochina.

APRIL 4   Q: Why are so many intellectuals sympathetic to left-wing causes?
   Velde: Because Soviet Russia has sought out our great thinkers for infiltration.
   Q: Do you think the press offers a good field for investigation?
   Velde: I do not. The reading public can judge lies and untruths in print.
   Q: How does a good, honest, decent American have the crust to hide behind the Fifth Amendment?
   Velde: I don't feel that anyone has a right to hide behind the

Adam Clayton Powell, Jr.

1953

Fifth Amendment. It was not provided for persons who come before congressional committees—we aren't a court and we don't convict anyone. No person has a right to use it as a cloak to hide high treachery and deceit.

Q: Would you say that I am a communist sympathizer if I say that your committee is more un-American than anything it has yet investigated?

Velde: Regardless of how much you hate the committee, it is bound and determined to investigate subversives.

—Question-and-answer period following the speech of Harold H. Velde, Republican congressman from Illinois and chairman of the House Un-American Activities Committee

APRIL 22 *Mayor Thomas A. Burke is holding back any reelection candidacy announcement until after the...Anvil Revue. It's a personal favor by his nibs to...[Revue author] Friebolin.... Any announcement earlier would have spoiled the show.*

—News

APRIL 25 There are men in Russia today intelligent enough to know that the main need...is peace. Possibly there were men who saw that Stalin's policies were ruinous...and decided to eliminate him. ...The sole reason for the Iron Curtain is to conceal Russian weakness. There are going to be a lot of red faces among our army brass if that curtain ever comes down, and it is revealed how weak Russia actually is.

—Louis Bromfield, *Pulitzer Prize-winning novelist, weekly newspaper columnist and owner of Malabar Farm in Mansfield, Ohio*

JUNE 19 **Convicted of spying for the Russians, Julius and Ethel Rosenberg are executed for treason, the first Americans to be so punished during peacetime.**

NOVEMBER 14 The President is entitled, I think, to a little recreation. Just the same as everybody else. But if anyone thinks he doesn't devote everything he has morning, noon and night to the welfare of this country, he is badly informed.

—Arthur S. Flemming, *director of defense mobilization, responding to a question from the floor about Ike's avidity for golf*

DECEMBER 5 One of the greatest and yet least noted accomplishments of [Ohio's] sesquicentennial...will be the virtual completion of the award[ing] of contracts for Ohio's and the world's greatest highway. When Ohioans assemble to celebrate Ohio's tercentenary, the pattern of this turnpike and the architectural forms which have developed about it will be noted as among Ohio's proudest accomplishments in the second century of her existence. This turnpike project will some day be revered as a form which will have left an impact on highway construction as great as the roads of the Caesars....

—James W. Shocknessy, *chairman of the Ohio Turnpike Commission, which poured its first concrete for the 241-mile road in October*

Abba Hillel Silver

DECEMBER 12 In the days to come, there will be many political adventurers and unscrupulous demagogues who may wish to ride into power, like Hitler did, on the issue of fighting communism.

They will stop at nothing. They will not limit themselves to routing out communists from government. They will wish to rout out everybody whom they do not like from our educational system, from our universities and colleges, from our churches and from the press.

These people will rally 'round themselves, as Hitler did, all of the reactionaries, all of the enemies of social liberalism in this country, and ultimately they will exploit racial and religious animosities to serve their political ends.

The time to speak out against them is now.

—Abba Hillel Silver

1954

Early in the year Secretary of State John Foster Dulles announces a new American defense strategy of "massive retaliation." He continues to plead unsuccessfully for U.S. air support to prevent the fall of Dien Bien Phu, the base in northern Vietnam where the French have chosen to make a major stand against the communist Vietminh—a foreign policy question that is debated at the City Club. In September the United States joins seven other nations in the signing of the Southeast Asian Treaty Organization (SEATO), a pact that will later be used to justify American military intervention in the war in Vietnam.

Another decision that will dramatically affect life in America is the Supreme Court ruling in *Brown v. Board of Education of Topeka* (Kansas), striking down the doctrine of "separate but equal" schools for whites and blacks and calling for desegregation with "all deliberate speed."

FEBRUARY 6 I want to see every man and woman in the nation a capitalist. I want to see an end to hostility between management, ownership and the workers. My solution is to let all the workers be stockholders and share the risks as well as the profits. Common stocks owned by the citizenry and common sense exercised by business and political leaders would be the most effective antidote against communism and the best guarantee of dynamic and flourishing capitalism. That's a better way to defeat communism than witch hunting and wiretapping.

—Cyrus S. Eaton, *Cleveland financier and industrialist and internationally known advocate of rapprochement with the Soviet Union*

1954

FEBRUARY 4 **Senator McCarthy denounces the Roos-evelt and Truman administrations as "20 years of treason."**

FEBRUARY 13 President Eisenhower should get on the radio and TV and tell the American people what Indochina means to the free world. The Indochina situation is far more dangerous to the security of the United States than Korea was or is. Every military man of standing will tell you that if we lose Indochina, we lose Asia, and if we lose Asia, it is only a question of time until we lose the free world.
—**Stuart Symington,** *freshman Democratic senator from Missouri and former head of the National Security Council*

FEBRUARY 20 Quit smoking, if you want to reduce your chances of lung cancer.
—**Dr. Leonid S. Snegireff,** *associate professor of cancer control, Harvard School of Public Health*

APRIL 10 It wouldn't be wise to discuss Senator McCarthy at this stage. A Senate committee is about to hear all the facts.
—**Leonard W. Hall,** *chairman, Republican National Committee*

APRIL 17 We are spending $1.2 billion this year to keep the war in Indochina going. I think we should continue this aid, but I am against dispatching troops or furnishing air aid.
After all, this is really a war of brother against brother now. Neither the French nor the Americans are going to win it. It will be won by the natives, and I hope by the anti-communist forces.
—**Mike Mansfield,** *Democratic senator from Montana and member of the Senate Foreign Relations Committee, which toured the Far East the previous fall*

APRIL 22 **A Senate subcommittee begins televised hearings on whether Joseph McCarthy has tried to win preferential treatment for a former assistant who had been inducted into the army.**

MAY 1 ...the man to watch....
—**Thomas P. Whitney,** *former Russian correspondent of the Associated Press, on Nikita Krushchev, first secretary of the all-powerful Central Committee of the Communist Party*

MAY 7 **Dien Bien Phu falls after a 55-day siege, forcing the French out of Vietnam.**

JULY 20 **Vietnam is partitioned into northern and southern zones, with the 17th parallel as the dividing line, at the 1954 Geneva Conference.**

NOVEMBER 11   I really think the state of scare is on the way out.

    —Bernard DeVoto, *Pulitzer Prize-winning historian*

DECEMBER 2   *McCarthy is formally censured by his Senate colleagues for his conduct during the Army-McCarthy hearings.*

1955

Aweary Rosa Parks refuses to give up her bus seat to a white man in Montgomery, Alabama. Her arrest leads to a 54-week bus boycott by Montgomery's Negro community that brings a young local pastor named Martin Luther King, Jr., into national prominence as a civil rights leader.

JANUARY 22   The grand project ahead is the adoption and carrying out of guaranteed universal disarmament. The project is difficult, but not impossible. It is enormous in scope and implications, but it can be accomplished within the next six years. A groundswell of comprehension and determination is the sure foundation.... When this arises from the hearts and minds of people in this and other nations, their governments will follow.

    —Ralph E. Flanders, *Republican senator from Vermont*

FEBRUARY 15   *The Atomic Energy Commission releases a report on the H-bomb, stating that it has the capacity to devastate a 700-square-mile area.*

FEBRUARY 19   If enemy bombers headed for Cleveland today, radar warning would give Clevelanders only an hour to evacuate this city, Val Peterson, federal civil defense chief, said today.

    ...With advance planning, with which he urged the city to proceed at once, Peterson said he thought Cleveland could be evacuated effectively in an hour...to concentration points in designated small towns, where [evacuees] would be fed and cared for by prearranged plan.

    He said the "fallout"...from a nuclear explosion decays from within hours to four or five days, so evacuees could expect to be away from their homes for at least that length of time.

    Peterson said no one could be sure, but to be on the safe side he suggested a 15-mile evacuation from the point of explosion.

    In reply to a question from the audience, Peterson said he did not believe there "is such a thing as an intercontinental guided missile, and maybe there never will be."

    —Press

FEBRUARY 26   I believe we will have atomic-generated power for industrial uses within the next three years.... Within the next 10 years it probably will be commonplace.

    —T. Keith Glennan, *president of Cleveland's Case*

1955

Institute of Technology and former member of the Atomic Energy Commission

Q: Has an effective program for the disposal of atomic waste been developed?

Glennan: Some waste can be used. Some probably will have to be taken out to sea and dumped.

APRIL 9 The dangerous thing about the stock market is not that people may lose money. It is the sovereign privilege of all citizens to get trimmed in any way they like. The harmful thing is the speculative episode. When such bubbles burst, they break more than themselves. If we have another big upsurge, it will be a question of curbs on the market or inevitable collapse.

—**John Kenneth Galbraith,** *professor of economics, Harvard University*

NOVEMBER 26 The situation in Vietnam has improved about 1,000 percent in the last year. There is every likelihood that the country which once looked like a certain victim of communism will soon be a showplace of democracy. We backed a winner who believes in democractic institutions, is strongly anti-communist and very popular with his people. That was a change in our usual policy.

—**Wesley R. Fishel,** *assistant director of the government research bureau of Michigan State University, recently returned from a mission to South Vietnam as special adviser to Premier Ngo Dinh Diem*

1956

Diem cancels the free elections provided for by the 1954 Geneva Conference because an estimated 80 percent of the South Vietnamese population would have voted for Ho Chi Minh, president of North Vietnam. The Soviet army crushes anti-government demonstrators in Hungary, and the United States opens its doors— slightly—to a flood of refugees. Dulles announces a new American foreign policy called "brinksmanship," suggesting that the United States will go to the brink of war to keep world peace. Poet Allen Ginsberg sets up a Howl, but most other Americans arc busy watching TV, which they now spend more time doing than any other activity. In November the Supreme Court invalidates the Alabama law providing for segregated buses.

FEBRUARY 18 The present law is...highly discriminatory [against] the people with the know-how, the people who built America. ...[It] is robbing the country of its future growth.

—**T. Coleman Andrews,** *former commissioner of the Internal Revenue Service, on the federal income tax*

FEBRUARY 25 Equality under the law will win eventually, if not immediately. Someone may go to jail in Montgomery,

Alabama; someone may be killed, but equal rights for all Americans are guaranteed by the Constitution and will prevail.
    —Charles H. Wesley, *president of Central State College, a black university in Wilberforce, Ohio*

MARCH 17   The Arabs want justice for the one million Arabs of Palestine who were the victims of the establishment of the State of Israel. ...In many cases the borders were drawn like the 38th parallel in Korea. Villages were divided—homes on one side, wells and farms on the other. Arabs going to their fields or homes are called infiltrators by the Israelis.
    ...There can be no peace [because] the Jews will not give up Jerusalem, will not consent to boundary changes and will not consider the refugee problem....
    —Fayez A. Sayegh, *deputy director, Arab States Delegation to the United Nations*

MARCH 24   On civil rights, the President did nothing until the issue had flared to conflagration proportions and even then he did virtually nothing. He not only didn't do his duty under the existing statutes, but he has remained inexcusably silent on the basic issues. ...By not setting a firm course [he has] encouraged the South to buck the Constitution.
    —G. Mennen Williams, *Democratic governor of Michigan*

MARCH 31   I recommend that the people of the North stop pressuring the people of the South to mix the races in public schools. You can't eradicate a master-and-servant relationship overnight. I urge Northerners to try to keep their heads and not foam at the mouth. If you really want to help, I suggest you use the only method that will alleviate the problem—migration.
    —Thomas R. Waring, *editor, Charleston (South Carolina)* News and Courier

    Q: If Negro health standards are unacceptable in Southern schools, how is it that they are acceptable in homes where Negro domestics are employed?
    Waring: You can screen it better on the home level.
    Q: How is it Negroes and whites can fight side by side in the army and yet not go to school together in the South?
    Waring: The proportion of Negroes to whites in the army is smaller. Besides, you've got discipline to control matters.
    Q: How can the Southern Negro improve morally and educationally if he is treated as an inferior?
    Waring: Whites of good breeding do not treat the Negro as an inferior.
    Q: How do you explain the fact that the recent Supreme Court decision has been welcomed all over the world?
    Waring: It has not been welcomed in the areas in which it applies.

1956

APRIL 7 At this moment the main issue facing the world in the Middle East is the danger that the Arabs, in possession of weapons supplied by Russia, feel that they are capable of carrying out their avowed intention of crushing Israel. Even as I speak, war may have broken out between Egypt, the Arab nations and Israel.

We need arms desperately. If the United States and the Western world callously stand aside and deny Israel defensive arms, they will be blamed nonetheless by the Arabs for the defeat the Arabs are sure to suffer. We are confident we can lick the Arab forces decisively, even at the crippling cost of 15,000 to 20,000 casualties among our young men and the bombing of our cities. The victory might be won over the ruins of Tel Aviv, but it would be won.

—**Colonel Katriel P. Salmon,** *military attache with the Israeli embassy in Washington, D.C.*

Albert S. Porter

APRIL 14 Q: Were you under the influence of chloroform when you traded Larry Doby [the American League's leading home-run hitter in 1953] to Chicago for Chico Carrasquel and Jim Busby?

Greenberg: I wasn't chloroformed. I was just in my usual state.

—*Question-and-answer period following the speech of Hank Greenberg, general manager of the Cleveland Indians*

JULY 26   **President Gamal Abdel Nasser of Egypt nationalizes the Suez Canal a week after the United States withdraws its offer of financial aid for the Aswan Dam in protest of Soviet arms sales to Egypt.**

OCTOBER 29   **Israeli forces invade Egypt, driving toward the Suez Canal. Two days later Britain and France, whose attempts to negotiate international operation of the canal have been frustrated, begin bombarding Cairo.**

NOVEMBER 6   **With both the United States and Russia poised to take action, Britain, France and Israel accept an American-instigated cease-fire enforced by U.N. troops.**

NOVEMBER 17 The world has been near, very near, to a third world war. If there had been no United Nations, I am convinced we would all be involved in that war right now.

—**George Thomas,** *Member of Parliament*

1957

Marilyn Monroe marries playwright Arthur Miller, while her fellow Americans fall in love with the newly invented Frisbee and the Volkswagen Beetle. Nearly 200,000 of the German imports are sold in the 12-month period that will see both the signing of the first civil rights legislation passed in 82 years (it provides penalties for the violation of the voting rights of any American citizen) and Governor Orval Faubus call

out the Arkansas National Guard to prevent the desegregation of a Little Rock high school. Nine black students
are finally enrolled when President Eisenhower orders
U.S. army troops to escort them into the school. Realizing
that the battle against segregation is far from over, Martin
Luther King helps to found the Southern Christian
Leadership Conference.

In Cleveland a dream of another sort dies aborning.
After taking four years to prepare it, Cuyahoga County
Engineer Albert Porter issues his feasibility report on the
proposed downtown subway. Though Porter's recommendation that construction be shelved is vigorously
attacked in a City Club debate, the county commissioners
ultimately accept his advice.

JANUARY 12   Those willing to stand in line from 4 a.m., those
with guts and hard elbows, are the ones who got visas. The
intelligentsia, not so inclined to push and fight with the mob, are
still behind, waiting.

   —Theodore Andrica, *nationalities editor of the* Press, *on
the impact of America's decision to place a 28,000-limit on the
number of Hungarian refugees allowed to enter the country*

FEBRUARY 16   We have followed a blind policy of making oil
our sole concern in the Mideast. That is why, whenever trouble
has arisen between Israel and the Arabs, we have always blamed
Israel and been careful not to antagonize the people who have
the oil.

   If we are going to impose sanctions against Israel for not
obeying the U.N. resolution to get out of Gaza, then why didn't
we impose them against Russia for not obeying the U.N.
resolution on Hungary and against Egypt for not obeying the
U.N. resolution in 1952 on opening the Suez Canal to Israeli
shipping?

   —Spencer D. Irwin, *foreign affairs columnist,* Plain
Dealer

MARCH 9   The heat is on in Washington over big spending.
The year 1957 may go down in history as the year when Congress
really did something to cut the budget.

   —Ned Brooks, *domestic news editor, NBC radio's "Three
Star Extra"*

APRIL 6   **Hyde:** During the month of October 1953, the
merits and demerits of a downtown subway were discussed,
described and debated in every newspaper and on every radio
and television station in Cleveland.

   We all know what happened on election day. The vote was
2-1 for the subway. No other county bond issue had ever won
such widespread support by so great a majority of the voters.

   ...[Yet] Porter's view on the subway remains as it always
was—he's against it. He was unimpressed, unswayed and

1957

unmoved by the thundering voice of this great metropolitan city and county.

...He was unimpressed, unswayed and unmoved by the $257,000 report made by...the county's carefully selected team of consulting engineers which states that the subway is feasible and practical; that it can be built within the $35-million bond issue.

...What makes Porter this way? I believe it is a blind prejudice against public transportation...and his wishful thinking that freeways alone can somehow solve the problems of traffic and congestion.

Porter: If you do get a subway you'll be the sorriest people that I know. They'll tear up the Public Square. They'll tear up Superior Avenue. They'll tear up East 13th Street. They'll tear up Huron Road. They'll cut off your water, your sewer, your lights, your gas, your telephone. Gas lines and water mains will be hung all over the sidewalks. Traffic will be blocked on every street downtown.

It will look like the Battle of the Bulge, and after this has gone on for two or three years Cleveland will be a ghost town. When it is all over you know what you'll have? A hole in the ground and a $50-million headache.

...I am trying to save downtown Cleveland from itself. The central business district has been stagnant for 25 years because you can't get to it with an automobile and you can't find a place to park when you get there. Now let me suggest a way in which downtown Cleveland can be revitalized.

Build an underground parking garage under the Mall and build another under the Public Square. Build a series of bus terminals around the Inner Belt and keep all buses out of the central business district except loop buses.

...Complete the Heights, Central, Willow, Medina and Northwest Freeways and build parking lots next to bus terminals. Then people could come downtown by either bus or car, and if they desired public transportation they could use a loop bus and if not they could find a place to park.

The parking facilities would pay for themselves and the whole plan could be built for a lot less than $50 million without tearing up downtown Cleveland.

—*Debate between Donald Hyde, general manager of the Cleveland Transit System, and Albert S. Porter*

Bill Veeck

APRIL 13   It is unfortunate that baseball, a most entertaining competitive sport, is sold through the win and loss columns. It should be and is good entertainment whether the contest is between the two top teams or the two bottom teams. ...When you emphasize first place as your selling point for baseball, it means that 14 of 16 teams in the major leagues are doing an unsuccessful job.

—**Bill Veeck,** *former president of the Cleveland Indians*

MAY 2   *Senator Joseph McCarthy dies.*

OCTOBER 4   *The U.S.S.R. launches* Sputnik, *the first satellite in space.*

OCTOBER 19   We now can have few doubts about the Russians. We doubted they had the H-bomb. We doubted they had the intercontinental ballistic missile. Now you cannot doubt that thing spinning up there above us at 18,000 miles an hour.

This does not mean the end of the world. ...[*Sputnik*] will be useful in giving us information about cosmic rays and the weather, but there are many other things scientists would like to know more about—cell growth and the mystery of cancer, for instance.

...Nor does it mean that Russia is necessarily first in the missile race. But there is now little question that our top officials have grossly underestimated the value to being the first to get the satellite up in the sky.

—**Ralph E. Lapp,** *former director of the Manhattan Project, calling for the immediate creation of a Department of Science with cabinet rank and a seat on the National Security Council*

NOVEMBER 16   We...can stop [Khrushchev if we] speed up our work...be the first to send mail and freight by rocket, because later you can send military supplies that way; be first to rocket to the moon; be first with interplanetary platforms; be first to send men to outer space and bring them back alive. It may be a stunt at first, but it will draw attention to us. We desperately need to impress people the way Russia has impressed them.

—**Albert Parry,** *professor of Russian civilization and language, Colgate University*

1958

Krushchev becomes the Soviet premier, and unrest in colonial Algeria returns Charles De Gaulle to power in France. In July Eisenhower signs a bill creating the National Aeronautics and Space Administration. Less than three months later NASA launches its first rocket, and that very morning City Clubbers are treated to an insider's account of the heart-stopping liftoff. A full-blown recession also makes headlines, with unemployment by summertime at 7.5 percent, the decade's peak.

FEBRUARY 15   In 10 years or perhaps much less a rocket will be sent to the moon.

—**Walter Sullivan,** *science writer,* The New York Times

MARCH 29   Historically Americans were willing to sacrifice anything to provide educational opportunities for their children. Unfortunately, through the years this kind of support and concern has been worn away. The power and privilege of education we have come to take too much for granted.

We now find the Russians taking a page out of the American

1958

history book and applying unprecedented vigor and resources to their educational system. It is their plan to beat us in the classroom.

—**Lawrence G. Derthick,** *commissioner of education, Department of Health, Education and Welfare*

APRIL 26 We are inclined as a nation to talk big. When we go abroad, all of us tend to become Texans. We talk about our great number of cars. Everything in the United States is bigger and better than anything elsewhere, we are inclined to say. And so we irritate people, and they welcome the chance to laugh at us when we err. ...People like to see the big fellow stub his toe once in a while.

—**George V. Allen,** *director, U.S. Information Agency*

MAY 13 *On a good-will tour of Latin America, Vice President Nixon encounters hostile, stone-throwing mobs in Caracas, Venezuela.*

OCTOBER 11 **Thor,** *the first propulsion rocket to escape earth's gravity, is launched at Cape Canaveral.*

We heard the order for ignition. Then we heard the main stage liftoff. It was described as normal.

One of the colonels connected with the project began to cry. There was a great sigh. You could just feel the great sense of relief.

—**Murray Snyder,** *assistant secretary of defense, describing the scene that morning at the Pentagon, where he had watched* Thor's *launch on closed-circuit TV after an all-night vigil*

OCTOBER 18 Big steel, auto and rubber are not to be found in the forefront of this battle [to pass a right-to-work amendment to the Ohio Constitution]. They recognize that weakened unions mean lower wages, and lower wages mean less purchasing power. This would hurt the corner-store merchant, the farmer, the factory worker and the small businessman. In states where [right-to-work laws have] been enacted, the economy of the state has suffered.

—**Howard Metzenbaum,** *counsel for the Ohio AFL-CIO, arguing against a November 4th ballot issue that will in fact go down to defeat*

NOVEMBER 22 Since the "persuaders" have learned how to trigger our responses we have become overcommercialized as a nation, besieged at every point by more than 1,500 sales messages a day. We have become standardized, homogenized, sterilized and hypnotized. By appealing to our hypochondria, inferiority, anxiety and frustrations, advertising experts are trying to sell the American people on things they really don't need. While this is being done by a corps of 150,000 professional

Cyrus S. Eaton

persuaders, we are losing ground on some of the key tenets of the American creed cherished by our founding fathers. These include respect for the dignity of the individual, freedom of choice and freedom from conformity.

—**Vance Packard,** *author of* The Hidden Persuaders, *a 1957 study of the use of the principles of psychology by mass-marketers*

DECEMBER 13 Getting ready for World War III has become the chief preoccupation of our government, not just our generals. The warlike exhortations from Washington are reported so frequently and prominently on page one that the angry face of our secretary of state has become more familiar than [that of] any cover girl. These official utterances are swiftly followed by inflammatory editorials, reeking of bravado with their dire threats of slaughter to the Soviets. Not only is this constant clamor courting destruction...but it is also leading us to the abandonment of our most cherished principles of freedom of thought and expression.

...This, I am certain, can be mainly blamed on the insane fanaticism of John Foster Dulles, who, by default, has been permitted to dictate American policy for...six years without hindrance from any quarter. In his every decision and declamation, Dulles demonstrates that he so detests communism that he would rather have the human race exterminated than permit communism to exist.

...The disastrous Dulles domination of our foreign policies is the product of default that runs right through practically the whole roster of men the American people have elected to federal office. And the greatest and most glaring default must, I think, be laid to America's industrial giants. Were these business leaders to urge an accommodation with the communist world, our government would have but small choice to change its policy.

—**Cyrus S. Eaton**

1959

On New Year's Day Fidel Castro's guerillas capture Havana and overthrow the regime of dictator Fulgencio Batista y Zaldivar. The United States promptly recognizes the new government, which is described to the City Club by a congressional fact finder as democratic at heart. The hula hoop takes off, and the TV quiz show and radio payola scandals break. Alaska and Hawaii become, respectively, the 49th and 50th states. After resigning in ill health, John Foster Dulles is awarded the Medal of Freedom.

As Cuyahoga County voters prepare to vote once again on the issue of metropolitan government, the City Club examines the parallel question, "Is Cleveland a Dying City?", and witnesses one of its most lively mayoral debates.

JANUARY 10 **Besse:** With 1 percent of the nation's popula-

1959

tion, the Cleveland area provides 2 percent of the nation's industrial production...and has invested $3 billion for industrial plants and equipment since World War II.

One billion dollars has been spent for commercial expansion, including the erection of 16 buildings in a four-block span between East 22nd and East 40th Streets. Our major bank capital has increased from [$65 million] in 1939 to four times that sum 20 years later.

Greater Cleveland's average family income in 1957 was $7,572—second highest (behind Washington) of the 12 largest metropolitan areas—and retail sales per family are highest here.

This area is now the fourth largest research center in America, with 375 companies maintaining 400 laboratories employing 15,700 persons with total wages of $120 million.

...If this be dying—give me death!

Benesch: [Suburbanization has] transformed Cleveland from what Tom Johnson envisaged as a city on a hill to what is almost a village on a shamefully neglected lake front adjacent to a valley which was once a beehive of industrial activity and from America's sixth city to America's seventh.

Many owners of downtown real estate—trust companies or estates or investment trusts—feel immediate income is more important than the future development of the city. Apparently New York and Boston investors are more acutely aware that the central city is, in the final analysis, the basis of municipal well-being. Have we not the right to assume these "foreign" investors—life insurance companies in particular—have as competent a staff of appraisers as any of our local banks, which are reluctant to finance substantial local undertakings? Are these insurance companies not as vitally interested in protecting their policyholders as are the banks in protecting their depositors and stockholders?

—*Debate on the health of the city between Ralph M. Besse, vice president of the Cleveland Electric Illuminating Company, and Alfred A. Benesch, attorney and member of the Cleveland Board of Education*

FEBRUARY 28   Castro and his men are as decent as Batista and his men were indecent. ...The Castro men never looted, they never raped, they never tortured or killed prisoners. I have met many of them. Never have I seen one who swaggered or was loudspoken. They are not a rabble in arms. They are disciplined and restrained, dedicated but not fanatical....

The Cuban revolution was not a change of the palace guard. It may not achieve all its noble ends. It may even degenerate into a police state of the left or the right, but I don't think it will. The determination of the Cuban heart to establish honest and democratic government is too intense and too universal.

—**Charles O. Porter,** *Democratic congressman from Oregon, recently returned from a tour of Cuba*

MARCH 14   If federal action had not been taken, it seems to me entirely likely that school segregation voluntarily would have been abandoned by now in such states as Kansas, Missouri, Oklahoma, Kentucky, Maryland, Delaware and possibly Tennessee and Texas. To those of you who may be incredulous, I would recall that once many of the Southern states imposed poll taxes as a device to minimize Negro voting. Slowly but steadily, these taxes were abandoned. Even South Carolina, oldest and deepest state in the old and deep South, voluntarily amended her state constitution five years ago to abolish her poll tax.

—**James J. Kilpatrick,** *editor, Richmond* News Leader

APRIL 11 Isn't that a beautiful sight? They are like sails billowing in the wind.

—**Dr. Willem J. Kolff,** *director of the department of artificial organs of the Cleveland Clinic, operating the valves on a metal-polyurethane artificial heart developed at the Clinic that he says could be ready for use in three years*

MARCH 21 I was in Russia and Poland in the spring of 1956, and I am not trying to say Russia and our country are the same. But there are many parallels. The difficulty is to calm people down so that we can look at the mote in our own eye.

Each country thinks of itself as an idealized image and of the enemy as a caricature. We are a bunch of Thomas Jeffersons and they are a bunch of labor slaves.

...[America] criticizes...Russia's treatment—censorship—of Boris Pasternak and suppression of his *Doctor Zhivago*. And yet the motion picture industry runs the biggest blacklist of our own Pasternaks. How in this case do we differ from Russia?

We chase the world's greatest comic—Charlie Chaplin—out of the country. And when one of your own Cleveland theaters runs an ad in the newspapers for old Chaplin movies it feels it must carry a note of apology. ...We wouldn't give Paul Robeson a passport because we didn't like his ideas. We blacklist movie artists and writers, ban Charlie Chaplin and harass Robeson because we are afraid of communists. Well, the Russians are afraid of capitalists.

—**I.F. Stone,** *editor and publisher of* I.F. Stone's Weekly, *a gadfly newspaper, covering national politics and the press, based in Washington, D.C.*

OCTOBER 31 Q: What is your position on the hotel proposed for the Mall?

Ireland: I'm against the Mall hotel. It's the biggest land grab since the Dutch bought Manhattan Island from the Indians for $20 worth of trinkets. This New York promoter doesn't even want to put up $20.

The city of Pittsburgh now is involved in tearing down buildings to get a mall. Why, after 50 years of preserving this land, should we give it up? This is illegal, in violation of the Constitution, this shoebox-on-end rising 26 stories that they propose to build. It's ugly, monstrous.

1959

Celebrezze: This is not a giveaway. We're going to get a rental of $100,000 or 1 percent of the gross income, whichever is greater. ...It will mean 1,000 new jobs and $4 million a year into our economy. Not one cent of the taxpayers' money goes into this. It burns me up to hear this talk of "giveaway." ...If anyone will come forward with a constructive plan to build a hotel, after we have waited for 30 years, I'll help.

—Traditional mayoral debate between millionaire Republican businessman Tom Ireland and Democratic incumbent Anthony Celebrezze, seeking his fourth term

Q: Aren't you running for mayor in the wrong city, since you live in Shaker Heights?

Ireland: Will the questioner identify himself?

Q: Dan Winston [Democratic nominee for Congress in the 23rd district in 1958].

Ireland: Where do you live?

Q: University Heights.

Ireland: Well, if you would stick your head out of University Heights once in a while, you would find that I have lived in the city since the primary campaign began, that I have slept and lived in the city every day since.

Q: But where are your children going to school?

Ireland: None of your damn business.

NOVEMBER 3 *The voters return Celebrezze to office, defeat the Mall hotel proposal and, for the second time in 10 years, reject a county charter form of government.*

NOVEMBER 21 Though Senator John Kennedy is now in front and campaigning very effectively as I saw him a half dozen times stumping Wisconsin recently, I believe Adlai Stevenson will emerge on top from a deadlocked Democratic convention. Kennedy is young. He can afford to wait. ...My hunch is he will be happy with the number two spot this time.

—Morris H. Rubin, *editor,* Progressive *magazine*

1960

Krushchev's announcement that an American U-2 spy planc has bccn shot down ovcr Russia makes world headlines. Though the U.S. initially denies the charge, pilot Francis Gary Powers is said to have confessed to spying. The sit-in is born in Greensboro, North Carolina, when four black students sit down at a Woolworth's lunch counter to protest its "whites only" serving policy. Within 12 months 50,000 persons will participate in similar demonstrations across the country, which represent only the first stirrings of a nationwide civil rights movement, the executive director of the NAACP makes plain to a City Club audience. Other of the year's inventions: oral contraceptives, the Twist and the Student Non-Violent Coordinating Committee (SNCC).

FEBRUARY 6   On my first day here, I was being shown about by a real estate man, and we commented that a certain apartment house was not unattractive. "Very nice place" was the response, "but unfortunately they don't take Jews."

The cold-water shock of the un-Christian unfriendliness, the revelation that medieval attitudes persist in modern Cleveland, left a chill that has not yet quite worn off.

The proper amenities from group to group are expressed, their ambassadors go back and forth, they even meet in committee and council, in voluntary agencies and organizations and on the top level of academic institutions. But the people do not really know one another. Indeed, they manifest no great desire to know one another. They prefer to sit smugly in the midst of their secure prejudices.

In Cleveland the five o'clock shadow is deep and complete. The after-dark social dividing lines constitute an "iron curtain...."

—**Arthur J. Lelyveld,** *newly named rabbi of Cleveland's Fairmount Temple*

FEBRUARY 13   *France explodes her first A-bomb.*

FEBRUARY 20   The significance in Tanganyika's move for independence is that it will give us a chance to give the lie to fears of some Europeans that an African-controlled democracy means the end of white men's rights. This is nonsense.

The fears of Europeans about Africans governing stem from something that is, to them, logical. They reason: "This is how we have treated the Africans. What happens when control passes into the hands of Africans? Are they not going to retaliate?"

We say, "No, the Africans are not going to retaliate."

—**Julius Nyerere,** *who will become Tanganyika's prime minister when Britain grants it independence later in the year*

FEBRUARY 27   We hear people say that they wish they were living in another age, where they might escape today's anxieties and tensions. Yet examination of fossils thousands of years old in the Nile Valley indicates those ancient people suffered just as we from the stresses and strains of their times.

—**Dr. A. Dixon Weatherhead,** *psychiatrist, Cleveland Clinic*

Q: What is the effect of *The Three Stooges* on children?

Weatherhead: This is a very valuable [TV] program. It keeps children contented [and] makes for peace in the home.

APRIL 16   In the six years since the Supreme Court decision, 6 percent of Southern schools have been desegregated. This blinding speed of 1 percent a year is what the South is screaming about and what the North has accepted as going too fast.

...Negroes are convinced that a welter of technicalities are being used against them. To fight back, we must mobilize as

1960

many kinds of pressure as we can in our behalf. The message of this movement is plain and short: Negro youth is finished with racial segregation, not only as a philosophy but as a practice.
　　—Roy Wilkins, *executive secretary of the NAACP, indicating that sit-down demonstrations are only the beginning of a massive civil rights campaign*

SEPTEMBER 26　The first of four hour-long debates between the presidential candidates is televised.

OCTOBER 1　Both Kennedy and Nixon are good actors, cunning and shrewd politicians and capable performers before their audiences. But both men are cold and lack the natural warmth of an Eisenhower or a Roosevelt.
　　...Nixon is shy but good at a news conference. In a receiving line he appears more interested in what he is doing than Kennedy. ...Kennedy just repeats the same words over and over again when meeting people at a reception. But when Kennedy speaks, his audience soars with him.... Audiences do not soar with Nixon.
　　—John F. Day, *vice president in charge of news, CBS*

OCTOBER 8　I am not in favor of the TV debate idea for presidential candidates. I think such appearances are all right on the state level or for lesser offices. But the really big issues can't be properly dealt with in the way the TV debates are being presented. ...There are too many small things which distort the images of these candidates, such things as studio lighting and face powder, as in the first debate.
　　—Eugene McCarthy, *first-term Democratic senator from Minnesota*

V.K. Krishna Menon

OCTOBER 22　There is no major economic group on the average that is not earning more, producing more and living better than ever before in America's history. A nation whose Republican administration has been able to register this kind of across-the-board dollars-and-cents accomplishment since 1952 cannot be stampeded into running in reverse in a misguided effort to revive the outdated economics of the New Deal.... If this is what Senator Kennedy has in mind—as he has implied many times—then he would lead us to a new frontier which is in reality the lost horizon.
　　—Jacob K. Javits, *Republican senator from New York*

DECEMBER 14　Why are you Americans always assuming that everyone who is not for you is against you?
　　—V.K. Krishna Menon, *defense minister of India and special ambassador to the United Nations*

1961

John F. Kennedy takes office, becoming the country's first Catholic President and, at age 43, its youngest. The new administration makes several fateful decisions: to proceed (on April 17th) with President Eisenhower's secret plans to have a CIA-trained force of Cuban exiles invade Cuba and to increase significantly the American military presence in South Vietnam. In April Soviet cosmonaut Yuri Gagarin becomes the first man to orbit the earth; shortly thereafter America boasts its first man in space—Alan B. Shepard. Ernest Hemingway commits suicide and, after a lengthy trial in Israel, Nazi Adolf Eichmann is found guilty of crimes against humanity and sentenced to death. Democrat Ralph Locher is elected mayor of Cleveland, perpetuating his party's longtime hold on city politics.

JANUARY 3   Just before he leaves office President Eisenhower breaks diplomatic relations with Cuba.

JANUARY 14   The huge unpleasant image of Fidel Castro hinders our seeing the Cuban people in the shadow of that image. We have wrapped up the Cuban problem in the personality of Castro and dismissed both.

    —**Kyle Haselden,** *managing editor of* Christian Century, *recently returned from a 12-day visit to Cuba*

Q: If Castro is doing so much for Cubans, why are they leaving?

Haselden: There are a lot of unhappy people in Cuba, and if I lived there I might be, too. It is the common people who are benefiting from Castro's policies.

The forum speaker advised the U.S. not to:
• Invade Cuba under any pretext.
• Try to return Cuba to the Batista era.
• Continue propaganda depicting Cuba as a villainous little boy tormenting a neighbor.
• Cut off trade with Cuba.
    —Press

FEBRUARY 11   Males want to do he-man's work, and there is no simple solution to this problem of unemployment like saying all married women should give up their jobs.

    —**Ewan Clague,** *U.S. commissioner of labor statistics*

FEBRUARY 13

CALLOOH, CALLAY, OH FRABJOUS DAY
THE LADIES WILL BE HERE!
Because the ladies consume more than anyone (who will deny), we've decided to open our manly and virile quarters to the gentle but consumptive sex for this meeting. All husbands who are confused by the Rube Goldberg abominations in our houses and garages and who are constantly nursing sore thumbs and checkbooks brought on by so-called repairs are urged to

1961

come and bring their gentle consumers.
    —*Announcement in* The City *of the "Ladies Day" speaker, Colston E. Warne, president of the Consumers Union*

MARCH 18   Who murders our daughters? Their fathers, 20 to 1.

Who murders our wives? Their husbands, 10 to 1. Or their brothers, 8 to 1.

Only 5 percent of the total number of murders of women in this country over a five-year period were done by persons outside the family.
    —**Donal E.J. MacNamara,** *dean of the New York Institute of Criminology and president of the American League to Abolish Capital Punishment, in response to a statement from the floor that capital punishment deters violence against women*

MAY 6   For the first time we are living in an age when material comfort is possible for almost everyone. But if this, because it is so much more available, is sought not in addition to emotional contentment, but in lieu of it, then there is the danger of our becoming addicted to it. We will need more and more goods, more and more technological progress to cover up our emotional want and discomfort.
    —**Bruno Bettelheim,** *psychologist, educator and author*

MAY 13   Castro...was hailed by us when he began to make his move. ...Some of our most distinguished newspapers began to lionize Castro. He was called an agrarian reformer.

We imposed an embargo on Cuba. Batista fled and Castro took over. We paid him twice the world price for his sugar; we brought him to the United States for a red-carpet welcome while he insulted us and expropriated American property.

And now Cuba is available as a communist launching pad in this hemisphere.
    —**Robert Morris,** *former counsel to the internal security subcommittee of the Senate*

Bruno Bettelheim

MAY 14   In Alabama a vehicle carrying Freedom Riders protesting interstate bus segregation is burned and its passengers attacked.

MAY 19   *There'll be a change in the Blue Room;*
    I'm going to paint it green.
    I'll do things Raymond Loewy's never seen.
    My hairdo is different and so is my hat,
    Might as well be ditto with my habitat.
        —*Solo by "Jacqueline Kennedy," sung to the tune of "There'll Be Some Changes Made" in the 48th annual Anvil Revue, "That New Jack Magic, Bennie in Blunderland"*

AUGUST 13   *East Germany closes the border between East and West Berlin by building a wall between the city's two sectors.*

SEPTEMBER 23   Until the Freedom Riders dramatized the situation, many Americans suffered from the illusion that all was going well with the program of integration, that the problem was solving itself.
—**James Farmer,** *director of the Congress of Racial Equality (CORE) and founder of the Freedom Riders, speaking the day after the Interstate Commerce Commission ruled against interstate bus segregation*

Farmer is a veteran of 40 days in a Mississippi jail, one of the first Freedom Riders to win what he called "this badge of honor."

"If the road to freedom goest through the jail," he told his City Club audience, "I must abide in jail for awhile."

Freedom, he said, is at least the world's second most important problem, the first job being to prevent a world conflict.

"Or we may all be equally dead."
—Plain Dealer

OCTOBER 7   The wall in Berlin is not a victory for Russia. It proves Berlin already is a defeat for communism.
—**Richard H. Rovere,** *staff writer,* The New Yorker

DECEMBER 2   If the best creative minds in the country had recognized the potential of television at the start, and the obligation to develop it as a public service, business would not have taken over. In their disinvolvement, in their arrogant abstinence, they bear a heavy responsiblity for the medium's sins and stupidities....
—**Marya Mannes,** *television and theater critic for* Reporter *magazine, criticizing intellectuals who refuse to have a television set in their homes*

DECEMBER 22   *Specialist Fourth Class James Davis of Livingston, Tennessee, is killed by the Viet Cong. Later he is cited by President Lyndon B. Johnson as "the first American to fall in defense of our freedom in Vietnam."*

1962

The world is poised on the brink of war in mid-October when the United States discovers the presence of Soviet missile bases in Cuba and President Kennedy responds by ordering a naval blockade of the island. After a week of intense negotiations the Soviets agree to dismantle their bases in exchange for the United States' public promise not to invade Cuba. The confrontation awakens both sides to their vulnerability. The following year a telephone hotline linking Washington and Moscow is installed, and both countries and Britain sign a nuclear test-ban treaty. Meanwhile, the City

1962

Club welcomes two noted right-wing representatives.

JANUARY 20   Q: Why should America continue to spend millions on advancing the progress of emerging nations, and is it making us any friends?

Mead: Cleveland is living proof that underdeveloped peoples can be developed. Clevelanders took people from some very strange places and made them into Clevelanders. It didn't make any difference whether your grandfather could read or not, if you could. It didn't make any difference if your grandfather wore shoes or was a practicing pirate.

Bring the people to America, move them into a good slum, send them to American schools and the next generation they are Americans.

—Question-and-answer period following the speech by Margaret Mead, anthropologist and author of Coming of Age in Samoa

FEBRUARY 10   Suppose you were walking over a golf course with the president of the golf club, and you noted a lot of holes—divots—gouged in the green. You'd probably say, "Gee, you got a lot of lousy caddies here." But you wouldn't demand that the president name them.

—Robert Welch, *retired Massachusetts candymaker and president of the John Birch Society, on why he has consistently declined to name any of the several thousand "comsymps" he has charged are in the employ of the federal government*

Q: Do you think that the Southern Christian Leadership Conference is more intimately related to communism than Christianity?

Welch: I do.... The phrase "civil rights" has been tossed around so much and so incorrectly and with such wild thoughts attached to it that, in my opinion, it has been used to some extent at least as a slogan and a weapon to stir up trouble and to cover up other things.

Q: Were you quoted correctly in saying that democracy is mob rule?

Welch: Not exactly correctly, but I won't quarrel with it, it is that close. I have said in print and I will say over again that democracy is a weapon of demagoguery and perennial fraud. ...Our founding fathers did everything in the world they could to prevent us from having a democracy. ...In the last 100 years there has been a left-wing conspiracy to change us from a republic to a democracy.

Q: Do you believe wholeheartedly in what you say?

Welch: ...I have never drawn one penny of pay from our magazine or one penny of pay from the John Birch Society.... I am living on what little bit of savings we had. I tell my wife if she would stop eating so much we could live better. She sometimes objects to that.

I am working, I will assure you, 16 to 18 hours a day, seven

Margaret Mead

days and nights a week, with no chance of ever getting any peace from all the harassment or any leisure.... I assure you I would not be doing that if I didn't believe in its necessity.

FEBRUARY 24   The established foreign policy of our nation is based on coexistence so that the communists will have time to "evolve" into rational human beings. It means we sit on our hands...in the fond hope that the Soviets will turn...from arms...to consumer goods and get too fat, lazy and self-satisfied to be their nasty, vicious, depraved selves. It means we write off the captive nations for whatever period it takes the communists to "evolve," even if it's three centuries.
    —**Strom Thurmond,** *Democratic senator from South Carolina*

MARCH 17   We Germans are too eager to blame Eichmann for everything, because that way we escape our own guilt; not the guilt of actual murder but the guilt of originally tolerating Hitler's racial theories, the guilt that made the actual murders possible.
    —**Paul Danaceau,** *reporter who covered the Eichmann trial for the Westinghouse Broadcasting Company, quoting a German reporter he had met there*

APRIL 22   Cleveland's burden has been a long history of bad planning.... You decentralized your cultural centers away from the major portions of the city and also spread governmental buildings around the downtown area. It was once thought this was good, but we now find out it will not work. It is inexcusable to repeat the principles that have failed.
    —**Jane Jacobs,** *associate editor of* Architectural Forum *magazine, criticizing Erieview, the City of Cleveland's urban renewal plan to build approximately five million square feet of office space in the isolated northeast sector of downtown*

NOVEMBER 10   No matter what the Supreme Court has ruled, there will be segregation in education as long as there is segregation in housing.
    —**Algernon D. Black,** *chairman of the National Committee Against Discrimination in Housing, calling for Ohio to join 11 other states in passing fair-housing legislation*

    Q: Would a mixed, mongrel race be superior in intelligence to what we have?
    Black: ...I don't think people are going to run into each other's arms and mate just because a law is passed.

1963   The Supreme Court hands down two landmark decisions—that states must provide indigent defendants with free counsel and that prayer in schools violates the First Amendment. The latter decision is defended at the City Club by a high-ranking government attorney named Archibald Cox.

1963

Other of the year's important developments: The Diem government is overthrown in a military coup, and the Red Chinese explode their first atomic bomb. Kennedy visits the Berlin wall and Dallas. James A. Rhodes takes the oath of office as Ohio governor.

APRIL 13 Publishers [in one-newspaper towns] today can cut out news the same way the only saloon in town, in the old days, could cut out free lunch.... Most newspapers offer their readers only a few stale pretzels and moldy peanuts.
　　—**A.J. Liebling,** *press critic,* The New Yorker

Q: What steps would you suggest, by whom, to improve the quality of newspapers?
Liebling: The only one I can think of offhand is for organized labor to start up some newspapers. They would be biased in favor of labor, as most newspapers are biased against labor, but then each side would try to nail down the other's lies. The public could then choose between two versions and perhaps reach a middle conclusion.

MAY 4 Whether one agrees or disagrees with that decision, surely it was emotional nonsense to call the court irreligious or to call the decision an attack upon religion.
School prayers helped to inculcate a religious feeling, and many will regret their omission as well as doubt the Constitutional necessity. But the ruling also was consistent with the deepest kind of religious feeling—with the belief that religion is far too personal, far too important, far too fundamental to be mixed up with the affairs of government.
　　—**Archibald Cox,** *U.S. solicitor general who a decade later will be named special prosecutor in the investigation of the Watergate break-in and cover-up*

AUGUST 28 *In Washington, D.C., 200,000 civil rights marchers at the Lincoln Memorial hear Martin Luther King give what will become known as his "I have a dream" speech.*

SEPTEMBER 25 *The United Freedom Movement (UFM), a coalition of civil rights groups, begins picketing the Cleveland Board of Education building, demanding "meaningful integration" of the system by the opening of the following school year.*

OCTOBER 19 **Zuverink:** The United Freedom Movement believes these things can be done about segregated schools in Cleveland: ...introduce integrated teaching materials, establish an in-service teacher training program in human relations and minority group cultures, develop programs to increase inter-group contacts, recruit and place teachers on a non-discriminatory basis, develop a plan for the September 1964 maximum

A.J. Liebling

integration of classrooms.

McAllister: The greatest danger in this whole procedure of the UFM is that it ignores the principal of individual responsibility.

As I watched [them picket] the school board building, the thought occurred to me that these people could be doing much more to improve the environment in which much of the problem they were picketing about is spawned.

...I wondered [if] these pickets should waste their time walking about the school board building when they might have been collecting clothes for needy children or conducting classes for newly arrived immigrants.

—Debate between the Reverend David L. Zuverink, UFM spokesperson, and Ralph McAllister, president of the Cleveland Board of Education

NOVEMBER 5   Democrat Ralph Locher, who had been elected in 1962 to replace Anthony Celebrezze as mayor of Cleveland when President Kennedy named Celebrezze his secretary of health, education and welfare, is reelected without opposition. This is believed to be the first time in American history a major-city mayoral candidate has run unopposed.

NOVEMBER 22   John F. Kennedy is assassinated in Dallas.

NOVEMBER 23 Poison and hate have done their worst and left us desolate. But the American people, in remembrance of President Kennedy, will rise, I believe, in a mighty resolve to carry forward...his devotion to fulfilling the American dream.

—Frank P. Graham, *senior member of the secretariat of the United Nations*

1964-
1974

A

House

Divided

Heated protest marked the country's—and the club's—passage through the turbulent Sixties and Seventies.

1964

The Warren Commission concludes that Lee Harvey Oswald acted alone in the assassination of John F. Kennedy. His successor is given carte blanche by Congress in conducting the war in Vietnam after two U.S. destroyers are attacked by the North Vietnamese in the Gulf of Tonkin. Despite the passage of the so-called "Gulf of Tonkin" congressional resolution, which gives new President Lyndon Johnson the power "to take all necessary measures to repel any armed attack against the forces of the United States and to prevent further aggression," voices raised in protest of the escalating war can now be heard, including at the City Club. On the domestic front Johnson declares a "war on poverty" and asks Congress for $962 million to fight it.

JANUARY 4   The American government has been trying to persuade us we are winning the war [in Vietnam]. The people who have said this are either uninformed or misinformed and open to charges of gross incompetence or lying to the American people.
   —**Robert Trumbull,** *chief correspondent for China and Southeast Asia,* The New York Times

FEBRUARY 8   We jump to the conclusion that if we pull out of the Middle East and Far East and stop trying to influence the African nations that all those countries will automatically go communist. Even if they did—and I don't think they would—it is wrong to assume they would automatically be tied to Russia or Red China. In any event, it is better to run that risk than to get into untenable positions such as Vietnam.
   —**Fred Warner Neal,** *professor of international relations, Claremont (California) Graduate School*

FEBRUARY 19   Whether we like it or not, the white man is going to be driven out of Asia, even it takes 50 years. ...We simply cannot win a guerilla war in [South Vietnam].
   —**Wayne Morse,** *Democratic senator from Oregon*

FEBRUARY 25   Cassius Clay defeats Sonny Liston to gain the world heavyweight boxing championship.

MARCH 21   The neighborhood school was productive 50 years ago. Today it is largely destructive. It makes no difference whether it is the golden ghetto of the privileged, the shiny ghetto of the middle class or the dusty ghetto of the poor. It develops and strengthens the idea of a class society...and class struggle. ...When it should function as the child's image of his society and his future, it presents him with an unrealistic picture of both—a shining reality for some and another reality for others.
   —**Max Wolff,** *sociologist, calling for the creation of federally financed "educational parks" with as many as 15,000 students from kindergarten through high school*

1964

APRIL 6 *Twenty-one members of the United Freedom Movement begin picketing the building sites of three new schools in Cleveland's black community whose construction they claim will help to perpetuate segregation. During the second day of demonstrations the Reverend Bruce Klunder, a white Presbyterian minister, is accidentally crushed to death by a bulldozer at one of the sites.*

MAY 22 *Chairman [of a mythical Senate committee investigating civil rights]: Do you feel that you have ever been discriminated against?*

Negro: Only on occasion.

Chairman: On what occasions?

Negro: Well, on the occasions when I'm looking for work, on the occasions when I want to find a place to eat and on the occasions when I'm looking for a place to live.

[Senator James O.] Eastland [of Mississippi]: There! You see! This whole thing has been blown way out of proportion!

  —Scene from a skit at the 51st annual Anvil Revue entitled "This is the Show That Wasn't" because it takes the form of a testimonial dinner for Carl D. Friebolin

OCTOBER 2 *The City Club moves its Forum from Saturday to Friday in response to dwindling attendance.*

Well, people stopped working on Saturdays.... Television began to emerge as a communications factor and as an entertainment factor, and bear in mind that the City Club was, in addition to everything else—there might be some purists who take offense at this—entertainment. ...Downtown began to die. ...The club membership, which had always run around 1,200, 1,300 members—it was down to 900.

The club was running...about a $20,000 deficit in those years.... So [when] I rolled in there in January '65 [as club secretary], we got the Forum Foundation to make the City Club a $20,000 loan. ...We got a true count on our membership. It was more like 700. We raised dues. But the critical thing [that saved the club] was the 1965 mayoral debate.

The City Club [had become] caught up in worldwide issues. ...And this was a critical time for Cleveland. Pete DiLeone, who was the president of the club, really was the guy who said...we're going to focus in on what's going on in our town 'cause it's the Cleveland *City Club.*

  —Peter Halbin, in an interview with the authors

NOVEMBER 6 We'll be returning to the streets in ever greater numbers now that the election is over. This time, however, we must broaden the participation to include many more whites, and we must concentrate on economic measures and not so much on public accommodations. The right to use accommodations doesn't mean anything for the Negro if he doesn't have the money to use them.

If President Johnson is really interested in creating the Great Society he speaks of, then he should welcome the Negro's return to the streets. If there had been no Negro demonstrations for jobs, there would be no war on poverty for the Johnson administration. If there had been no Negro demands for school integration, there would have been no great debate on establishing 20th-century education in this country to supplant the 19th-century system we have. If there had been no Negroes in motion, there would have been no ecumenical religious movement concerned with social issues.

The Negro alone has been the catalyst in advancing social progress.

—**Bayard Rustin,** *assistant to Martin Luther King and deputy director of the civil rights march on Washington the previous year*

1965

A devastating riot breaks out in the Watts section of southwest Los Angeles, precipitated when a white policeman flags down a black motorist he suspects of drunk driving. When the burning and looting subside six days later, having caused $40 million in damages, 34 persons are dead, and many Americans are shaken by the realization that civil rights achievements in the South have not been matched in the West and North. Even so, a charismatic young black politician named Carl Stokes makes a credible showing in Cleveland's mayoral race, in part due to his performance at the City Club's primary debates, in part due to the city's burgeoning Negro population. By 1965 one of every three Clevelanders is black.**

JANUARY 7 If President Johnson moves decisively for peace, our people will support him. If, instead, he approves steadily expanding military involvement, he will please our militarists and war hawks in Congress. Then in the 1966 congressional elections and in 1968, as casualty lists mount, some Republican politicians, now urging acceleration of the war by bombing Hanoi and Haiphong and even Red China, will be first to denounce "Lyndon's war."

Can anyone claim that we would lose face and that our prestige in Asia would be damaged were we to withdraw from this conflict? A great nation like ours cannot lose face by withdrawing from a miserable war. ...We Americans should not be so much interested in saving face as in saving lives—the lives of Americans and Asiatics.

—**Stephen M. Young,** *Democratic senator from Ohio*

*MARCH 8 **Two battalions of Marines land in South Vietnam, the first American combat forces sent to that country.***

1965

MARCH 21 *After being blocked by Alabama state troopers on their first two attempts, more than 3,000 civil rights demonstrators begin marching under the protection of federal troops from Selma to Montgomery to protest voting rights discrimination.*

APRIL 26 Craig: You cannot find a moderate thinker in Selma. But that does not mean there are not moderates.

Krawcheck: I couldn't find the [alleged] sex orgies. I heard some folk singing and drank some very bad coffee.

—Bob Craig, managing editor of the Spartanburg (South Carolina) Journal, *and Julian Krawcheck, reporter for the* Press, *discussing their experiences covering the Selma march*

SEPTEMBER 10 Chips flew in the City Club yesterday as mayoral candidates Carl B. Stokes [Democratic state representative] and Ralph J. Perk [Republican county auditor] lashed at one another over the issue of Cleveland's municipal finances.

The chips were real—poker chips used by Perk to illustrate [that] at City Hall...Mayor Ralph S. Locher is saddled with the political friends of former mayors.... [Perk stacked] a new layer of chips atop the previous one as he mentioned each mayor.

"If I am elected, I will destroy this layerism," said Perk, smashing the stack to the floor.

—Plain Dealer

I remember when I debated Ralph Perk on finances in 1965, he had a stack of poker chips on the table and to make his point about the high number of persons on the city payroll, he set the poker chips up and then dashed them aside the way he would cut the payroll of the City of Cleveland. Quite effective for the moment until I rose to remind the audience that those poker chips represented people, working men with families, people who should not be arbitrarily dismissed by knocking down a pile of poker chips when there's no indication that their services haven't been needed and they haven't been of substantial worth to our city. I don't think Perk's stunt went very far.

[The debate] more than anything else illustrated that Carl Stokes, black man, understood municipal finances, first. Secondly, that he understood [them] better than the white man he was debating, and, thirdly, [it] helped to legitimize me as a candidate for mayor. Of course, nobody would think: Why should Carl Stokes, who had a bachelor's degree and a law degree from one of the Big 10 colleges and a juris doctor from Cleveland Marshall Law School—why would I [need to] legitimize myself, when Ralph Perk had only a ninth-grade education and nobody was questioning whether or not he could understand finances and manage a city?

—Carl B. Stokes, in an interview with the authors

Carl B. Stokes

My mistake in debating Stokes, I went there without notes, whereas Stokes read a beautiful, long 20-minute speech. It was

well-thought-out, well-written. I ran into Carl about a week before the debate at the Cleveland Hotel, and I said, "What are you doing here, Carl?" and he said, "I got a room here. I'm preparing for the debate." I said, "You're preparing? Is it going to be that hard?" ...I just spoke off the top of my head, which might have been a mistake. But the media called it a draw.
    —Ralph J. Perk, in an interview with the authors

OCTOBER 30 Things got hot early, when the audience, traditionally stacked by the candidates' backers, began answering the rhetorical questions salted throughout Perk's opening remarks. "Who can REALLY unite Cleveland?" asked Perk. "Is it Mayor Locher...."

"Yes!" interrupted the Locher partisans.

Undaunted, Perk went ahead with questions like: "Do you think a one-party government which has had control for over a quarter of a century will ever move Cleveland ahead?"

"Yes!" came the booming reply again.

It reached the point where Perk interrupted his train of thought to say: "You stooges of [Democratic party leader Albert S.] Porter in the audience can laugh. You're only taking up my time." ...The laughs, whistles, hurrahs and boos continued.

[Ralph] McAllister [an independent Democratic candidate, as is Stokes]...laced into Locher, charging the mayor with violating the public's trust by ducking some 40 earlier chances to debate with the other candidates.

...Locher was boiling by the time he got to speak.... He tossed out his prepared text and pounded the podium, saying, "I'll tell you where I've been, I've been taking my record to the people of this city."

...Stokes broke up the crowd with this quip: "Mayor Locher, I don't know who is going to win the election, but I did make some money today. I bet that you'd be here."

...[A] questioner tossed at Locher the hot potato issue of race relations. Why, he asked, did Locher refuse in June to meet with a delegation from the United Freedom Movement, the civil rights federation?

...Locher pounded the podium again and said, "If a labor group or a management group or a civic group comes in on that same basis [conducting a sit-down demonstration in his office], I won't see them, either. And no mayor worth his salt would."

Stokes took issue with Locher. "The very essense of government reflects pressure from all sorts of divergent groups," Stokes retorted. "The question is how best, with those pressures, to do what is in the best interest of all the people. A hard-nosed, podium-pounding attitude isn't helping any."
    —Plain Dealer *account of the mayoral primary debate*

That debate—interestingly enough—is a footnote on history. I think there are many people who feel that Carl Stokes's performance, and his subsequent performance in the general election, set the framework for his election in '67....

1965   *—Peter Halbin, in an interview with the authors*

NOVEMBER 19   The [world] population is expanding so fast that all of our efforts to keep pace are in vain. ...Real famine—broad-scale famine—will start by 1970. In Latin America, India and Africa it will affect billions of people. It will cause lunging social unrest and galloping political chaos.
—Ernest J. Hodges, *former U.S. marketing advisor in Latin America*

1966   **The death toll in Vietnam for the year surpasses 5,000. Congress enacts legislation mandating truth in packaging and conducts hearings on auto safety at which a young attorney named Ralph Nader becomes a star witness. The Supreme Court's Miranda protections start a new protocol with arrestees in police headquarters across the nation: "You have the right to remain silent...." The U.S. Civil Rights Commission, which has been conducting hearings throughout the South on the health, education and social problems of the American Negro, comes to Cleveland, the first big city in the North to be so investigated. An observation made at the City Club by a Commission investigator that tensions in the black community could erupt into violence proves prescient.**

Following the 53rd annual Anvil Revue, which, like its recent predecessors, has lost money, club directors reluctantly decide that the time has come to stop subsidizing public performances. They mandate that all future Revues be staged at the club.

FEBRUARY 18   To the often-repeated question, "Can [Ohio Governor] Jimmy Rhodes be defeated?", the answer is: That depends upon which Jimmy Rhodes you're talking about.

We have Jimmy Rhodes as his image makers view him, a sort of cross between Batman and the Good Fairy. Like the Good Fairy, he flits about, solving problems of the hard pressed and careworn. Like Batman, he has some mysterious source of income which enables him to perform his feats without acquiring the wherewithal for doing so.

There is the Jimmy Rhodes of the legend, the one we state senators hear about but never see. He's the super-administrator Jimmy Rhodes. He's super because while he is usually away dedicating schools and fishing on ice floes and invading Europe for industry, somehow he is also making magnificent executive decisions in the state capitol.

Then there is the Jimmy Rhodes the image makers don't talk about. He's the front man but not necesarily the real power. And what gets done in his name is neither high, nor noble nor wise.
—Frazier Reams, Jr., *Democratic state senator from Toledo and candidate for governor*

Ralph Nader

APRIL 15 Fathers in the inner city are likely to have received an inferior education in the South and [because of that] may be able to provide their families with housing that barely meets minimum standards and sometimes doesn't.

...Mothers on ADC [Aid to Dependent Children] sometimes don't have enough money to meet school fees and sometimes may keep their children out of school because they don't.

...Schools predominantly colored in enrollment are likely to be overcrowded.

...Housing codes are not enforced in urban renewal areas.

...Negroes feel they are the victims of discriminatory law enforcement.

   —**William Taylor,** *staff director of the U.S. Civil Rights Commission, reporting on the findings of five days of public hearings in Cleveland*

Q: Does the threat of violence exist here?

Taylor: I think we are seeing tensions growing out of grievances...that are unresolved.

MAY 13 Nothing is more beautiful than functional design. Any safety feature can be stylized if there is a desire to do so.

   —**Ralph Nader,** *attorney and author of* Unsafe at Any Speed, *the book criticizing the auto industry for its irresponsible preoccupation with aesthetics over safety, appearing at the City Club on the last day of congressional hearings on auto safety*

JULY 18 *A barroom argument between a white bartender and a black customer explodes into rioting in Cleveland's Hough neighborhood. After two days of violence, Governor Rhodes calls out the National Guard, who remain on duty there until the end of the month.*

SEPTEMBER 16 **Stokes:** The [county grand jury report on the Hough riots] gives a clean bill of health to an inept, leaderless and indifferent city administration. ...Out of the 38 riot-torn cities across the country this summer, only Cleveland [the grand jury report found] needed the communists to inform its Negroes that things here are bad.

   Hill: You members of the City Club, white and Negro, are just as much to blame as the city administration for the problems that beset the colored community. You are to blame because you are educated, high-salaried suburbanites who, by not getting involved in the problems of the inner city, have contributed to its failures.

   —*Louis Stokes, attorney for the Cleveland chapter of the NAACP, and Baxter Hill, local chairman of CORE, on the Hough riots*

SEPTEMBER 30 The situation in Southeast Asia has improved in all ways—military, political, diplomatic.... We have at this point secured our main base areas. We have enough troops,

1966

mobility and firepower to spoil major offensive efforts of the communists. What needs to be done now is to go into the Viet Cong's base areas, where they train, rest, recuperate and re-outfit themselves. We cannot accomplish this cleaning up…without roughly doubling our troops [to 600,000 strong].

—**Walter Friedenberg,** *Scripps-Howard editorial writer with 22 months of observation time in Vietnam*

NOVEMBER 8   *Rhodes beats Reams four to one, racking up a 700,000-vote plurality.*

NOVEMBER 25   There is a far greater likelihood of an innocent man being convicted because of a mistake by the jury than because of an error of law by the judge. While we review and review decisions of judges, there is no review of a jury's verdict.

…I would propose the establishment of some board or commission which would have the power to review a jury's verdict when the man's attorney was willing to say that, from everything he can learn about this case, the boy just didn't do it.

—**F. Lee Bailey,** *attorney who won a U.S. Supreme Court reversal of Cleveland doctor Sam Sheppard's conviction for murdering his wife (based on prejudicial media coverage of the first trial) and an acquittal in a second trial held earlier this year*

F. Lee Bailey

1967

The City Club remains at the center of local and national political developments. The Hough riots prompt a debate of the purpose and progress of Cleveland's urban renewal efforts. Carl Stokes, whose ongoing campaign to become the first black mayor of a major American city has taken on a new urgency because of the Hough riots, pulls a few surprises on audiences there. And George Wallace elicits an unexpected reaction when he uses the Forum to test the viability of his presidential aspirations.

FEBRUARY 24   With rare exceptions, cities have distorted the intent of [urban renewal], directing benefits to central business districts, expansion of universities and hospitals and displacement of the poor to make room for housing too costly for the poor. Too often renewal has risen over the ashes of what was a community in the best sense of the word—a community of well-established though poor residents.

—**Barton R. Clausen,** *community development director, City of Cleveland*

MARCH 3   I believe that American firms must either withdraw from South Africa or they must cease pouring more money into it. The danger is that your country may be forced into a fight on the wrong side, merely to protect its financial interests. That would be a tragedy.

—**Dennis Brutus,** *poet and South African exile who was*

imprisoned for his opposition to apartheid

APRIL 28   On the Vietnam war, I don't have any panacea. No one has. But the first thing I'd do, as President, would be to let Hanoi, Peking and Moscow know that the American people are solidly behind our servicemen, that the lunatic fringe is only a small part of our people. I would use every justifiable effort to stop people who are aiding and abetting the enemy. It isn't academic freedom to raise money, medical supplies and clothing for the Viet Cong. They are not exercising academic freedom. They are guilty of treason. If I were President, I'd take some of those professors, grab them by the hair of the head and have the justice department indict them.

   —George C. Wallace, *former governor of Alabama, making his first swing through the North in a test of his viability as a third-party candidate for President*

APRIL 29   *George Wallace ran into difficulty in Cleveland yesterday—silence.*

   He used the same speech that wowed the all-white Amen Corner in Pittsburgh Thursday and drew cheers and jeers at Syracuse University the night before.

   But yesterday, in this city of racial unrest, the venerable City Club gave Wallace the coolest reception of his Northern presidential test run so far.

   As his jibes and jokes about "big government" and his attacks on the federal judiciary fell flat, Wallace became flustered enough to talk about the state rights stand of the founders of Pennsylvania, instead of Ohio.

   —The Washington Post

MAY 27   **Ealy:** There is a new Negro who refuses to accept the system as it is. He says that if I have to live like my father lived, then I don't care whether I live.

   Some of Cassius Clay is in him, and he is not certain he wants to fight for a country in which he is not free.

   Some of Adam Clayton Powell is in him, too, and he will not be humble or apologize for what he has earned or what he thinks is rightfully his. [Accused of having used government money for personal expenses, Adam Clayton Powell, Jr., earlier in the year has been excluded by his House colleagues from the 90th Congress.]

   Now that he goes to Yale or Case Tech—instead of Alabama State College—he will not accept segregation. He expects and knows he should have what his white classmates have.

   Mason: Black power is a declaration of independence.... It calls for black control of the black ghetto and, as a first step, a change in thinking of black people about themselves. ...Cleveland can allow Negro leadership to speak in Negro interests without harassment, to be accountable to the black community and not to the power structure, the press or Negro flunkies. [Or] there can be a continuation of the status quo, of the get-tough policy by police, of the red baiting of the civil rights movement. But the Negro response will be disruption of the society and more intensified anger and hate.

—Reverend Jonathan Ealy, chairman of the United Pastors Association, and Phillip Mason, director of the Head Start program of the Council of Churches of Christ of Greater Cleveland, on the black nationalism movement

JUNE 10   I walked into a store 15 minutes from my home, asked to buy a gun, showed my driver's license and walked out with this revolver. And I could now kill someone with it.

—Carl B. Stokes, *sponsor of an Ohio House bill requiring licensing of all weapons except those used for hunting, brandishing a gun to demonstrate how easy it is to buy one*

[The reaction] was one that I had intended—horror, shock and surprise.

—Stokes, in an interview with the authors

SEPTEMBER 22   Q: How do you respond to criticism of your urban renewal program?

Locher: Urban renewal is bogged down in red tape. It's easier to get a foreign aid loan for Tasmania than it is to get our own dollars from Washington. Tasmania can get by with a three-page memo. We have to submit documents two and three feet high. I tell you there is something wrong with urban renewal, and it has to do with red tape in Washington and Chicago.

—Question-and-answer period following the campaign speech of the incumbent mayor

OCTOBER 3   Locher is defeated in the mayoral primary by Carl Stokes, who will face Republican attorney Seth Taft in the general election.

OCTOBER 17   One hundred fifty thousand persons, many of them the long-haired members of an emerging "hippie" counterculture, march on the Pentagon. Similar anti-war demonstrations are held in Chicago, Philadelphia, Los Angeles and Oakland.

OCTOBER 27   We accuse hippies of deviating from standards that are no longer relevant to our own behavior. [But] the instability of the hippie society reflects a breakdown in the so-called normal world, a breakdown of marriage and the family. Our own turning outward for pleasure via alcohol, tranquilizers and television is reflected in the hippie's drug-taking behavior. And the hippie's "dropout" kind of life is a reflection of the fact that our economy has shifted so that we are no longer a nation of producers but a nation of consumers.

—Edward Cliffel, *graduate student in clinical psychology, Western Reserve University*

NOVEMBER 4 [Taft] claimed that Stokes was not qualified because he was an absentee landlord, an absentee Democrat and an absentee legislator.... Stokes's final thrust came at the very end of the debate. In answer to a question about his record as a legislator, Stokes pulled out a letter and, waving it like a red flag, said: "Very quickly, I've just been told I have 30 seconds. Folks, you know that I have not only been endorsed by every leading newspaper and the Democratic party, but I'm going to give you what I think is the best attestation of Carl Stokes's service in the legislature....

([Moderator Richard] Campbell: "Our time is up. We're off the air. We thank you all. I'm sorry about the air. Now, we'll let Carl finish his answer for the people here.")

"The attestation that I have of the way that I have tried to serve the people of the City of Cleveland is furnished best, I think, by Seth Taft himself. And Seth, I'll hand to you the letter, that you yourself wrote me on June 7, 1967, and I'll read it to the audience here. 'Dear Carl: The reports I hear of your performance in Columbus are excellent, and I congratulate you on the job. With best regards, Seth Taft.'"

Richard Campbell thought the impact would be lost because the scheduled broadcast time had run out, but one television station stayed on the air long enough to televise the incident. The newspapers highlighted it: a picture of [Taft public relations manager] William Silverman's face and the utter dejection he revealed for all to see.

—Checkmate in Cleveland, *a 1972 Case Western Reserve University Press study of the Stokes mayorality by Estelle Zannes*

NOVEMBER 10 If [victor] Carl Stokes doesn't beat the system built up over 25 years by a few persons in critical positions, his administration will come and go with nothing accomplished. I'm certain he will beat the system.

—James M. Carney, *vice chairman, Cuyahoga County Democratic Party*

DECEMBER 1 The thing that will do more to shorten the war than anything else would be for all of America to back our team over there and quit giving the enemy any comfort or any indication that we are liable to pull out. ...I've talked to several defectors from the other side and many prisoners, and they don't believe they can win the war militarily. But they do believe that if they can hang on long enough and cause enough casualties, that they can win the war in the political and psychological arena here in the U.S. That is what they're shooting for.

—Lieutenant General Lewis W. Walt, *former commander of the U.S. Marine Corps in Vietnam*

1968

Peace talks between the United States and North Vietnam begin in Paris. Presidential politics take an unexpected turn: On March 12th anti-war senator Eugene McCarthy wins 42 percent of the vote in the

1968

Democratic primary in New Hampshire. On March 16th Senator Robert F. Kennedy declares that he will run for President. On March 31st President Johnson gives a televised address announcing his intention not to seek reelection. Gunfire silences two men of vision and brings Mayor Stokes's honeymoon to an abrupt end.

APRIL 2 *Requests poured in yesterday for tickets to Senator Robert F. Kennedy's speech Friday at a special City Club forum.... In a little more than eight hours...more than 1,400 of the 2,100 tickets [were sold]. Only members may buy tickets, but a member may bring guests. Nine persons joined the club yesterday to be eligible for tickets.*
　—Plain Dealer

APRIL 4　Martin Luther King, Jr., is assassinated in Memphis, Tennessee.

APRIL 5 *Senator Robert F. Kennedy, saddened and shocked by the killing...came to Cleveland today....*
　The New York senator...in deference to the memory of Dr. King, directed that all political phases of his visit be eliminated.
　...A speech prepared yesterday for delivery at the City Club meeting was scrapped. He and his aides worked into the early morning hours to prepare a talk that was keyed to the theme of Dr. King's life and civil rights leadership....
　—Press

　This is a time of shame and sorrow. It is not a day for politics. I have saved this one opportunity to speak briefly to you about this mindless menace of violence in America which again today stains our land and every one of our lives.

　It is not the concern of any one race. The victims of violence are black and white, rich and poor, young and old, famous and unknown. They are, most important of all, human beings whom other human beings loved and needed. No one—no matter where he lives or what he does—can be certain who next will suffer from some senseless act of bloodshed. And yet it goes on and on and on.

　Why? What has violence ever accomplished? What has it ever created? No martyr's cause has ever been stilled by his assassin's bullet. No wrongs have ever been righted by riots and civil disorders. A sniper is only a coward, not a hero; and an uncontrolled, uncontrollable mob is only the voice of madness, not the voice of the people.

　...Yet we seemingly tolerate a rising level of violence that ignores common humanity and our claims to civilization alike. We calmly accept newspaper reports of civilian slaughter in far-off lands. We glorify killing on movie and television screens and call it entertainment. We make it easy for men of all shades of sanity to acquire whatever weapons and ammunition they desire. ...Only a cleansing of our whole society can remove this

Robert F. Kennedy

sickness from our soul.

...Our lives on this planet are too short and the work to be done too great to let this spirit flourish any longer in our land. Of course, we cannot banish it with a program nor with a resolution.

But we can perhaps remember—even if only for a time—that those who live with us are our brothers; that they share with us the same short moment of life; that they seek—as we do—nothing but the chance to live out their lives in purpose and happiness, winning what satisfaction and fulfillment they can.

Surely this bond of common fate, this bond of common goal, can begin to teach us something. Surely we can learn, at the least, to look at those around us as fellow men. And surely we can begin to work a little harder to bind up the wounds among us and to become in our own hearts brothers and countrymen once again.

—Robert F. Kennedy

The most moving forum I was ever at was the one where Bobby Kennedy spoke the day after the death of Martin Luther King. ...This incredibly small figure, slight figure, walked in, followed by his wife. His face looked very drawn. He gets up and gives this incredible, very moving speech...and people were just held there. He spoke only for 15 minutes or so and then he walked away. Six weeks later he was dead.

There's a picture...of Kennedy speaking at the podium, with [his wife] Ethel behind him. The light was shining down, and it was as if you could see her foreseeing the future. You could almost see the shadow of death in the wings.

—Thomas F. Campbell, City Club historian and member, in an interview with the authors

MAY 10 When you start running out of white children in the city, you start running out of the potential for integration.

—Paul W. Briggs, *Cleveland public schools superintendent, explaining why Cleveland schools are not yet integrated*

JUNE 6 Robert Kennedy is shot while campaigning in Los Angeles and dies several hours later.

JUNE 17 It's time to throw out the welfare system and start all over. The present system discourages people who want to work. It does so by deducting everything they earn from the amount of money they otherwise would have received. That amounts to a 100 percent tax on income, and I can think of no better way to quash energy and ambition.

The system almost sponsors broken homes and illegitimacy. It does so by withdrawing benefits from any home that harbors an employable male. The effect of the rule is to discourage marriage, to encourage promiscuity and to establish a cycle of continuing deception.

—John V. Lindsay, *Democratic mayor of New York City*

1968

JUNE 18   The war protests and the civil rights protests were directed against public policy. But they also called into question the ability of the American system to respond to the needs and values of the people. ...I have said from the beginning that one objective of my campaign was to offer an alternative to the centralization of presidential power, which extends itself in a personal way into every institution of government.

—Eugene McCarthy

JULY 2   I come to you not as an expert but as a concerned American...deeply concerned about what's happening in our cities. Seventy percent of the population of this land lives in our cities, representing about 2 percent of the land area. ...How do we make these cities not only liveable, but how do we make them the best of the American experience and the fulfillment of the American dream?

...I call my proposal a Marshall Plan for America's cities.

Local initiative, careful planning, coordinated policy, strict priorities, massive commitment—these are the techniques that were effective in the most successful foreign aid program this nation has ever known. ...The vision was grand enough to inspire hope...that the job could be done and to generate the will of self-help which brought the peoples of Western Europe to self-sufficiency and prosperity. May I say these are the requirements for perfecting the American city?

—Hubert H. Humphrey, *vice president of the United States and candidate for the Democratic presidential nomination*

JULY 23   *The Black Nationalists of New Libya led by Ahmed Evans start firing at passersby from an apartment building in Cleveland's Glenville neighborhood. Seven persons including three police officers are killed and 15 wounded.*

SEPTEMBER 20   Schumacher: The only argument against [the papal encyclical forbidding Catholics to practice birth control] is the population explosion. Overpopulation is a myth. ...Population growth is generally beneficial and is a powerful spur that drives men on to greater economic progress in science, culture and political freedom. The promotion of contraception is a cause of social tensions and hatreds. What a mockery it is to tell the poor we love them and want to help them—but won't they please stop breeding?

Gerken: There was a time when the concept of papal authority was simply that of the ruler and the ruled. It was one in which the rulers made the decision and the subject obeyed. If obedience proved very difficult, the difficulty was overcome in contemplating Christ, obedient unto death. But...this theory is not good enough to meet the needs of the present moment. ...There are times when people should not have children, but

Hubert H. Humphrey

when they need marital love and affection. Nature demands a man use his intellect and interfere with the lower biological process.

—Debate between Monsignor Leo S. Schumacher, dean of philosophy of Cleveland's Borromeo Seminary College, and the Reverend Father John D. Gerken, associate professor of theology of Cleveland's John Carroll University

Q: What would you advise someone who in conscience disagreed with the encyclical?

Schumacher: The thing for him is to do some studying and practice self-control. We shouldn't throw out heroism.

SEPTEMBER 25 *The City Club "Cityzen" who pulled a fast one on the membership and signed a young lady for the all-male club on Short Vincent was Richard Miller of the community relations department of East Ohio Gas Company. The member he signed was Tracy Spuhler, a writer for the gas company. ...Secretary Fred Vierow says her first quarter membership dues ($8.50) will be returned.*

—Press

NOVEMBER 8 Americans seem to want a pause, a period of reflection, a chance to breathe a bit while figuring out where the nation has gone, how it got there and where it should head next. Don't expect a progressive movement in the next four years. But don't expect a regressive upheaval either. We're in for four years of cooling it.

—James M. Naughton, *politics writer of the* Plain Dealer, *analyzing the reasons behind Richard Nixon's defeat of Hubert Humphrey for the Presidency*

NOVEMBER 15 No public official has worked harder than Stokes to bring racial harmony to the city. And yet the city is as divided as it was a year ago. This is not the fault of Carl Stokes. The apparent harmony that prevailed in his early days in office was destroyed by a handful of lawless men in Glenville.

—Norman Mlachak, *city hall reporter,* Press

1969

Apollo 11 astronaut Neil Armstrong takes humankind's first inspiring step on the moon, while the darker side of human nature comes to the fore when the army reveals that it has charged Lieutenant William Calley with premeditated murder in the massacre of Vietnamese civilians at My Lai. The first draft lottery is held shortly after President Nixon's November announcement of the "Vietnamization" of the war—a policy of gradual delegation of responsibility to the South Vietnamese that will see America's fighting forces reduced by 110,000 men by the end of the year. Facing criticism of his administration from all sides, especially on the issue of law and order, Mayor Stokes nonetheless

1969   **manages to hang on to his job for two more years.**

FEBRUARY 28   Who's breaking the law here? I am convinced that an increasing number of Americans are convinced that the war in Vietnam is not just slightly illegal and immoral but totally illegal and immoral. The hope of America is its young people who are...willing to face the wrongs and willing to get their faces bashed in, if necessary, to right the wrongs.
   —**Dr. Benjamin Spock,** *noted baby doctor (formerly on the staff of Western Reserve University's medical school), author of* Baby and Child Care *and anti-war protestor*

MARCH 18   The Cuyahoga County grand jury begins an investigation of charges that the Cleveland Civil Service Commission is guilty of favoring blacks in its handling of Cleveland police recruitment and promotion examinations.

MARCH 28   Don't think I came here to ask for civil rights or jobs. For too long black people have cried for civil rights and now they realize it is a big hoax. You can't ask whites for civil rights because they have no rights to give. We are all born with human rights.
   I'm just going to explain black nationalism. We are trying to create black business, a black police force, a city within a city and a nation within a nation. We want to stay in Hough and build it up. We want to get the whites out who are exploiting black people. We might fail, but give us a chance to fail. You failed, let us do it.
   —**Harllel Jones,** *leader of Cleveland's Afro Set, a black nationalist youth group*

APRIL 11   We merely believe that God created whites to build great civilizations.
   —**Robert W. Annable,** *Ohio state president of the United Citizens Council of America, explaining why he will circulate petitions seeking the secession of the predominately white West Side from Cleveland proper should Stokes win reelection*

   Q: Why do you suppose that perhaps 95 percent of your listeners disagree with your views?
   Annable: They're not too intelligent.

AUGUST 15   Three hundred thousand youths attend a three-day music festival near Woodstock, New York.

SEPTEMBER 12   The grand jury issues a report censuring the Civil Service Commission for irregularities in its handling of Cleveland police examinations.

SEPTEMBER 9   **Kelly:** Who wants to do business in a city where fear has resulted in the closing of four major movie houses

Gus Hall

in less than two blocks of Playhouse Square? Who wants to do business in a city where conventioneers are warned against the use of downtown streets at night? Yet this is Cleveland's national image from the recently released FBI report of crime.

Stokes: There are some in this town, including the police themselves, who have questioned our record regarding safety on the streets. They have questioned our support for the police of Cleveland—not in true concern, I submit, for law and order, but out of base political motivation. And, I might add, if some of the members of our police department spent more of their time worrying about the rising crime rate and less time thinking about politics, we might be able to cut our crime rate.

—Traditional mayoral primary debate between incumbent Stokes and Robert J. Kelly, his challenger for the Democratic nomination

OCTOBER 3 Our mistake was in attempting to make changes in an area in which those affected relate change to subversion, see progress as a threat to self-interest and view civilian direction as outside interference. The real danger in the community is the police-county prosecutor team which has been able to...use the grand jury as their tool. The grand jury report is an undisguised effort to smear Mayor Stokes and his appointees to the commission in an effort to clear the prosecutor of responsibility for the delay in getting new policemen on the street.

—Marvin Chernoff, *vice chairman, Civil Service Commission of Cleveland*

OCTOBER 10 To view what is happening as a mere fad—an age gap, a drug cult, a sex revolution—or as some passing fancy of mini-skirts, beads and four-letter words is to hide one's head in the sands of time. These are but surface manifestations, tremors resulting from the political earthquake that is shaking the foundations of the old social order.

—Gus Hall, *general secretary of the American Communist Party, on the imminent rise of socialism in the country*

Outside the club...eight members of the John Birch Society protested the appearance. ...One of the protesters said the demonstration was not being conducted in the name of the Society, but was spontaneous among [its] members. They called for City Club members to dismiss those who arranged Hall's talk or to resign from the Club. Hall said he walked past the demonstrators apparently unrecognized.

—Plain Dealer

OCTOBER 21 *It is my considered judgment that these debates, entertaining as they usually are, do not afford voters an insight into the capacity or competence of the candidate seeking public office....*

—Ralph J. Perk, explaining why he is the first candidate for Cleveland's highest office since 1933 to turn down the City

1969   *Club's invitation to debate the opposition*

OCTOBER 23

> *IS PERK AFRAID TO DEBATE?*
> —Press *headline*

I was very ill. I had been in the hospital [with kidney stones] for three months prior to the election and there was no way I could engage in those kinds of debates without hurting the campaign. Because I looked so bad, I didn't want to get on television. I didn't want to face all those questions about my health. So I didn't debate Carl at the City Club. Because if you looked at me, you'd probably say: "He's a nice guy, but he's going to die tomorrow. Why vote for him?"
> —*Ralph J. Perk, in an interview with the authors*

NOVEMBER 3   I would prefer not to win if we had to depend on violence.
   —Cesar Chavez, *national director of the United Farm-workers Organizing Committee, on the 49-month-old grape boycott California farm workers have chosen as the best tool to win the right to unionize*

NOVEMBER 7   Stokes, an incumbent mayor with two newspapers, the Democratic organization and organized labor [behind him], beat Perk, who had only the Republican organization, by only 3,753 votes. It's obvious that a low turnout [due to rain] saved Stokes.
   —Richard L. Maher, *politics editor,* Press

DECEMBER 18   Let the grape boycott succeed and no perishable produce will be safe from boycott in the name of labor union organization. Shouldn't the American housewife have the right to purchase what food she wants, without being intimidated or without having to go from store to store because her favorite market has knuckled to the boycott pressure?
   —N. Lorraine Beebe, *national chairperson, Consumers' Rights Committee*

1970   In the same year that 18-year-olds are given the right to vote, James Rhodes justifies using force to quash campus protest in an explosive debate at the City Club. Two days later the Ohio National Guard fires into a crowd of anti-war demonstrators on the campus of Kent State University, killing four and wounding nine.

JANUARY 2   This nation in which we live was born in revolution. A part of its priceless heritage is the right to dissent. If this nation ever permits the President or any other person, organization or combination of the same to permit the quelling of dissent, this nation will have lost its very reason for existence.

James A. Rhodes

—**Louis Stokes,** *Democratic congressman from Cleveland, on President Nixon's admiration for the so-called "silent majority"*

APRIL 30   Nixon announces that he will order American troops into Cambodia to attack Viet Cong supply bases.

MAY 2   The way I handled the situation at Ohio State points up the sharp difference of opinion and philosophy between my opponent and myself. [In calling out 1,200 National Guard troops to quell protest at the university], I followed my frequently stated views that rioters, regardless of age or social philosophy, will not be permitted to take over any state university campus by force or violence.

[My opponent] said he would have gone much more slowly and obtained a court injunction against the rioters [at Ohio's Miami University, where Rhodes had also called out the National Guard after students occupied the Army-Air Force Reserve Officers Training Corps headquarters on campus in protest over the war]. By the time an injunction is obtained campus buildings could be burned to the ground and people maimed or killed.

My opponent's soft attitude on campus violence is not surprising since in 1968 he voted against an amendment to the higher education bill requiring colleges to deny federal funds to students who participate in serious campus disorders.

—**James A. Rhodes,** *on Ohio congressman Robert Taft, Jr., his Republican challenger for the Senate seat being vacated by Stephen M. Young*

Rhodes and...Taft climaxed their senatorial campaign with a shouting match so wild that at one point the moderator appeared to be the man under attack.

...[They] squeezed and elbowed City Club President Thomas F. Campbell at the podium as they argued nose-to-nose....

Campbell, acting more like a prizefight referee than a moderator, broke up the clinch between the two coldly smiling Republicans.

—Plain Dealer

I was president when Taft and Rhodes debated, and I remember at the end they almost came to blows. As the last 30 seconds [of the time alloted for speeches] ticked away, Rhodes...shook Taft's hand and said: "No matter what happens in the primary, come November we'll have harmony in the party." And I looked at the two of them and I said: "That kind of harmony we call a donnybrook in Ireland."

And then I heard Rhodes say: "Well, there's some trouble down in Kent. I've got to go down there and deal with it." I asked him to continue on [with the question-and-answer period] for a little while, but he said no and he stormed out and he went on to make that speech that many people feel set the

1970

emotional tone for the [Kent State University] killings.
—Thomas F. Campbell, in an interview with the authors

MAY 9   My patience wears thin when I hear these railings and condemnations [of the Peace Corps because of its administration by the federal government]. I do not believe, as some young revolutionaries apparently do, that it is wrong to accept money from your parents if you convert that bread to good use. I do not believe in letting something that is needed in this society go under simply because young people cannot accept the thought of a federal agency actually doing something groovy.
—C. Payne Lucas, *special assistant to the director of the Peace Corps*

OCTOBER 24   Salvador Allende Gossens is elected President of Chile.

DECEMBER 11   The university officials seemed paralyzed and uninformed. The guard seemed zealous and uninformed. The students were simply angry and uninformed.
—Michael D. Roberts, Plain Dealer *reporter and coauthor of* 13 Seconds, *a book on the Kent State killings, blaming the tragedy on a total lack of communication*

1971

After 41 years at the same location, the City Club prepares to move into joint quarters with the Women's City Club. Each organization stages a sentimental moving-day parade, in which members carry furnishings and memorabilia over to what is being called the new Cleveland Civic House, and the final forum in the old Short Vincent building is devoted to assessing the lessons of the past. Meanwhile, President Nixon makes an historic break with tradition, announcing that he has accepted Premier Chou En-lai's invitation to visit mainland China. And, in a decision that will have strong reverberations in Cleveland, the Supreme Court upholds busing as the most effective means to accomplish desegregation of public schools.

FEBRUARY 5   It means that we have at last decided to clamp the leash on the CIA and to abandon our outworn strategy of trying, by force or by bribery, to interfere with and even overturn foreign governments that do not completely suit our liking.
—Cyrus S. Eaton, *recently returned from a visit to Chile, on President Nixon's announcement of continued friendship with that country*

Q: Will the people of Chile have a chance to vote the new government out of office if they wish?
Eaton: The idea that the Allende government is the end of democracy is the bunk. ...Allende is not a communist but a

socialist and a Catholic. I would pigeonhole him as no farther to the left than the leaders of the Labor Party who recently ruled Britain.

FEBRUARY 12 The South Vietnamese government has a million men under arms and 600 military planes we supplied to them. They can't stand off even one fifth that number of enemy troops. There is only one explanation. The people there don't support the war.
> **—Leonard Woodcock,** *president, United Auto Workers union*

MAY 31 *The table is 106 inches in diameter. ...Somewhere on the table there is supposed to be a swastika carved by an enraged lawyer whose pro-Hitler views were not well received. Surrounding the star [in the center] in circling rows are the painted names of 114 Soviet Table members...[from] some years ago, when the table was rather formally organized....*

Lawyer A.H. (Harry) Zychick, a City Clubman for 45 years...provided the black plaster bull that stands pawing a plaster base in the center of the table. It is not only a fitting symbol but also a memorial to [Jack] Raper, who used [a similar] device in his Press *column. The table also supports a wooden hammer formerly used to call loud disputants to order and a wooden figurine somewhat resembling a laughing Buddha. According to a small [name]plate, it came from Jerusalem in 1935.*

"It looks like Golda Meir taking a shower," suggested a...member. As the remark perhaps illustrates, standards for table membership are looser today than in the days when editors and political leaders shaped civic policy at the Soviet Table.
> *—Plain Dealer feature about the Soviet Table, which members plan to carry to the club's new headquarters on the day of the move*

> *You're talking about a lot of men who would make sacrifices to get Cleveland going. Now you've got people who won't get involved, [while] all they wanted at the Soviet Table was to get involved. They thought that was the only way to make democracy work. That's the only way you could have a city with character. They would write letters, they would talk, they would go to meetings, they would do any darn thing. They would go over and sit in council meetings so that [council] people would know who was interested.*
> *—William T. McKnight, former law director of the City of Cleveland and club member since 1940, in an interview with the authors*

JUNE 4 Black people have no alternative except to adopt the political philosophy that "we have no permanent friends, no permanent enemies, just permanent interests." That, gentlemen, is what black politics is going to be about in the 1970s. Unless and until black communities coalesce their vote power with other similiarly situated groups such as Mexican Americans, Spanish-surnamed people, poor whites, liberal whites and other minorities, our gains will continue at a disproportionate percentage.

—Louis Stokes, *one of 13 blacks in Congress, on the advantages of coalition politics over party politics*

JUNE 25 It is primarily because of our healthy trade surplus in technology-intensive products that we have managed to hang on in our trade balance. [But] we are losing the technological advantage.

—James T. Lynn, *undersecretary of commerce, predicting that unless American business invests more in research and development imports of high-tech products will soon exceed exports*

JULY 9 **Stokes:** People blamed [Locher] for what hadn't been done in Cleveland. I was among them. If you ran today I could make a speech for you. Being there yourself makes a difference.

Locher: I want to convey one thought: Let us all unite; all people of the entire county in a crusade to save the central city. The next mayor of the City of Cleveland must not only try to form a consensus between those groups that are now at a complete or virtually complete stalemate. By that I mean the council and the mayor, the county and the city, the suburbs and the city.

...We should have in this city a new spirit. One that will recognize statesmanship rather than gamesmanship. The infighting must go....

—Carl Stokes, who earlier in the year had announced his decision not to seek reelection to a third term, and Ralph S. Locher, in the final forum held on Short Vincent to which all five of Cleveland's living mayors had been invited to address the subject "Learning From the Past"

OCTOBER 30 *Robert E. Hughes, Republican county co-chairman, today resigned from the City Club because, he said, he resents the treatment of GOP mayoral candidate Ralph J. Perk.*

Hughes criticized Carl Spangenberg, club president, for his introduction of Perk at yesterday's debate of the mayoral candidates. Spangenberg referred to the fact that Perk had not accepted an invitation to debate Mayor Stokes two years ago and quipped: "We have here the man representing Ralph Perk."

—Plain Dealer

NOVEMBER 5 **Maher:** Stokes had his prestige riding on this [mayoral] election. If [Stokes protege] Arnold R. Pinckney had won, [Stokes] would have proved to the nation that he had a bloc of votes that he could turn on and off at will.

Burdock: I don't think Stokes lost Tuesday because he was black. He lost because in addition to being black he was a bad mayor. He had become thin-skinned and arrogant. ...I think Cleveland has had a bellyful of charisma, and with Perk it won't have to worry about that.

—*Richard Maher, political writer of the* Press, *and Robert Burdock, political writer of the* Plain Dealer, *analyzing why Republican candidate for mayor Perk defeated independent Pinckney and Democrat James M. Carney*

NOVEMBER 18 The people have voted for honesty and unpretentious problem-solving....

—Dennis J. Kucinich, *Democratic councilman who nonetheless supported Perk, arguing that his candidate's election is representative of a national shift towards a politics free of ideology*

1972

Nixon kicks off a presidential election year with an historic eight-day visit to Peking in February; both powers agree to work for a "normalization of relations." Despite the continuation of peace talks between national security adviser Henry A. Kissinger and the North Vietnamese, begun in secret the previous June, in March the Viet Cong attack South Vietnam in the biggest communist offensive since 1968. In Congress another battle is joined the same month, when the House and Senate approve the proposed Equal Rights Amendment (ERA), giving the women's movement until 1979 to persuade three fourths of the country's state legislatures to ratify it.**

The City Club gets a new logo: two Cs placed back-to-back to indicate its devotion to airing both sides of an issue—a creed that is mightily tested by a painful and prolonged debate over whether to admit women members.

JANUARY 14 *Until three years ago, the City Club was open to all citizens of good repute, a commendable open-door policy.*

...That was until one citizen of reportedly good repute, Tracy Spuhler, joined. The club's constitution was changed because of Tracy. The constitution now states, in effect, that membership is open to all men of good repute.

You don't have to be hit over the head to figure out what happened. Tracy, of course, is a woman.

...The Tracy episode was followed by the generous decision to open the club's forums to women. City Club members are now resting on their laurels...confident they bought time and the situation is now under control.

It isn't and here is why. Women like me are going to cajole, reason, shame, debate and lobby until we are admitted. ...Why bother? Personally, I need to join. As a former political reporter, now a fledgling editorial writer and columnist, I now have to wait for my boss and most of the other editorial writers, all

Ralph J. Perk

1972

men, to come back from lunch at the City Club and tell me what's going on in Cleveland.
—Plain Dealer *column by Judith McCluskey*

JANUARY 18   I know both men. I've met them many times. I've eaten with them. I've talked with both of them in the back rooms. Nixon will be lucky to get out of there with his pants on.
   —Jack Anderson, *author of the syndicated newspaper column "Washington Merry-Go-Round," on the President's forthcoming trip to China and his meeting with Premier Chou En-lai*

JANUARY 26   ...*The City Club Forum speaker Friday is to be Georgie Anne Geyer,* Press-Chicago Daily News *foreign correspondent. The club thought it would be a fine idea to invite members of Sigma Delta Chi, journalism society, to come hear her. So the letters of invitation went out and concluded with the offer: "If you are not now a member of the City Club, we invite you to take this opportunity to join...."*

Sigma Delta Chi used to be a men-only organization, too, but finally saw the light a few years ago and has initiated numerous women journalists. So when the SDX gals on The Press *editorial staff received invitations to join the City Club they hastened to write its officials: "...We welcome the opportunity to share in and contribute to the City Club's tradition of free expression of ideas on social, political and economic issues."*

...They are waiting for an answer.
   —Press

FEBRUARY 4   I've taken no poll. But considering the fact that more people work for a living than do not, and almost all of them belong to unions, they have to understand the players' desire to protect their rights in a labor situation.
   —Marvin Miller, *executive director, Major League Baseball Players Association*

FEBRUARY 7   *The board of directors has called a special meeting of the entire membership to be held at noon on Wednesday, February 16th. The purpose is to debate and then vote on a proposed change in our bylaws.*

At present Article III, Section 1, reads, "Membership shall be open to all men of good repute...." The proposed change would read, "Membership shall be open to all persons of good repute...."

Needed to change the bylaws is a two-thirds vote of the membership present....
   —The City

FEBRUARY 16   **Davis:** Women participate in the financial, legal and business management of the Cleveland Civic House. There is a precisely equal board, three men, three women. Women may attend our forums by virtue of their membership in the Women's City Club. They may ask questions at our forums. They may dine on identical menus.

...[This] really amounts to a raid on the Women's City Club's base. Both clubs need large memberships to keep fees modest so that people can join.

Campbell: When the City Club was founded before the First World War, this country was not yet awakened to the concept of equality for women. President Wilson's America, which was preparing to save the world for democracy, was not yet ready to give American women the right to vote.

But our world has changed. Women are nearing the end of their long march to equality. We can no longer remain half restricted, half free. Opening our forums, but refusing to break bread. We are too sensitive, too sophisticated to stand in these portals and say to half the members of this community: Thus far, and no further, shall ye come.

—Debate on whether women should be admitted as members between City Club members James B. Davis and Thomas F. Campbell

FEBRUARY 17 *After a democratically held forum debate yesterday, the male chauvinists voted to keep the City Club a men's club.*

...The vote was 65 for admitting women and 63 against. Passage would have required a two-thirds majority of the 128 votes cast, or 86 votes. The club has 1,100 members, but only those present at the luncheon meeting could vote on the issue.

—Plain Dealer

MARCH 3 Blacks have won their basic civil rights. The chief issue today is economic. We've earned the right to go to any college—but we can't pay the tuition. We've won the right to live in most residential neighborhoods—but we can't pay the mortgage. We've got to begin to march on the treasury department, the commerce department, the Office of Management and Budget.

—Reverend Jesse Jackson, *national director, Operation PUSH (People United to Save Humanity)*

I remember when he started, it was as if he were speaking to a group of businessmen. He was giving a speech he thought was befitting a place like this, and he wasn't getting much of a response. Then he went into his ''Jesse Jackson'' delivery, and everybody perked up and started taking notice. He got a standing ovation.

—Lillian Anderson, associate director of the City Club, in an interview with the authors

SHOULD WOMEN JOIN THE CITY CLUB?
THE DEBATE CONTINUES
...Which has greater priority? Being a luncheon club, with women excluded from membership? Or sponsoring one of the

1972

nation's most important forums, devoted to problems we face as a city and nation?

...Ultimately, possibilities of fewer speakers from which to choose, of fewer members and of lawsuits all may shrink the meaning of what we attempt.

   Larry Robinson, president [of the City Club]

The only real function, other than as a social meeting place, which the club has is the forums. Although these are open to women, few attend and fewer participate. Membership for women would most certainly result in the end of the Women's City Club (who, given the choice, would join it?) and a less effective club for the men....

   Michael F. Ward

...As I understand it, only about 10 applications have been received from women for membership in the club. This is a small minority stirring up trouble. On the outside are a lot of "big mouths" voicing opinions....

   Peter C. Eby
      —Letters to the editor of The City

MARCH 24   The President has assembled around him the most arrogant group of advisers and leaders that we have seen in the past 20 years.

   —John M. Ashbrook, *congressman from Ohio, citing one of the reasons why he had decided to fight Nixon for the Republican presidential nomination*

APRIL 10

WOMEN IN THE CITY CLUB
THE DEBATE CONTINUES

I...urge the City Club to...initiate new discussions immediately with the Women's City Club for the purpose of consolidating the two clubs. In the event of consolidation, I would hope that private dining areas for men only and for women only will be preserved somewhere on the premises for the misguided among us of both sexes who do not regard absolute unisex as either the wave of the future or the ultimate fulfillment of human aspirations on earth.

   Robert D. Storey

I have signed the petition asking for a new meeting relative to the question of admitting women to membership. I never thought for a moment that the issue wouldn't pass in the first instance. I think this has become an unnecessary cause celebre, and the sooner we open the doors to the sexes, the sooner we will have reached the right decision.

   Howard M. Metzenbaum
      —Letters to the editor of The City

Muhammad Ali

APRIL 28 *U.S. Senator George S. McGovern...abruptly cancelled...an appearance this morning at the City Club because of the club's men-only membership policy.*
—News item in the Plain Dealer *on the presidential candidate's change of heart about renting the club facilities to make a private speech*

MAY 1 *In response to petitions and to the 71 percent majority vote favoring admission of women [the results of a questionnaire mailed to the membership], the board of directors has called a meeting regarding the admission of women to be held on Friday, June 2nd.*
—The City

MAY 15   While campaigning for the Presidency in a Maryland shopping center, George Wallace is shot and partially paralyzed in an assassination attempt.

JUNE 2 *By a vote of 228 to 97, 11 more than the required two thirds, the City Club voted today to accept women as members for the first time in the club's 60-year history.*
—Press

[The campaign to admit women] really was a lot of hell to go through. I had no idea that would be the case; at the outset it seemed clear to me that the change ought to be made, and I thought it would be a simple matter of taking a vote. ...A lot of us worked very hard [on] it and were amazed at the strenuous opposition we had from many people who characterized themselves as so-called liberals. I was threatened with misfeasance and malfeasance and that I'd be thrown out of office.
...I remember that [immediately after the second vote] Norma Huey, who was head of the Women's City Club, said she would like to join...so I picked her up and carried her across the threshold.
—Larry Robinson, *in an interview with the authors*

JUNE 17   White House-directed "burglars" break into Democratic National Committee headquarters in Washington's Watergate office towers.

AUGUST 22 *When I get through with you, you'll think you were caught in Vietnam with a BB gun. You'll feel like you slid down a razor blade into a bucket of turpentine. Fightin' me is worse than trying to shave a mountain lion with a dull razor.*
—Muhammad Ali, *former heavyweight boxing champion, kidding one of his opponents in an upcoming benefit exhibition in Cleveland while lunching at the City Club*

SEPTEMBER 14 Kissinger would have to go to the moon to divert people's attention from Watergate.
—Shirley MacLaine, *actress and co-chairperson of the*

1972

McGovern Advisory Council on Women's Rights, referring to the many Kissinger peace missions abroad

SEPTEMBER 22 Richard Nixon believes that it is by force and violence that you secure what you want. That may have been all right for the caveman, but it won't work today.

How will history justify Richard Nixon as a man of peace when he is a man who has dropped more bombs than anyone else in history?

...America must renounce violence as a problem solver or we will destroy ourselves. I commend [Democratic presidential nominee] George McGovern to you as a man who will stop that bombing.

—**Ramsey Clark,** *former attorney general under President Johnson*

OCTOBER 3 We can't afford to have a Walter Mitty as President of this country.

—**George Romney,** *secretary of housing and urban development, on McGovern*

OCTOBER 5 Our foreign policy must avoid the reflexive interventionism that has foolishly involved us in the internal political affairs of other nations in the past. The kind of interventionism I would favor as President would be agricultural and technical assistance, the building of roads and schools, the training of skilled personnel, in concert with other nations and through multilateral institutions. The problems of 2.5 billion poor people in the world are insistent and demanding—and President Nixon has done nothing.

—**George S. McGovern,** *Democratic presidential nominee*

OCTOBER 9 You have one chance every four years, by voting for a President, to influence national policy. ...So when people say to me, between Nixon and McGovern they do not have a choice, I say to them they are defaulting on their responsiblity to make a choice.

...I don't know how many times in the last four years I have had people come to me and say, "If we had only known, we would have voted in 1968, and then Senator Humphrey would have been President and you would have been vice president." ...Yet I see so many millions of them on the threshold of doing the same damn thing all over again. And they are going to be saying, "If we had only known...."

—**Edmund S. Muskie,** *senator from Maine and former Democratic front-runner*

OCTOBER 26 *Returning from secret peace negotiations with North Vietnam, Kissinger informs the nation that an end to the war is "within reach in a matter of weeks...."*

Why all of a sudden 10 days before the election will we finally have peace?
—**Mike Gravel,** *Democratic senator from Alaska*

NOVEMBER 3 *At the end of the [forum], the club took a secret-ballot poll for presidential preference. The traditionally liberal City Club voted 55 percent for McGovern [and] 42 percent for Nixon....*
—Plain Dealer

NOVEMBER 8 **Nixon wins in a landslide, with 60.6 percent of the vote to McGovern's 37.5.**

DECEMBER 18 **Peace negotiations having stalled over South Vietnam's unhappiness with the draft settlement, the U.S. resumes bombing of North Vietnam.**

1973

The Vietnam peace treaty is signed in late January; the first prisoners of war come home to California's Travis Air Force Base in mid-February; and by the end of March the last American troops have left South Vietnam. But President Nixon's headaches are far from ended. In a televised address on April 30th he takes responsibility but not the blame for the acts of those "people whose zeal exceeded their judgment." One of them, White House counsel John Dean, later testifies before the Senate Watergate committee about Nixon's complicity in an alleged cover-up, and talk of impeachment begins to rumble at the City Club and across the land.

In October Nixon asks Attorney General Eliot Richardson to fire special Watergate prosecutor Archibald Cox for refusing to halt judicial proceedings to obtain tape recordings of White House discussions of Watergate. Richardson and his assistant, William Ruckelshaus, resign instead. The day before this so-called Saturday Night Massacre, the Organization of Petroleum Exporting Countries (OPEC) declares a ban on oil exports to the United States because of its support of Israel during the Yom Kippur attack launched against that nation by Egypt and Syria the week before.

In Cleveland, Mayor Perk forms a five-detective Smut Squad to crack down on retailers of hard-core pornography as the Supreme Court rewrites the obscenity laws to allow states to judge, according to local community standards, if certain films, books or plays appeal to prurient interest. But it is a case filed in the federal courts in December by the NAACP, charging the Cleveland Board of Education with illegal segregation, that will preoccupy the city for many years to come.

FEBRUARY 13 President Nixon, who broke every decent,

1973

divine human law by ordering the massive bombing before Christmas, shows himself to be frighteningly hypocritical in keeping the law with regard to war resisters.
  —Father Philip Berrigan, *anti-war activist recently paroled from federal prison where he was serving a sentence for burning draft records*

FEBRUARY 27   Russell Means and 200 other members of the American Indian Movement take over the hamlet of Wounded Knee, South Dakota, in protest of the federal Bureau of Indian Affairs' treatment of 11,000 Oglala Sioux living on Pine Ridge reservation 15 miles away. The siege ends 71 days later, with the Senate promising to investigate alleged civil rights violations on the reservation.

MARCH 7   *A White House memo urging him to make a speech before the Cleveland City Club during the presidential campaign came back to haunt Acting FBI Director L. Patrick Gray III yesterday.*
  Gray made the speech on August 12th, but acknowledged yesterday during his confirmation hearings that the White House made a "gross mistake" in asking him to make the appearance.
  ...The memo...states: "With Ohio being crucially vital to our hopes in November, we would hope you will assign this forum some priority in planning your schedule...."
  —Plain Dealer

MARCH 8   *If this is embarrassing to Gray, it should be more disconcerting to the American public and taxpayers who had come to look upon the FBI as staunchly independent, serving no party or President except in the direct line of duty.*
  —Plain Dealer *editorial*

APRIL 18   [Russell Means'] costume was a curious blend of old and new. He wore a red work shirt and Levis and there were braids and feathers in his pigtails. He wore a Timex watch, but the band was made of Indian beads. So was his belt, which had "Russ Means" stitched across it in two-inch-high letters.
  Means speaks with force and intelligence, but his remarks are seldom adorned by humor, and he gets bogged down in the intricacies of Indian problems.
  Means received a rousing ovation when he was finished, then met well-wishers in a receiving line. Several women gushed and told him they were thrilled with his speech. "Where can we contribute to your cause?" one asked. "Can we send money?"
  —Plain Dealer

MAY 4   The fight is not between the girls, but a test to see whether the American public will let a small percentage of noisy women libbers overthrow our social structure or whether they

Russell Means

Jane Fonda

will stand up and protect their American heritage.

 —Evelyn Pitschke, *Indianapolis attorney and legal advisor to the national Stop ERA Committee*

MAY 17 Hearings by a Senate committee investigating Watergate begin in Washington under the chairmanship of Democratic Senator Sam J. Ervin, Jr., of North Carolina.

MAY 18 Watergate is not a Republican problem. As a party, it had nothing to do with it, nor are the Republican politicians responsible. Not a single person thus far implicated, with the exception of President Nixon, ever ran even for dog catcher.

 —Joseph R. Biden, Jr., *Democratic senator from Delaware, warning that partisan handling of the scandal could bring down the two-party system*

SEPTEMBER 11 Chilean President Salvador Allende is killed by the military in a violent coup ending 46 years of civilian rule.

OCTOBER 26 Miss Fonda walked into the jammed auditorium for lunch. Sitting at the head table with club president Bertram E. Gardner, she ate only about half of her fish and almost none of her macaroni. Gardner entertained her with a stream of conversation and then asked if he could have her autograph.

 "I'd rather not," said Miss Fonda. Gardner smiled and kept talking to her.

 "I don't believe in autographs," Miss Fonda said later. "I want people to realize that all names are important and that nobody's name means more than anybody else's."

 She got a rousing ovation when introduced. She responded...with a passionate indictment of the situation in Vietnam.

 She said South Vietnam was the most massive police state in the world, and it had been created by U.S. dollars in the name of peace with honor. She said there is no freedom of speech in South Vietnam, no elections and that the regime executed 40,000 political prisoners without trial and with U.S. sanction. She called Henry Kissinger, the U.S. secretary of state who just won the Nobel Peace Prize, "a killer with blood on his hands."

 Afterward Miss Fonda was besieged with well-wishers. "I thought it would be a waste of time coming here today," said a man who looked like a retired banker. "I thought she was a nut, some kind of dope fiend. But now I'm glad I came."

 —Plain Dealer

DECEMBER 14 The hatred and cruelty they unleashed have never before been seen in our country nor anywhere in Latin America. They speak of liberty while they open concentration camps throughout the country where leaders and intellectuals are tortured and murdered. Thousands of students and profes-

1973

sors have been expelled, while half-literate army officers are named deans. They burned books, not just by Marx but by Shakespeare. They even burned books on Cubism because they thought it is related to Cuba.

—Hortensia Bussi de Allende, *widow of the Marxist president of Chile, on the country's new military leaders*

Although the audience appeared largely friendly to Mrs. Allende's cause, the first three questions were hostile. One club member asked whether she thought it might be possible for a refugee from a communist country to make a similar speech in Moscow. The other two questioners…asked about the unstable economy under the Allende regime.

Mrs. Allende answered the questions calmly, but ended the answer to the third question with the announcement, "We have just come from Detroit. Our delay was not our fault, but the fault of the airplane, and therefore we have a right to rest and eat now." …She abruptly terminated the traditional question period.

—Plain Dealer

DECEMBER 21 It will be a stick in the image of American journalism for a long time to come that after the *Washington Post,* and later CBS, delved into the background to Watergate, no one else would air it or write about it. The fact that Americans were permitted to go to the polls without knowing the facts about Watergate will be something that journalism students and scholars 100 years from now will write about.

—Fred W. Friendly, *former president, CBS News*

1974

Streaking becomes a national craze…Atlanta Brave Hank Aaron socks No. 715 out of the park, surpassing the Babe in career home runs…32-year-old Muhammad Ali wrests the heavyweight crown away from George Foreman in Zaire…and Jack Benny passes away—none of which serves to divert for long the country's attention from gasoline lines, inflation headed toward double digits, 6.5 percent unemployment and the inevitable denouement of Watergate. James Rhodes regains the Ohio governorship, and the first cracks in the City of Cleveland's financial house of cards appear.

JANUARY 4 I've been doing a lot of tossing and turning at night lately trying to come up with new ideas on keeping a balanced budget without cutting services or raising taxes. The more I think about it, the less sleep I get. Your city administration will be hard pressed in 1974 to keep its budget in balance without raising taxes.

—Ralph J. Perk, *on how to resolve the difference between the city's anticipated revenues of $110 million and its proposed budget of $140 million*

JANUARY 11 Ralph Perk not only lacks the answers to

Cleveland's problems, he doesn't even have a clear idea of what the problems are. Perk's greatest achievement was balancing the budget without an increase in taxes. But he went out and overspent that budget to the point that Perk now admits that the city is facing the same financial crisis that he claims to have solved two years ago.
    —George Forbes, *Cleveland's first black city council president*

JANUARY 12   Move over, Dick Gregory, here comes George Forbes.

Forbes did not intend his City Club Forum talk to be a comic hour yesterday. He prefaced his speech with: "There won't be any jokes today." But once unshackled from his prepared speech, he turned on the humor during a question-and-answer session that left the jam-packed audience in stitches.

...On his political enemies: "I don't want you to think that all my political enemies are white. If you don't believe me, you read this week's *Call & Post* [Cleveland's black weekly newspaper]. If you don't have this week's *Call & Post*, read last week's *Call & Post.* In fact, just pick up any *Call & Post.*"

On Mayor Ralph J. Perk's expected candidacy for the U.S. Senate: "It would be a good way to get rid of him...."

On how Perk spends city funds, in response to a question from W. Kiely Cronin, former Cleveland ports director: "They have a way of hiding it, of putting it in secret funds—well, you know (turning to Cronin). You were down there...."
    —Plain Dealer

JANUARY 19   I intend to walk softly, talk persuasively and work effectively to make the voices of Ohio heard in the U.S. Senate.
    —Howard M. Metzenbaum, *newly appointed to fill the Senate seat vacated by William B. Saxbe upon his acceptance of the position of attorney general*

FEBRUARY 1   Impeachment—like radical surgery—is not unthinkable when the alternative is more dangerous. Can we not agree that a three-month trial would be better than a three-year period of little leadership and much uncertainty?
    —Leon Shull, *national director, Americans for Democratic Action*

MARCH 1   *[Exiled Russian poet Alexander Sergeyevich Yesenin-Volpin] was like a stereotype of a typical Russian—big head of hair, big beard, quite stocky, I would have guessed he was maybe in his seventies. I learned later he was more like 42. He had been [detained] in one of these psychiatric hospitals.*

He started to give his speech—he had an accent but he was speaking good English—but then as he went on a bit he became more and more difficult to understand. And people began to look at each other—there was sort of an undercurrent of

1974

reaction—and it got worse and worse and some people got up and left. ...He was literally having a breakdown right in front of our eyes. He was just shaking and sweating as he was recounting what he had been through.

From my point of view it turned out to be a terrific forum because it was like Exhibit A of what happens to a person. We tried to have a question period but finally gave up. He just collapsed right in front of us.
  —*Alan Davis, in an interview with the authors*

MARCH 4   *Each Friday noon [since last November] we have [had] as our Forum guests 40 social studies students from Cleveland [area] high schools. ...Following each Forum address the speaker meets with the students for an additional seminar session.*
  —The City

MARCH 15   Why did we impose the oil embargo? We did it as a disincentive for the United States to...avoid underwriting Israel's objectives in the Middle East, Israel's conquests. We [felt we] were marketing the oil, seeking the oil, directly or indirectly...for the war machine of Israel.
  —Clovis Maksoud, *special envoy of the League of Arab States, speaking three days before the embargo suddenly ends*

MARCH 29   Many people have the idea that the President is sulking in the White House, waiting for impeachment, but that's not so. He's one of the toughest men I've ever known.
  —John J. Rhodes, *House minority leader and Nixon apologist*

[Rhodes] had a tough assignment coming here, but he handled the questions pretty well during the forum itself. And then he went into the students and I guess they really let him have it. No fooling around—they gave him a hard time. So here he comes out and I ask him my standard question, "Well, how'd it go?" He's all flushed in the face and his jowls are shaking and he says, "Those smart-ass kids, what do they know?"
  —*Alan Davis, in an interview with the authors*

James Hoffa

APRIL 19   James Hoffa, the ex-convict who aspires to regain the presidency of the Teamsters Union, was in Cleveland today. ...The five-foot, five-and-a-half-inch Hoffa, who spent nearly three years in prison for jury tampering and mail fraud, proved at 61 that he is still at no loss in picking a fight.

...Clad entirely in black except for a white shirt (even the face of his wristwatch is black), Hoffa...charged that John Dean and Charles Colson, former White House lawyers, "flimflammed Nixon" into signing restrictions into Hoffa's commutation from prison [that] forbid Hoffa from engaging even indirectly in union affairs until 1980. "Colson worked out an agreement with [Frank] Fitzsimmons...so he could be the lawyer of the international at

$150,000 a year and Fitzsimmons would be perpetuated (in the presidency).''
—Press

Time was when James R. Hoffa came to town—any town—everybody who was anybody in the Teamsters Union would flock to him like disciples. Yesterday Hoffa addressed the City Club Forum and the local Teamster leadership was conspicuously absent. Only James Trusso, not exactly of the Teamster establishment, took time out from his battle with the city on behalf of his striking (Local 244) city truck drivers to look up an old friend. Hoffa rewarded Trusso's loyalty with a public statement of support and acid criticism of Mayor Ralph J. Perk's handling of the garbage driver's strike.

"...There is a headline this morning that the mayor of this city is going to bring out the National Guard to drive garbage trucks [because] the citizens of this community say, 'Pick up our garbage.' Well, the hell with your garbage. What about [the fact] that [the strikers] are entitled to live like human beings...entitled to a decent wage, that the Constitution is their Constitution also, that they are supposed to be protected, not destroyed and harassed by the so-called elite management of city, state and federal government?''
—Plain Dealer

MAY 3 [Former Marine Corps combat pilot and astronaut John] Glenn drew the biggest cheers from his supporters when he responded to a comment two weeks ago by Metzenbaum [his opponent in the Democratic senatorial primary] that Glenn "never held a job.''

"You go with me to a veterans hospital, see their mangled bodies and tell them they didn't hold a job. Go with me and tell a Gold Star mother her son didn't hold a job. Go to Arlington National Cemetery..., watch those flags, stand there and tell me those people didn't have a job. I tell you, Howard Metzenbaum, you should be on your knees every day of your life thanking God that there were some men, some men who held a job!''
—Press

Let me make it clear, John. I was talking about a job in private employment.
—Metzenbaum, *who will go on to lose the primary*

Glenn was never more effective than in how he answered that charge by Howard. Up to that time he had been the typical poised-but-dull John Glenn. We found out that Glenn did have a streak of fire in him, and it had a very profound impact on the audience. We all said, "By God, there is another John Glenn, but you have to get the bellows and blow a hell of a lot on him.''
—Herb Kamm, former editor of the Press *and former president of the City Club, in an interview with the authors*

JUNE 21 **Berkman:** In [neither] historical perspective and

1974

legal experience nor in empirical research [is there justification for] the suppression of words or pictures in a free society.

Boylan: Why are books written? They're written to influence. It may be true that not everyone who reads the Bible becomes a Christian or that everyone who reads Karl Marx becomes a socialist, but its foolish to say that the Bible and Marx had no influence. Hitler's *Mein Kampf* may not have caused Naziism, but it certainly contributed to it.

I submit that the reader and viewer of hard-core pornography and smut is influenced—just how much depends upon the person and to some extent upon his previous experiences.

—Debate between Bernard A. Berkman, president of the Legal Aid Society, and Richard L. Boylan, head of Mayor Perk's Smut Squad, on whether the First Amendment guarantees of free speech extend to pornography

JUNE 28 Justice Oliver Wendell Holmes once said that wiretapping was dirty business. I won't argue the point, but I will simply suggest that sometimes it is the last resort of decent men striving to protect our freedom against activities that are far, far dirtier. [However], electronic surveillance will not be employed by the justice department during my time as attorney general as some sort of easily obtained hunting license.
—William B. Saxbe

JULY 24 *The Supreme Court rules that the White House must turn over its tapes to special Watergate prosecutor Leon Jaworski.*

JULY 27 *The House Judiciary Committee votes 27 to 11 to recommend the impeachment of Richard Nixon on a charge of obstruction of justice. On August 9th President Nixon resigns.*

SEPTEMBER 8 *President Ford grants Nixon a full pardon.*

SEPTEMBER 19 I support the end result...but I don't agree with the way the pardon was reached.
—Eliot Richardson, *former attorney general, suggesting that a full public accounting of the charges against Nixon should have preceeded his pardon*

Q: Why do you favor the pardon?
Richardson: Would any significant public interest be served by sending him to jail? Nixon will be remembered...as the only President to suffer the disgrace of resigning in mid-term.
Q: Do you think there was a deal between Nixon and Ford?
Richardson: I don't think so. Whatever we may think of [Ford's] judgment, his integrity has not been questioned.

Eliot Richardson

SEPTEMBER 27 The clock is just beginning to tick away. We are going to have to repay that borrowed money, and it will put a still greater stress on our budget.

—**John Burke,** *professor of economics at Cleveland State University, on the city practice of financing its operating expenses through the sale of bonds not approved by the voters*

OCTOBER 25 **Perk:** According to FBI standards, Watergate is considered a victimless crime. No one was hurt and nothing was stolen.

Glenn: Calling Watergate a victimless crime is the biggest travesty of justice I've ever seen.

—*Debate between Ralph Perk and John Glenn, candidates for Senate*

1975-1986

Time for a Change

As the country sought to bind its postwar and post-Watergate wounds, a maverick Cleveland mayoral candidate by the name of Dennis Kucinich pushed his reform platform during frequent appearances at the club.

1975

The problems of Northern cities grab the headlines early in the year, when New York City Mayor Abraham Beame announces $100 million in cuts in an attempt to balance a city budget more than $1.5 billion in the red. Later New York narrowly avoids defaulting through a state-engineered bail-out that takes fiscal control away from the mayor. Struggling with his own budgetary problems and an image tarnished by his losing Senate bid, Mayor Perk initiates a $327-million antitrust lawsuit against the Cleveland Electric Illuminating Company, charging the utility with conspiring to put the Municipal Light Plant out of business. This move will inadvertently provide Dennis Kucinich, who is elected clerk of courts in November, with an issue to use against Perk in the 1977 mayoral race.

At the City Club, one of the country's most controversial white supremacists gets a fair hearing.

FEBRUARY 14 The multitude of anti-poverty and other programs popularly considered "black programs" benefited far more whites than blacks. More whites got housing under federal subsidy programs, entered open-enrollment colleges, got jobs in companies that formerly discriminated, took part in community-action programs and received food and welfare assistance than did blacks.

—Vernon E. Jordan, Jr., *executive director, National Urban League*

FEBRUARY 22 From the standpoint of homicide prevention, it is meaningless whether the gun is registered, licensed or inspected. The mere presence creates the statistical probability for homicide.

—Dr. Emanuel Tanay, *Detroit psychiatrist and homicide expert, linking the number of guns in a community to the probability of accidents and killings*

FEBRUARY 28 I want a commitment from [Secretary of State] Henry Kissinger that the United States will stop dealing and trading with nations that do not give equal status to women. If it is proper to attach riders to a trade bill concerning the rights of Soviet Jews, why can't the same be done for women? Of course, the ban may mean we have to stop all interstate commerce, too.

—Karen DeCrow, *president, NOW (National Organization of Women)*

APRIL 18 They say I am on an ego trip. Of course, I have an ego, but my ego wasn't questioned when I made a deal with Heinrich Himmler to save Jews during World War II. I was an advisor to the War Refugee Board. Was I on an ego trip then?

—Rabbi Baruch Korff, *Nixon confidant and supporter, responding to critics of his leadership of the National Citizens*

1975   *Committee for Fairness to the Presidency*

APRIL 24   *City Club officials are attempting to make sure that Dr. William Shockley, Nobel Prize-winning physicist from Stanford University, is given an opportunity to speak during tomorrow's City Club Forum.*

Dr. Shockley was shouted down at Case Western Reserve University last September when he attempted to debate Roy Innis, national director of CORE [Congress of Racial Equality], on Shockley's theory that blacks may be genetically inferior to whites.

W. Kiely Cronin, City Club president, has contacted police to alert them about Dr. Shockley's appearance.

 —Press

APRIL 25   My thesis is not inferiority, but the failure of the intellectual community to look at the problem of dysgenics [the disproportionate growth of groups with a low intelligence].

 —William Shockley, *suggesting that welfare encourages large families among blacks, who he claims have an average IQ about 15 points lower than the average IQ of whites*

Q: What is your solution?
A: If you want me to say "genocide," I'll say I'm in favor of genocide of a low-IQ population over a long haul by methods of limited population growth.

 —Shockley on his Voluntary Sterilization Bonus Plan, which would pay those with certain mental or physical defects to undergo voluntary sterilization

William B. Shockley drew more criticism and skepticism from a small group of high school pupils than he did from an overflow crowd of 350 at the City Club—the largest audience the club has attracted this year.

Shockley, who talked with Cleveland youngsters for more than an hour after his City Club discussion, threatened at one point to walk out "because I have not found an intellectual interest here."

A white adult moderator appeased Shockley by saying he thought the 27 pupils—20 of them black—"are perplexed, concerned and genuinely interested."

The Stanford professor, who says statistics prove blacks are on the average less intelligent than whites, told the pupils he realized, "This is a very painful thing to look into, I'm sure."

...Shockley was asked by a black girl whether his statistics took into account that "blacks in the ghetto have insufficient diets," that IQ tests can be culturally biased and that many blacks receive inferior educations.

"These families live in the ghetto all of their lives. They eat maybe once a day—beans and cornbread," she said. "A child may be coming to school practically starved."

Shockley looked around the small room.... "Did you yourself

Donald Johanson

suffer from this? Are there students in this room that grew up under these adverse dietary conditions?''

The pupils looked at each other. Some laughed. "Maybe we didn't, but some people do," one said.

Shockley then plunged into an involved study which, he said, showed through experiments using "hundreds of thousands of people" that children can be born from starving mothers and still develop a normal IQ. He was annoyed when the discussion moved to other topics and nobody seemed to care to hear where the study had been done.

...Probably the single bright moment came when Shockley held up pictures of blocks, circles and other symbols that he said represented a culturally unbiased IQ test. The pupils outshouted each other in correctly guessing which symbols fell into the appropriate blank spaces on Shockley's charts—while a reporter tried unsuccessfully to unravel the patterns.

—Plain Dealer

MAY 2 Intelligence tests are racist instruments. They are only given and relied on in nations where there is a minority which the majority wishes to discriminate against and suppress. America is not morally, psychologically, intellectually or politically fit to determine innate racial intelligence. It is highly unfair and prejudicial to have educational values, standards and goals for blacks set by whites.
    —Roy Innis

JUNE 13 People ask me what sort of implications for modern people can be found in all these old, dry bones. I tell them that all of it points to the fact that survival for these creatures was based on one thing: cooperation. If we want to learn something and survive for another million years, we have to do what they did. We have to cooperate.
    —Donald Johanson, *curator of physical anthropology at the Cleveland Museum of Natural History and discoverer of "Lucy," the fossil skeleton of the earliest known human ancestor*

JUNE 20 How many barrels of oil is a jet engine worth? Do you want us to triple the price of our armaments, or do you want a 40 percent reduction in the price of oil? These are the types of questions we should be asking the OPEC countries.
    —Eliot Janeway, *economist and syndicated columnist, on how America can break the Arab oil cartel, which doubled its prices at the end of the previous year*

SEPTEMBER 12 If I could live the last five years over again, I would urge the board not to hire the gladiators to fight the desegregation case.
    —Audrey V. McCutcheon, *executive deputy superintendent, Detroit public schools*

SEPTEMBER 19 Does the publicly subsidized splendor of

1975

[new] downtown offices really do much for a city's economy? I think the answer has to be no. Our study in St. Louis indicated the businessmen were just moving from older office buildings that paid full taxes to new buildings that were often given partial tax abatements.

—**Norton Long,** *director, Center of Community and Metropolitan Studies at the University of Missouri*

DECEMBER 28   The Census Bureau announces that Greater Cleveland's population has slipped below two million and that Houston has replaced Cleveland as the country's 15th largest city.

1976

As the country prepares to celebrate its 200th birthday, the City Club reluctantly announces that the Anvil Revue will be discontinued in its 62nd season; instead the club will cosponsor (with the Cleveland Area Arts Council) a production of an original bicentennial comedy, *Black Horse Tavern,* by Cleveland novelist Thomas P. Cullinan. On May 21st Roy Hattersley, the British minister of state, addresses the City Club in London, marking the first time the Forum has been held outside Cleveland and the start of a new tradition: regular Forum broadcasts from abroad. The scheduling of desegregation experts from around the country serves to elevate the quality of the local dialogue on that inflammatory subject.

JANUARY 9   With 15 million people out of work, with the country facing the greatest unemployment problem it has had since the Great Depression, this is hardly the time to celebrate.

—**Charles B. Rangel,** *chairman of the Congressional Black Caucus, on the bicentennial*

FEBRUARY 6   Unfortunately, urban rot is not visible from the windows of Air Force One. President Ford, in his State of the Union address, made no mention of the cities and the problems that confront them. In the year of the near-collapse of New York, this omission is incredible.

We must not sweep the financial crisis of New York City under the rug. This is not New York's problem alone. It could happen to almost any big American city.

—**Charles Mathias, Jr.,** *Republican senator from Maryland and as-yet unannounced candidate for President*

APRIL 2   [Desegregation has] resulted in emphasis on what is at the end of the bus ride rather than on transporation itself.

—**R. Jerrald Shive,** *chairman of the department of secondary education of Cleveland State University, citing evidence of the improvements in curriculum that have accompanied desegregation of schools in Minneapolis and Boston, among other districts*

Jimmy Carter

APRIL 9 I see nothing wrong...if you have a neighborhood that is primarily black, primarily Polish or primarily German. I would not be in favor of the federal government trying to break up such a neighborhood. I think it would be counterproductive.

—**Jimmy Carter,** *former governor of Georgia and Democratic presidential aspirant, clarifying his controversial remark, made earlier in the week, about protecting the "ethnic purity" of neighborhoods from forced public housing*

MAY 28 It takes a slick politician to come out on both sides of important issues—and they don't come any slicker than Jimmy Carter. For Carter to advocate voluntary busing is like offering voluntary Yom Kippur services in Cairo. ...I am here because I believe when the people of Ohio get the chance to find out what lies behind the smile and the talk of love and trust and all the press attention, they will decide that it's not enough to do the job they want done.

—**Morris Udall,** *congressman from Arizona and candidate for the Democratic presidential nomination*

AUGUST 31 *After nearly three years of hearings on the NAACP's case against the Cleveland Board of Education, U.S. District Court Judge Frank J. Battisti rules that the Cleveland schools are illegally segregated and orders the board to work with a court-appointed expert to prepare a desegregation plan within 90 days.*

SEPTEMBER 10 Our preoccupation with traditional manufacturing jobs—as important as those are—misdirects our attention away from the real dimensions of the challenge facing Ohio's economy: our failure to capture a full share of the rapidly developing high-technology industries and to generate the related research and service activities that attract and sustain this type of investment.

...We must identify those areas for research and development that hold special promise in our state. ...We must develop mechanisms to ensure that our best ideas are brought to the attention of potential investors—both public and private—who can take new concepts and reshape them into useful and saleable products.

—**Richard F. Celeste,** *lieutenant governor of Ohio and possible Democratic gubernatorial candidate in 1978*

SEPTEMBER 14 *Judge Battisti appoints Cleveland attorney Daniel R. McCarthy as special master for desegregation to act as the court's liason with the school board.*

SEPTEMBER 24 For the most part school desegregation works, and it works without violence. It is replacing despair with hope in the lives of thousands of young people and their parents. ...In Tampa, where busing started six years ago, schools in

1976

minority communities had textbooks which were copyrighted in 1935 and were in very inferior condition. After busing, suddenly these conditions changed.
     —**Arthur Flemming,** *chairman of the U.S. Civil Rights Commission, describing the conclusion of his agency's recently released study of American school desegregation efforts*

OCTOBER 2   In his second debate with Democratic presidential nominee Jimmy Carter, President Ford claims that "there is no communist domination of Eastern Europe."

OCTOBER 15   What's in serious disrepair after eight years of the present administration is a sense of national unity, national confidence, national purpose. We have become in many ways a nation of strangers, suspicious of our neighbors and, more important, suspicious of our government.

During the 21 months Jimmy Carter has been campaigning, he has been open and accessible to the people and to the press, almost to a fault. He has talked to small towns and to big magazines, and he has made mistakes. He is a human being, and it seems to me that what we want in the man who is our President is a human being rather than a god who takes six days to realize that Eastern Europe is indeed under communist domination.
     —**W. Hodding Carter III,** *editor of the Greenville (Mississippi)* Delta Democrat-Times *and spokesperson for Concerned Americans for Good Government, who will become assistant secretary of state for public affairs under Jimmy Carter*

NOVEMBER 13   If [inner-city blacks] steal your pocketbook or automobile, just remember that it was your school system that kept [them] in school for 12 years and then turned [them] out unable to read and without job-oriented training.
     —**W.O. Walker,** *editor and publisher,* Call & Post

1977

Jimmy Carter enters office with a show of modesty, beginning his inauguration day by attending a Baptist church service and ending it by dancing at seven $25-a-ticket inaugural parties. Three months later the honeymoon ends when the Carter administration announces its controversial energy program, which calls for, among other things, a gasoline tax and more nuclear power plants in a conservation campaign the President likens to "the moral equivalent of war."

With his race for a fourth term still ahead, Mayor Perk clings to the promise of no new taxes that resulted in his first election victory in 1971. Instead, to raise desperately needed operating funds and maintain the city's Triple-A bond rating, he proposes the sale of the unprofitable Municipal Light Plant and $35 million in property tax abatements for two Cleveland corporations

planning to build new headquarters downtown that he claims will generate additional jobs and revenues from city income taxes. Opponent Dennis Kucinich's adroit manipulation of these issues at the City Club and elsewhere strikes a responsive chord in the city's voters that fall.

While the politicians do battle, the club also takes a look in March at the growing urban crisis and sponsors a Human Rights Week in December.

JANUARY 7 It is a matter of record that CEI has waged an intensive behind-the-scenes campaign to steal Muny Light from the people of Cleveland...thereby winning acclaim perhaps as the biggest bulb snatcher in history.

—Dennis J. Kucinich, *clerk of Cleveland Municipal Court, lambasting Mayor Perk's proposal to sell Muny Light, which provides low-cost power to 50,000 city residents*

JANUARY 8 *Dennis Kucinich proved one thing in his impassioned speech...that he is a clever orator. Kucinich...an unannounced candidate for mayor, made a strong pitch for not selling Muny Light Plant to the Illuminating Company. Anyone seeking office, whether he admits it or not, likes to have a villain to run against. Kucinich is attempting to create two...Mayor Perk and CEI.*

The Perk administration was asked to supply someone to debate Kucinich, but politely declined the invitation. Apparently Perk's allies feel going one-on-one against Kucinich is a no-win contest, like walking into a buzz saw.

—Press editorial

Any speech that I gave before the City Club was the product of hours and sometimes days and weeks of intensive preparation and research.... I understood...that the City Club audience was a litmus test. If you had an idea or a position on an issue and you could get through the intellectual gantlet at the City Club, you then had credibility to take the issue to the community at large. ...The City Club audience was just the initial audience, but then the media provide each speaker with an audience of millions. Needless to say, I was always cognizant of that.

—Dennis J. Kucinich, in an interview with the authors

FEBRUARY 4 *The Carter administration announces reductions in U.S. aid to Argentina, Uruguay and Ethiopia because of human rights violations, but South Korea, Chile and other strategically important allies are sheltered from such cuts.*

MARCH 4 As a starter, we need to get rid of the dominant economic idea of the last eight years that more joblessness is the way to fight inflation.

—Henry S. Reuss, *chairman of the House Committee on*

1977

Banking, Finance and Urban Affairs, on the need for a national urban policy that would limit federal economic development grants, investment tax credits and tax-free municipal industrial revenue bonds to low-employment central cities

MARCH 7 The fiscal crisis of cities is deeper than generally acknowledged. In addition to the short-term financial crisis, there is good evidence that cities are allowing their capital stock—water and sewer systems, roads and streets, public schools—to deteriorate. Reacting to financial pressures, many cities have chosen to defer maintenance and repairs. This will either throw a very large investment burden on future generations or lead to the scrappage of a lot of facilities—along with the functions they serve—in the older cities.

  —George Peterson, *director of public finance, National Urban Institute*

MARCH 9   President Carter ends restrictions on travel to Cuba, Vietnam, North Korea and Cambodia.

MARCH 15 I don't share the gloom which has been expressed by the other speakers. The so-called [urban] fiscal crisis was primarily New York's. We have come out of the worst of it.

  —Warren Riebe, *finance director, City of Cleveland*

MARCH 28 You're going to have to give up some of your concern for environmental matters if the city is to rebuild its capital plant. You have to put economic development first. Otherwise, you're not going to be able to save the environment or equality for anybody.

  —Roger Starr, *former New York City housing administrator now a member of the editorial board of* The New York Times, *noting that the choice for industrial cities may come down to "hot lunches for school children or bridges"*

JUNE 9 [Jimmy Carter's] administration has been marked far more by style than by substance. His imagery may buy him some time, but ultimately he'll have to perform substantively.

  —James M. Naughton, *Washington bureau correspondent,* The New York Times

JUNE 25 Carter promised a lot to the neighborhoods. He campaigned in the neighborhoods; he got votes there and raised the people's expectations so they expected something fast. But we're waiting for his first hit or home run for the cities.

  —Gale Cincotta, *founder of the National Peoples Action, a coalition of Chicago neighborhood groups*

SEPTEMBER 16 The bus is going to roll [in Cleveland]. We can delay it, but it will roll.

  When it rolls, it will drive us to opportunity, but it stops at the door. It will neither give us the will to learn nor the urge to excel, and it cannot revive a dead attitude. It is a means of transportation. The challenge lies beyond the door.

—Reverend Jesse Jackson, *calling for parents, the church and the media to join hands with the school to teach children a sense of responsibility*

SEPTEMBER 9   Kucinich: Cleveland's failure to keep and maintain a sewer system, a port, a zoo, a hospital, a light system, water system, stadium and convention center is the work of crooks, political hacks and incompetents....

Feighan: We don't need a poll [distributed] by garbage men [a Perk administration innovation] to tell us that pornography is garbage. The most obscene thing in this city is that people can run for public office and be guilty of the worst kind of intellectual dishonesty. I do not intend to become a political prostitute to be elected mayor of this city.

Perk: City government, having laid the groundwork for increased employment in business and industry and the coming revitalization of the neighborhoods, will require no increase in taxes in the foreseeable future.

—Mayoral primary debate between Democrats Dennis Kucinich and State Representative Edward F. Feighan and Republican incumbent Ralph Perk

OCTOBER 27   Special master Daniel McCarthy presents the federal court with his desegregation plan to bus 30,000 students the following September.

DECEMBER 16   Human rights today are violated in the majority of countries all over the world. All major regions, all political and ideological blocs, are involved. In spite of the universal declaration of human rights adopted by the United Nations in December 1948, as many as 117 countries are cited in the Amnesty International report of 1977....

It is all too easy when listening to such a catalogue of political imprisonment or torture or execution to forget that these brutalities and indignities have been suffered by individual human beings...because they are communists and because they are not; because they seek social change and because they do not; because they speak out and because they remain silent; because the regime has undergone change and because it has not; because they have not taken up arms against their fellow men and because they have come to the defense of the poor....

For the sake of practical achievement, Amnesty International has deliberately chosen to limit its investigation and its activities to human-rights violations suffered by prisoners. ...Any truly adequate survey of the state of human rights conditions in today's world would have to be much broader in scope.... It would have to cite and include the whole realm of economic, social and cultural rights....

—Andrew Blane, *the only American member of the executive committee of Amnesty International, which was*

1977

1978

Dennis Kucinich, age 30, takes office as Cleveland mayor and installs several equally youthful advisors in key cabinet positions. The administration's inexperienced handling of a major snow storm, among other first-year crises, prompts a recall election from which Kucinich narrowly escapes by 236 votes.

The City Club, at the instigation of journalist member Sidney Andorn, launches a summer series of outdoor forums in the Eastman Reading Garden of the Cleveland Public Library downtown in order to foster public discussion on (among other pressing topics) "Is Cleveland Broke?" The question is firmly answered when in December the city slides into default. Forced to lay off 2,000 workers, including large numbers of police and firemen, Kucinich calls for a special election in February 1979 to ask voters to raise city income taxes and determine once and for all whether to sell Muny Light.

Elected to the presidency of the City Club is Annette Butler, the first woman and only the second black to be so honored.

MAY 5   In the heat of the argument, Rabbi Rosenthal turned from the podium and lunged with a sweeping motion toward Haiman, who was seated, as if to slap his face. There were gasps from the audience as the back of the rabbi's hand stopped short of Haiman's cheek.

"If I came up to attack you like this, you would certainly have a right to defend yourself," Rabbi Rosenthal said. Haiman, who had not flinched, used the rabbi's action to illustrate his own argument.

"I had no way of knowing whether or not you were going to hit me," he said. "As a matter of fact, I thought you were going to. But I do not have a right to react with violence until after you attack me, although some people would resort to violence before that."

Rabbi Rosenthal argued the right of free speech should not protect an intentional provocation to violence.... Haiman, however, said that one cannot be selective about who should be protected by the rights of free speech and assembly guaranteed in the First Amendment.

—Newspaper accounts of the debate between Rudolph M. Rosenthal, rabbi emeritus of Cleveland's Temple on the Heights, and Franklyn S. Haiman of Chicago, national secretary of the American Civil Liberties Union, on the right of American Nazis to parade in Skokie, Illinois, whose sizeable Jewish community includes many survivors of the Holocaust

JUNE 9   Bonda: There is a sickness in City Hall...there has been for a long time now. That is why I wish there were no recall. A recall is not going to help the sickness. Kucinich is

Simas Kudirka

likely to emerge from it even more arrogant abrasive.

Campbell: When 50,000 people sign petition for a recall election, an election should be held.

—Debate between Alva T. Bonda, former president of the Cleveland school board and a former supporter of the mayor, and Thomas F. Campbell, a leader of the recall movement

JUNE 16   In 1970 [Simas] Kudirka, a Lithuanian sailor, fled from Soviet clutches by jumping from a fishing trawler onto the deck of a U.S. Coast Guard cutter off the Massachusetts coast. In the ensuing furor, he was returned to Soviet control and eventually to prison. But he was freed four years later and came to the U.S. when it was learned that he had U.S. citizenship through his mother, who was a natural-born American.

...Kudirka described how...as the U.S. ship approached, the Russians were fearful, imagining that the Americans were all armed "like Al Capone."

Then, he said, the sailors were smiling and shouting greetings and waving their caps. Some threw packages of cigarettes to the Russians. Meanwhile, the KGB forbade the Red crew to wave or return greetings.

One U.S. sailor brought up magazines which he threw to the Russians, and two Red sailors picked them up to take to their cabin. The KGB officer ordered one of his men to go after the two and arrest them.

"Something exploded within me," Kudirka said, "and I knew I could not go back. And then I jumped to the U.S. ship."

—Press

JULY 1   If [Charles Leftwich's] attitude about desegregation could be summed up in one sentence, it would be this:

"Let's get on with it."

Let's quit hoping that a higher court will overturn the desegregation decision. Let's quit speculating that a lack of funds or a lack of buses—or a combination of those circumstances—will stop the plan to have most white and black children go to school together in Cleveland.

...It is time to stop arguing about...who's to blame and start concentrating on the remedy....

Children, if left alone, are best able to respond to change.

There is nothing in transportation that is intrinsically dangerous to anybody.

...It was encouraging to hear Leftwich describe the desegregation plan for Cleveland schools as one that deals 85 percent with the quality of education of youngsters and 15 percent with the mechanics of how to get them to school.

—Press editorial on the speech by the deputy superintendent for desegregation implementation

JULY 7   **Russo:** Dennis Kucinich in eight months' time has succeeded in placing this city on the brink of bankruptcy. For six months the mayor refused to even admit a problem existed, and

1978

now he is making only futile last-minute accounting changes that offer us only temporary solutions in hopes of delaying the impact beyond August 13th [the date of the recall election], so that he will not have to account to the voters for his disastrous policies.

In May, the mayor found the financial situation bad enough that he endangered the city water system to temporarily obtain cash to pay current operating expenses. The administration raided the waterworks construction fund, took $17.8 million, much of which belongs to taxpayers who live outside the city—monies which were to construct a new water division plant—and he placed the money in the general account because the administration didn't have enough money to issue payroll checks to city employees. Despite this, Kucinich still says there is no money problem at City Hall.

Tegreene: As I now monitor cash flow on a daily basis, I do not foresee any time when the city will be unable to honor its operating or capital improvement obligations.

    —*Open-air debate on the seriousness of the city's financial crisis between Basil Russo, majority leader of Cleveland city council, and Joseph Tegreene, Cleveland finance director*

JULY 28 *Political debates do not significantly add to the opportunities already available to communicate with the voters of Ohio.*

    —*James Rhodes, explaining to the press why he turned down the City Club's invitation to debate his gubernatorial rival, Lieutenant Governor Richard Celeste*

AUGUST 4 **Mottl:** Had there been a referendum, the proponents of forced transportation would have discovered that a majority of blacks as well as a majority of whites are unalterably opposed to court-ordered busing.

Tolliver: A lot of black people don't believe in busing. A lot of black people don't believe in desegregation. We do believe in following the law, even if we don't believe in [what the law dictates].

    —*Open-air debate between Ronald M. Mottl, Democratic state representative from Cleveland, and Stanley E. Tolliver, Cleveland attorney and head of the NAACP's local political action committee*

OCTOBER 6 **The Senate votes to extend the deadline for the ratification of the Equal Rights Amendment until June 1982.**

OCTOBER 13 The businessman not only receives no phone calls from the mayor, but he hears that the mayor may occasionally refer to some businessmen as "corporate crooks." He is told this is the only American city generating the impression of an anti-business atmosphere at a time when most cities are battling for business and jobs and tax income.

—Larry Robinson, *on how corporations considering new locations for expansion are treated by the current Cleveland administration*

NOVEMBER 3 Jim Rhodes is trying to take credit for everything under the sun. But he couldn't be here today. Why? I believe it's because he simply can't defend his 12-year record of broken promises, and so he's hiding behind a $2-million campaign of false accusations and outright lies.
   —Richard F. Celeste, *debating an empty chair at the club's traditional gubernatorial debate*

NOVEMBER 17 The biggest problem of the women's rights movement is to awaken people that there is a problem.
   —Eleanor C. Smeal, *president of NOW, explaining why ERA has stalled*

DECEMBER 15   Cleveland defaults on $14 million in loans when M. Brock Weir, chairman of Cleveland Trust bank, refuses to rollover the notes.

DECEMBER 22 Cincinnati does not gloat over Cleveland's plight. We in Cincinnati find no humor, smugness or false sense of satisfaction in your problems. The "you" we laugh about today could become the "us" we cry about tomorrow.
   Your city is in deep trouble ahead of other cities, not instead. The fact is, cities are in trouble—all of them.
   The increasing concentration of poor people within city boundaries and the flight of the rich to the suburbs has left cities unable to pay for their upkeep.
   ...Even though the bulk of our taxes are sent to Washington, most of the services that touch us are local. We're already paying enough to do the job, but we're sending it to the wrong place.
   —Gerald Springer, *Cincinnati councilman and former mayor*

1979

I**n the Middle East Egypt and Israel sign a treaty ending nearly 31 years of war; the pact is immediately denounced by the Palestine Liberation Organization (PLO) and the Arab nations, who sever diplomatic ties with Cairo. With that historic milestone and the growing anti-nuclear movement stealing the headlines from the urban crisis, Cleveland voters act decisively to solve their city's problems. They vote for a tax increase, veto the sale of Muny Light and oust Mayor Kucinich in favor of Republican George Voinovich. Before temporarily leaving the political scene, "Populous Man" puts in an appearance at the City Club's newly revived Anvil Revue, an old-time radio broadcast produced by WCLV-FM program director and club member Robert Conrad.**

JANUARY 5 The present administration has done an excellent

1979

job in only one area—blaming others for its own incompetence. It's time the mayor was forced to become a statesman, whether he likes it or not. If he refuses to act promptly and responsibly, then the state should take over the finances of the city until a new mayor can be elected.

    —Ralph J. Perk, *former Cleveland mayor*

JANUARY 19   If the United States had spent $12 billion on civilian needs in Iran instead of armaments, perhaps that country would be much more stable today than it is. Instead, it is in open and total political tumult. The least we should have done is learn from recent experience that equal attention must be given to economic and political development of a country instead of arming it to the teeth.

    —John J. Gilligan, *administrator of the U.S. Agency for International Development and former governor of Ohio*

FEBRUARY 9   I've seen a great city destroyed. I've seen a great city controlled by a cult as dangerous as anything Jim Jones ever had in Guyana.

    —George Forbes, *comparing the Kucinich administration to the notorious suicide cult*

FEBRUARY 16   The entire story of my 15 months in office is a story of CEI and their corrupting influence on the power structure of this community. They control everything except the people. Now they're demanding that the people sell their souls.

    ...If Muny Light is sold, not only will it mean higher electric rates and higher street lighting bills, it will mean that the people of Cleveland are granting a general pardon to CEI for its crimes against our community. And, incredibly, an economic analysis will show that Muny Light is actually being given to CEI. The people of Cleveland will, in time, be paying CEI to take Muny Light off of our hands.

    —Dennis J. Kucinich, *claiming that CEI will be able to pass along the $158.5 million it has offered for Muny Light should the voters decide to sell the utility February 27th*

CEI has used its influence to destabilize the municipal government in a manner reminiscent of greedy, ruthless, immoral corporate oligarchs in Latin America.

    —Kucinich, *noting during the question-and-answer period that four persons sit on the boards of both CEI and Cleveland Trust*

FEBRUARY 17   A surprised audience watched Mayor Kucinich climax his City Club speech with a theatrical flair that had him calling on the most unlikely of people to help him dramatize his administration's 15-month war with the Illuminating Company.

    The lights...dimmed and there, flashed on a giant screen, was council majority leader Basil Russo being interviewed by Channel 3 newswoman Cheryl Browne.

George Forbes

The mayor explained to the startled crowd of close to 1,000 that they were being shown a tape of a news broadcast from December 15th—the day Cleveland went into default.

The camera zoomed to a close-up of Russo [announcing] that Cleveland Trust chairman Brock Weir would single-handedly solve the city's financial woes with a $50-million loan if only Mayor Kucinich would sign a special resolution.

Browne: "That is to say if he will...sell Muny Light?"

Russo: "That is correct."

—Press

During his presentation the mayor was asked repeatedly what his plans are for helping the city solve its many problems, and each time he avoided a definitive answer—apparently he has no answer and is simply trying to take attention away from his own inadequacies and focus it unfairly on the business community.... His use of these red-herring tactics has...only succeeded in causing the loss of jobs, the loss of major construction projects and the flight of business from the city.

—Karl H. Rudolph, chairman of the board of Cleveland Electric Illuminating Company, in a written statement responding to Kucinich's City Club speech

Then and now there has been a kind of civic amnesia about that point that Muny Light was integrally involved in the default and the bank's demand for the sale of Muny Light was the crux of the issue. Many people had missed that moment when it occurred in December of 1978. When I played a videotape at the City Club...for all to see, there was an audible gasp of shock and surprise; people could not believe that it had actually happened. In that election of 1979 I think the Forum appearance was extremely important to the outcome.

—Dennis J. Kucinich, in an interview with the authors

MARCH 28 **The nation's worst accident at a nuclear power plant occurs at Three Mile Island near Harrisburg, Pennsylvania.**

MARCH 30 It takes some intestinal fortitude for a country boy, like I am, and freshman state legislator to come to the city of Cleveland, which is as full of carnivorous political animals as it is...[such as] Cleveland Electric Illuminating Company, Cleveland Trust, the *Plain Dealer* and, because I know he'd hate to be left out, Mayor Dennis Kucinich.

I'm one downstater who feels Cleveland is a great city important to the state of Ohio and the United States. I would vote funds to help Cleveland. I'll even give you a blank check on any legislation [on which Ohio House chairman] Harry Lehman [Democratic state representative from Cleveland], Governor Rhodes and Mayor Kucinich can agree.

—Wayne L. Hays, *former Ohio congressman for 14 terms who resigned his seat following disclosures that his mistress,*

1979   *Elizabeth Ray, was on the congressional payroll*

APRIL 13   One thing I learned from my years of opposing the Vietnam War was that [government leaders] are fantastically stupid and blind. I raise my voice [in protest of nuclear power] because we won't protect ourselves until we get over the crazy notion that the government knows what it is doing. The government does not know what it is doing. When they tell you not to worry, that all will be taken care of in the peaceful use of nuclear power, do not believe them.
     —Dr. Benjamin Spock

MAY 11   I am convinced that with an attitudinal change on the part of the city government, there would be an outpouring of commitment and initiative on the part of the private sector which would be astounding.
     —M. Brock Weir, *chairman of Cleveland Trust bank*

JUNE 15   *Narrator: The scene is the sparsely appointed office of the young mild-mannered mayor of a large Midwestern city.*
     Mayor: Well, Ms. Medvic. How much money do we have in the city treasury?
     [Mary T.] Medvic [newly appointed 31-year-old city finance director]: Five, 10, 15, 30...about 60 cents, Mr. Mayor.
     Mayor: Holy Tom Johnson!
     —Scene from the all-new Anvil Revue, this year entitled "Anyone for Dennis?"

JULY 13   **Williams:** Almost 250,000 engineers and scientists have endorsed nuclear power as safe. Would you rather believe [those] who are betting their lives they are correct or Nader, Fonda and a few of the "anti's? "
     McCormack: No one must underestimate the power of large government working with a large industry, where a great deal of money is involved, and no one must assume the public interest will be met.
     —Open-air debate between Paul C. Williams, engineer and former chairman of the northern Ohio section of the American Nuclear Society, and J. Timothy McCormack, Democratic state senator

SEPTEMBER 7   I hope what they can supply, we don't have to use.
     —Peter P. Carlin, *superintendent of Cleveland Public Schools, announcing that the city safety director has assured him that there will be adequate police protection when the elementary schools open the following Monday in their first year of court-ordered busing*

SEPTEMBER 28   **Kucinich:** All I had to do in the past two years to gain the favor of the media, the praise of editors, the laurels of the Growth Association was to remain silent—

I.F. Stone

And let Muny Light be quietly sold.

And grant tax abatements without a whisper.

And shut up when the banks and the Republicans tried to engineer a state takeover.

And keep my lips sealed as dozens of dirty deals danced across my desk.

If I had done these things, I wouldn't be up here this afternoon facing an uphill battle against the quiet onslaught of corrupt corporate powers secretly funneling cash into the campaign of the Republican, in order to steal back the city quietly, like thieves in the night.

Voinovich: The mayor has warned that things will be quiet at City Hall if I'm elected, but I'm telling you that my administration will not rest until every problem facing our city has been...thoroughly addressed.

You'll hear noise from City Hall, but it will be constructive noise, useful noise—the noise of mature, experienced, professional city officials going to bat for every single resident of Cleveland. It will not be the harsh, destructive, self-serving shriek we've heard for two years that humiliates or degrades people and institutions, simply because they don't happen to agree with the mayor.

—Traditional primary debate between mayoral candidates Kucinich and Ohio lieutenant governor George Voinovich, who will go on to win the general election

NOVEMBER 4   Inspired by the anti-American rhetoric of the Ayatollah Ruhollah Khomeini, 500 militant students seize the U.S. embassy in Tehran, Iran, taking 65 Americans hostage. The students vow to hold their captives until the deposed shah, who is undergoing medical treatment in the United States, is extradited to stand trial for alleged torture, murder and robbery.

DECEMBER 14   Ayatollah Ruhollah Khomeini is a saintly man, but he makes a poor ruler. Saints have made poor political guides throughout history. [Nonetheless, it is the United States that] is responsible for driving these people into fanaticism and paranoia, [having installed the shah] on the throne as our puppet and the puppet of the oil companies and Chase Manhattan Bank. Twenty-five years of deep freeze under the Savak [the Iranian secret police]...didn't prepare them for democratic rule.

—I.F. Stone

DECEMBER 25   Following a Marxist coup, the Russians airlift 5,000 troops to Afghanistan to shore up the new government against Islamic resistance. Three days later 15,000 Soviet tank troops invade the country.

1980

In response to the Afghan invasion, President Carter declares that no American athlete may participate in the summer Olympics to be held in Moscow—an

1980

unpopular decision that no doubt contributes to his drubbing by Ronald Reagan that fall. Also suffering a defeat at the polls is the local county government issue—the fourth time such a proposal has been outvoted since 1949.

The City Club gains a national audience when 21 radio stations across the country join via satellite a WCLV syndicate offering rebroadcasts of each week's address. Though this new programming focus will make parochial forums more rare in the future, Cleveland's "little people" are given a platform early in the year.

JANUARY 4   They can't afford it so they are going to *take* it.
    —Michael K. Evans, *nationally known econometric forecaster, explaining the Soviet invasion of Afghanistan as part of a pincer movement to take over Middle East oil fields*

FEBRUARY 3   The press discloses that 31 public officials, including a senator and seven congressmen, have been the subjects of a two-year investigation of political corruption by the FBI. Indictments follow in the wake of "Abscam," as the undercover operation is dubbed.

FEBRUARY 29   **Sedlacek:** Our neighborhoods did not deteriorate overnight. There have been long patterns of disinvestment and neglect that have combined to create our current plight.... Bankers started not lending; insurance companies started not renewing insurance policies; and City Hall began neglecting the delivery of basic city services.... It's a vicious cycle.

Brown: We held meetings with public officials to find out why, and we learned from those meetings that we were being ignored because there was no politician or bureaucracy pushing the money our way. All we had was one another, so we got as many of us involved as we could—whites, blacks, Hungarians, Slovenians, Italians, young people, senior citizens. All of us had the same problems; none of us had anything to lose but our neighborhood.

Kidd: Vacant houses, vacant lots and dying business strips were obvious evidence to us that the banks were not giving us our fair and rightful share of money. We felt that our hard-earned money which was on deposit at banks all over the city was being used...for the suburbs, the downtown merchants, every place but in our neighborhoods.

It was one thing to know this and yet another to prove it. [Thanks to] the Home Mortgage Disclosure Act [HMDA, requiring] that all lending institutions report where their loans are going...we had cold, hard facts to prove the unfair practices of the banks. The important thing here is that if it hadn't been for an eight-year struggle of neighborhood people...there never would have been an HMDA.

Dostal: We were tired of being mugged and beaten...so 500 of us...came with our demands for a special police unit just for senior citizens. ...We came from the high rises, from the meal sites, the church clubs and the senior centers. We came from the neighborhoods, where we have to live on $276 a month. And when a mugger steals our Social Security check, we have to suffer through a month of beans, limited heat and no health care. We walked with our canes on our sore and tired feet. We came with our hearing aids and arthritis to negotiate for better protection, because we want to live out our lives in peace.

—Panel discussion on neighborhood activism in Cleveland by Marlane Sedlacek, president of Citizens to Bring Broadway Back; Felix Brown, president of Buckeye-Woodland Community Congress; Hugh Kidd, vice president of Union-Miles Community Coalition; and Theodore R. Dostal, vice president of the Senior Citizens Coalition

APRIL 11 [President Carter's greatest] desire [is] to [do] the right thing with a capital R. He sees the biggest challenge of the office as the need to make the right choices rather than seeing that they are effective.

—James Fallows, *former chief speech writer for the President, now Washington editor of* Atlantic Monthly *magazine*

MAY 16 What we have experienced in Washington over the past three and a half years is what might be called a Dennis Kucinich administration at the highest level of government—an administration where the only experience lies in the field of running political campaigns. And, just as the Kucinich administration lasted only one term in Cleveland, I predict that Carter will last only one term in Washington.

—George Bush, *Republican presidential candidate*

George Bush called me after he had spoken at the City Club, about three or four weeks later, and said, "I'm coming back [to Cleveland] and I know that there was some conversation in the audience [about] my policies towards minorities." He said, "Well, I'm going to have to do something about it when I get there; so where do you suggest?" ...[I] took him to Karamu House [a black community theater, where] he spoke on minorities, spoke to minorities about what he was going to do. He had not even been aware that...he should cover [the subject] and then came the forum, and [so] he came back and cleaned up his act. ...He made a lot of friends [at Karamu] and he knew it. He'll never forget the City Club.

—Annette Butler, in an interview with the authors

MAY 30 The boycott [issue] transcends the Olympics. It strikes at the freedom we purport to have here in America. Athletes are being forced to make a sacrifice that won't benefit them or the country. The issue has only divided this country and divided countries around the world.

—Harrison Dillard, *Olympic gold medalist in track in*

1980 *1948 and 1952*

JULY 25 [The proposed charter amendment would] create a position of power between those of the mayor of Cleveland and the governor. It is not too far-fetched to suppose that the county executive will daily have his countenance on TV while placing one foot in the face of the mayor of Cleveland and the other foot on the rung of the ladder hopefully leading to governor.

Further, many of those who have no stomach for the thankless job of mayor of Cleveland would see in the county executive an easier, more rewarding road to political stardom—probably at the expense of peace, quiet and progress in Cleveland.

—**Robert Hughes,** *chairman, Cuyahoga County Republican Party*

SEPTEMBER 19 [The federal government is] not going to rebuild your schools; we're not going to make them into models of educational excellence that this community wants and deserves. Nobody can do that but the parents, the educators and the civic leaders.

...I am frustrated and angry myself about letting any [Cleveland] youngsters drop through the cracks because the adults for years have not been able to get their act together. I think that's appalling. But the idea that there is somebody on a big white horse in the sky who is going to come galloping along and change [things] without forfeiting at the same time the whole concept of having municipal governments and school boards and state legislators—I don't know how you do that without changing the whole mechanism.

—**Shirley M. Hufstedler,** *secretary of education*

SEPTEMBER 26 Obviously, neither Mr. Carter nor Mr. Reagan is advocating nuclear war, but both of them, nonetheless, propose programs which in effect endorse the idea that nuclear wars can be won. Both have proposed building missiles aimed at destroying the Soviet Union's missiles. But I submit to you this is the wrong response. With our missiles aimed at theirs and their missiles aimed at ours, the result will be a hair-trigger situation in which each side will be tempted to shoot its missiles quickly. In other words, "use them or lose them" will be the doctrine that will come to be employed by both sides.

—**John B. Anderson,** *former Republican congressman from Illinois and independent candidate for President*

OCTOBER 10 The emphasis must change from making government more open and honorable, which was the battle of the 1970s, to making government more effective, which I think will be the chief battle in the 1980s.

—**Archibald Cox,** *chairman, Common Cause*

OCTOBER 22 Let us assume that...the technical defense of entrapment prevails. Where does that leave the public official who was so weak and so vulnerable to temptation as to let his influence be bought even under circumstances of artful enticement. His moral wrongs remain the same. He is unfit for public office whether it be because of a corrupt heart or weak spirit.

—Leon Jaworski, *former special Watergate prosecutor, justifying the FBI's tactics in the Abscam investigations*

1981

Minutes after President Reagan is inaugurated, the 52 Americans still held hostage by Iran are released after 444 days of captivity. The country barely has time to celebrate before it is plunged into acrimonious debate over the first Reagan budget, which proposes cuts—called heartless and disastrous by critics—in federal human services programs in order to stem the deficit hemorrhage. Later in the year Reagan wins kudos for his nomination of Sandra Day O'Connor as the first woman member of the Supreme Court. A speech at the City Club describing the horrors of nuclear war brings another woman national attention.

JANUARY 9 We have succeeded in putting Cleveland back on an even, rational keel. We have stopped the downward negative slide we experienced during the Seventies and replaced it with a very positive "can-do" attitude.

—George Voinovich, *mayor of Cleveland*

Since George Voinovich took office there has been an attempt to project a city-wide front of agreement. It's my impression that the City Club has been a part of that, wittingly or unwittingly. ...If the City Club had continued to be a forum for [local] debate and ideas, I think that George Voinovich would find the requirements [of being] mayor to be a bit more stringent. ...As a result, the political spirit of a community, which needs to be kept enlivened with ideas and discussion, [has] become atrophied. Since it's taken the responsibility for being the premier forum in the city, the City Club has to take some responsibility for that.

—Dennis J. Kucinich, in an interview with the authors

APRIL 3 My confidence in the future of this newspaper is unbounded.

—Joseph E. Cole, *chairman of Cole National Corporation and new owner of the failing* Press, *which the Scripps-Howard chain sold to Cole after threatening to shut it down*

APRIL 10 What happens if a 20-megaton bomb should drop on Cleveland? It would form a crater a mile and a half wide and 300 feet deep so that everything within that volume would be converted to radioactive fallout. All people up to a radius of six miles from the center would be vaporized, turned into gas, and most buildings. All people out to a radius of 20 miles would be either lethally injured or dead. If you were looking at the blast,

1981

just looking, 40 miles away, you would be instantly blinded....

It would form by its immense heat a firestorm of 3,000 square miles in area, so everything would spontaneously ignite, even burning concrete and sometimes steel. And if you were in a fallout shelter you would not survive, because the fire would use up all the oxygen and you'd be asphyxiated.

What would happen if you lived in a rural area? I am describing now an article from the *New England Journal of Medicine* in 1962. You would have to be awake, not asleep. You would have to be listening to the radio. ...They would probably say, "Run very fast to the nearest shelter, you have 20 minutes." Remember, you won't probably have time to collect your family, your children, those you love. Now, medically, when you're in the shelter you cannot reemerge for two weeks or you would die. When you come out, this is what you will see. There will be millions of corpses, and the bacteria multiply in the dead bodies and mutate in the radioactive environment to become more lethal. The immune mechanism in our bodies that fights infection is depleted by radiation, so all of the diseases we medically now control—polio, typhoid, plague, dysentery—will be epidemic....

What about the doctors? Most hospitals, almost all, will be destroyed; most doctors will be dead. Those who are alive will have no drugs. Except that last year the Boston *Globe* reported that President Carter was stockpiling huge quantities of opium just in case there's a nuclear war. I guess we'd have to know where it was, and if we had it we could inject it into the dying people to give them some peace. That's euthanasia.

It is thought that so much ozone will be destroyed that if you stayed in the sun for three minutes you'd develop third-degree sunburn, which is lethal, and be blinded, so you'd have to live underground. There would be nobody to help. In Hiroshima there were people to come and help. In this instance civilization as we know it will be totally destroyed. All the music, the architecture, the literature, the art—gone. People will die of starvation. They'll die of a synergistic combination of starvation, acute radiation illness, infection, sunburn, blindness and grief.

It would be the grief that would kill me.

—**Dr. Helen Caldicott,** *president of Physicians for Social Responsibility, an anti-nuclear weapons lobbying group, cassettes of whose address become the most requested in City Club history*

MAY 16 I may be the last of a generation of moderates. My children can't accept the conditions. It's a new generation of young blacks who are determined to be free. We are threatened with a bloodbath—a black-white confrontation—like no one has ever seen.

—**Percy Qoboza,** *former editor of the Johannesburg* Post, *one of only two black newspapers in South Africa*

Helen Caldicott

JUNE 10   *Major League baseball begins a 59-day*

strike, the longest in sports history.

JUNE 11 Whatever one feels about the unmet social needs of this country—and many needs are still unmet—it was impossible to meet these needs until the country had some relief from inflation.

—**David S. Broder,** *syndicated political columnist of the* Washington Post, *claiming that inflation was the most important issue behind the 1980 Republican landslide*

JULY 10 **Mottl:** Look around at the Cleveland Public Schools today and ask yourselves, "Have we destroyed a school system in the name of saving it from the supposed evils of racially imbalanced classrooms?" The answer to that question is, unfortunately, yes. What was once one of the finest public school systems in the nation is now one of the worst. The system lurches from one financial crisis to another, while attempting to budget $40 million per year not to educate kids but merely to move them around.

Hardiman: That position is obviously an attempt to inflame the passions of people who have children in Cleveland schools. The Cleveland Public Schools have been in financial difficulties for well over 10 years. When he concentrates on revenue, he begs the ultimate point. The point is that in Cleveland we have got an illegal system. If it costs money to eliminate segregation, so be it.

—*Open-air debate between Ronald M. Mottl, Ohio congressman and sponsor of a constitutional amendment banning busing, and James L. Hardiman, lawyer for the Cleveland NAACP, on whether the $23 million in federal funds spent so far on desegregation could have been put to better use*

OCTOBER 6 *Following his criticism of Islamic fanatics, Egyptian President Anwar Sadat is assassinated by extremist Moslem soldiers as he reviews a military parade near Cairo.*

OCTOBER 9 We do not dare slap the second most powerful friend in the region in the face at this crucial time. If, by 1985, say, Arabia succumbs to a radical revolution or force from without the country, there will be cause for larger concerns than the AWACS [falling into unfriendly or terrorist hands].

—**Richard B. Secord,** *Air Force major general assigned to the defense department (who will later help to divert funds to the Nicaraguan contras from the Reagan administration's arms-for-hostages deal with Iran), arguing in favor of the sale to the Saudis of an $8.5-billion arms package including five Airborne Warning And Control Systems planes*

1982

The Census Bureau announces that the United States has a poverty rate of 14 percent, the highest since 1967. Another record—a federal budget deficit of

1982

$110 billion—is reached. These and other seeming consequences of "Reaganomics" are roundly condemned at the City Club, which will mourn the loss, along with the rest of the community, of *The Cleveland Press*, which ceases publication in June. State law prevents Governor Rhodes from seeking a third consecutive term, which signifies, among other portents, that the City Club's national radio network, now 83 stations strong, will not have to broadcast yet another debate between a Democratic politician and an empty chair.

JANUARY 5   *A federal judge in Arkansas overturns a state law requiring that both creationism and evolution be taught in public schools.*

JANUARY 8   **Cearley:** There is no shred of scientific evidence in support of "scientific creationism."

Thompson: Show me a watch without a watchmaker, show me a building without a builder.
    —*Debate between Robert Cearley, attorney for the American Civil Liberties Union in the Arkansas trial, and the Reverend Dr. Roy Thompson, founder and pastor of the Cleveland Baptist Church*

Hi, brother!
    —Thompson, *greeting club member Peter Halbin, who crashes the Evolution vs. Creationism debate dressed in an ape costume*

FEBRUARY 12   Q: You spent half your time discussing [the specter of] women in the military. Are you insensitive to the needs of millions of traditionally feminine women who are alone, widowed or divorced and who seek support and care for their children?

Schlafly: I'm not insensitive to those needs. But I might ask, what do you want me to do?

The Equal Rights Amendment doesn't help those women in any shape or form. It doesn't do anything for them, whatsoever. But I might ask why are those women who are in the job force, widowed, divorced or whatever, trying to force my daughters to be drafted? I'm not forcing the widowed or divorced women to do anything in this world.
    —*Question-and-answer period following the speech of Phyllis Schlafly, crusader against the Equal Rights Amendment, whose deadline for ratification has been extended until June 30th of this year*

Mrs. Schlafly, her hair piled high in a teased, wavy hairdo, wore a red blazer, blue skirt and pumps and a white shirt with red polka dots. The matching bow stood starched and tight under her chin.

Her opponents parodied her. Barbara Winslow, chairwoman

Jerry Falwell

for "Ladies Against Women," an offshoot of the Pro-Choice Action Committee and other women's groups, pranced about in a lacy pink dress, a frilly white apron and a pillbox hat, all vintage 1945.

Before Mrs. Schlafly's "Do We Want a Gender-free Society?" lecture, about 30 ERA advocates, some sporting pillow pregnancies and waving dainty handkerchiefs, rallied in front of the City Club.

"Roses not raises," they chanted. "Keep our nation on the track. One step forward, three steps back." One pseudo-pregnant woman led a cheer—"What do we want? Nothing. When do we want it? Now."

—Press

FEBRUARY 25 Obviously, I would have liked to mediate between the owners and the players, but the players weren't about to let the commissioner of baseball mediate with them.

—**Bowie Kuhn,** *defending himself against some club owners' dissatisfaction with his low profile during the previous year's strike*

MARCH 5 Because a country is a victim, it feels it has the right to make others victims.

—**Moorhead Kennedy,** *one of the American hostages in Iran, explaining how his captors justified their actions*

MARCH 19 Are we as a nation so impersonal, so blind, so callous that we turn our backs on the children? Is a missile more important than milk? Is a tax credit for a mega-corporation more vital than Salk vaccine?

—**Barbara Mikulski,** *Democratic congresswoman from Maryland who will be elected to the Senate five years later*

MARCH 26 The nation started on its downward trend in 1973, when the Supreme Court ruled in favor of abortion on demand. This has brought on a biological holocaust and led to between 10 and 12 million deaths. More Americans have died by abortion than in all the wars in 206 years of our history.

—**Reverend Jerry Falwell,** *fundamentalist Baptist minister and founder of the Moral Majority*

MARCH 28 *The Reverend Jerry Falwell came to Cleveland...with all the trappings of a potentate. He flew in on a Jet Commander, was chauffeured in a Lincoln Continental, called his own press conference and was girdled by his own security force, all of them wearing walkie-talkie earpieces. When club director Alan Davis (himself a minister) remarked that it looked like a political extravaganza, one of Falwell's aides said with a sly smile: "No, sir, this is show business."*

—Press

MARCH 31 **Gordon:** My husband...was taking the children

1982

to school on February 8th, 1978, and went out to the car as usual. I...watched them drive out to the road. Suddenly there was an explosion and the window I was standing at collapsed on me.

I saw the car was wrecked. I saw my husband inside and my daughter Leslie with her head leaning on his shoulder. I think they were already dead.

I couldn't find Richard at first. He was like a bundle of clothes across the street. His eye was hanging out of its socket. He lost the sight of that eye and his legs were badly hurt.

Deacon: My husband left a message to say he was going out to get shampoo. That was the last I heard from him. They found him two days later. He was hooded, badly gagged. He had been shot six times, one of the last in the groin. ...He was thrown by the roadside.... You wouldn't do that to a dog. We have four children.

—*Georgina Gordon and Sylvia Deacon, members of the Widow's Mite, an organization of the spouses of victims of Irish Republican Army killings (predominantly security officers) organized in 1981 to raise the awareness of American IRA supporters about the consequences of their financial aid*

JUNE 12   An estimated 500,000 march in New York City on behalf of nuclear arms control.

JUNE 18 About 30 polite but persistent picketers greeted Glenn.... The demonstrators carried homemade signs saying "Stop the Arms Race Now," "Jobs, Not Bombs" and "Sen. Glenn: Please Support Kennedy-Hatfield Freeze!"

When Glenn [author of the Nuclear Non-Proliferation Act] saw the demonstrators, he said, annoyed, "I've got a better freeze than the Kennedy-Hatfield freeze. Yet they want me to sign on that or else."

David Hoehnen, a leader of the demonstration...asked Glenn why he will not support an immediate freeze on nuclear weapons. Glenn said, "I have a better program of my own. You ought to read it."

"I have," Hoehnen said.

...At the City Club, Glenn said the Kennedy-Hatfield freeze and other freeze resolutions are long on rhetoric and short on substance. "They call for a beautiful end without the means of getting there," he said. "I support the end and I'm offering a practical way to get there."

...Flyers distributed by the pickets asked people to call or write Glenn's office, urging him to support an immediate freeze, but Glenn suggested the mail ought to go to Moscow.

...As Glenn...walked out, Glenn again was confronted by Hoehnen, 42, a former City Club president, who asked, "Why should we write letters to Soviet citizens? Why should we write letters to Brezhnev?"

"Don't write letters if you don't want to," Glenn bristled. "I just don't want [the nuclear freeze movement] to be the fad of

John Glenn

the spring of '82."

"It will not be the fad of the spring of '82, I promise you that," Hoehnen said.

—Plain Dealer

I was working with a coalition of people at that time who were very concerned about the arms buildup in this country.... We [decided] we would have a demonstration in front of the City Club, not protesting Senator Glenn's right to speak there—that would be the last thing on our minds—but an opportunity for us, quite frankly, to get some media coverage.... I think we got our point across. In fact, the peace community in Ohio has turned Senator Glenn around. ...When the nuclear freeze movement first started, he was absolutely dead-set against it. As of two years ago roughly he had turned around and supported the nuclear-weapons freeze.... We got him to oppose the MX missile, which, again, originally he had supported. And I think it's because of confrontations like the one that occurred at the City Club.

—David Hoehnen, in an interview with the authors

JUNE 30 **Three states short of the 38 needed for ratification by this date, the Equal Rights Amendment dies.**

SEPTEMBER 10 Every time I propose a change you tell me about Battisti, the state, buses...those things are just convenient excuses. The mission of the board of education is clear to me and very, very simple.... We will teach children to read, write, compute, think, behave and get a job.

—Frederick D. Holliday, *new superintendent of Cleveland Public Schools*

We began [the year I was City Club president] with Frederick Holliday. When he finished it was hushed. And then people stood up and gave him a standing ovation and cheered! He was going to be the messiah for Cleveland.

Our last speaker was George Forbes. In between [we had] Karen Horn, [who] was new president of the Federal Reserve Bank; Dick Celeste gave his first [City Club] address as governor; George James gave his first speech as the new director of Cleveland Metropolitan Housing Authority.

I think the club must continue to be part of the urban scene in Cleveland and be the meeting ground, not only for the famous...and the gurus from on high, but it must also make sure that it is a setting for people coming together to solve and discuss Cleveland problems. ...One of the things that bothers me about the Forum from time to time is that it's a passive thing. We eat our lunch and we listen and then go home or go back to the office and that's the end of it. ...That's why I'd like to see a lot more of a local think-tank kind of approach, using the City Club, not to take sides, not to present a solution, but to

1982

say, *"Look, why don't we convene all these people and talk about this?"* And they *go out and do whatever [needs to be done.]*
—Nancy Cronin, director of the Cuyahoga County Department of Community Development, in an interview with the authors

NOVEMBER 5 I'm not suggesting that the U.S. should legislate hothouse protection for our basic industries of autos, steel or electronics. Instead the Congress and the administration must make it clear to the Japanese that the day when they could get a free lunch in our market is over. No major company, auto or otherwise, should expect to participate importantly in a foreign market if its only strategy is to sell products and take profits home, without investing in the host country.
—**W. Paul Tippett,** *chairman, American Motors Corporation*

1983

President Reagan announces his Strategic Defense Initiative (SDI) to "intercept and destroy strategic ballistic missiles before they reach our own soil or that of our allies." But to help the Lebanese government keep the peace in Beirut, where warring religious factions are in daily battle, he sends in the Marines—a decision that is closely scrutinized by the City Club.

FEBRUARY 25 We intend to see that Cedar [Estates, America's first public housing, built in 1937 in Cleveland] is so improved that people will want to come and live there and be proud of what it is.
—**George James,** *director, Cleveland Metropolitan Housing Authority*

MARCH 25 Wreckonomics.
—**Philip Berry,** *vice president of the Sierra Club of San Francisco, on Secretary of the Interior James Watt's environmental policies*

MAY 20 Q: We...Americans...believe in one person, one vote. Will this prevail in South Africa peacefully or violently?
A: This will not occur within the next 30 years. Our nation is far too complex for this one man, one vote.
—*Question-and-answer period following the speech of Gert J. Grobler, South African consul general based in Chicago*

JUNE 17 Dennis Kucinich screwed everybody in this town for two years. And when he comes back downtown, there's a whole line of people waiting to screw him, including me. ...The brother is going to get it. He deserves to get it and he should get it.
—**George Forbes,** *on the former mayor who is now running for city council*

JUNE 20   *It's disappointing to see the City Club being used as a forum for violence and racism. It was even more disappointing to see club members who were present appear to enjoy the remarks. The audience's response was shocking. I really feel the City Club owes me an apology for not censuring the council president's remarks.*

—Kucinich, explaining to a reporter why he cancelled a scheduled August appearance before the City Club

SEPTEMBER 21   **Describing an advisory panel of his department, Secretary of the Interior Watt says, "I have a black, I have a woman, two Jews and a cripple."**

OCTOBER 7   A problem we have in Washington that is pointed out by [Watt's remark] is when we make employment decisions, or appointive decisions, we have to consider race and sex. ...People are not treated as individuals, but as representatives of particular groups.

   —Clarence Thomas, *chairman, Equal Employment Opportunity Commission*

OCTOBER 9   *Watt resigns.*

DECEMBER 9   If we have a definite advantage to gain for our freedom, our citizens or our property, them I'm for using troops, but I don't know what's in Lebanon for us. We're not protecting anything over there of great value to us. In fact, we don't even know who's fighting who, or why or what. ...I'm half Jewish. I don't want to see anything happen to Israel, but I also don't want to see...half a million American boys shot up in that sandy old desert over there.

   —Barry Goldwater, *Republican senator from Arizona*

DECEMBER 23   What is the interest of a free West in an independent Lebanon? We do not want Lebanon to fall under the aegis of Syria. ...We don't want a radical state allied with Iran and the Soviet Union having any longer of a seacoast on the Mediterranean.

   —Daniel J. Silver, *spiritual leader of The Temple and son of the late Abba Hillel Silver*

DECEMBER 30   One of the primary obstacles for most Americans in understanding the nature...of problems in the Middle East is the...risk of raising reservations publically about policies of the Israeli government or America's relationships with Israel. In these areas rational discussion most often leads to emotional rhetoric and the questioner being considered pro-Arab, anti-Israeli or worse. In effect, there has never been in our country any broad, significant public debate on the basic issues of Arab-Israeli relations and how our country might contribute most productively to improving them.

   Are the wisdom and justice of all Israeli policies vis-a-vis the

1983

Arabs, and our role in support of these positions, so clear that we have no alternative courses of action to serve better American national interest and Israel's long-range security? ...I am convinced that continued full and unquestioned support of Israel by the United States is the surest way to encourage existing and expanding Soviet influence in the Middle East. When our policies in this area become more balanced, Arab reliance on Soviet assistance will decline, along with its influence.

—**James Lipscomb,** *executive director of Cleveland's Gund Foundation and former Ford Foundation representative in Egypt*

1984

It is a year of political firsts. For the first time a black man mounts a serious run for President and a woman is nominated for vice president of the United States. Not since 1972 will so many presidential campaigners take advantage of the club's high-visibility Forum.

FEBRUARY 10 I personally, and a lot of women, feel an urgency about presidential politics that I haven't felt since 1968. My God, the national debt will be doubled by the end of the Reagan administration. ...Ronald Reagan has said that any candidate he appoints to the Supreme Court will be against the right of women to control their bodies. ...The kind of obscenity now going on in Lebanon—we must stop it. I love men [but] they think it's impossible to get rid of this reactionary.... We are not that hopeless.

—**Betty Friedan,** *author of* The Feminine Mystique *and founder and first president of NOW*

FEBRUARY 14 Lebanon is on everyone's lips; the Iran-Iraq war isn't but should be. That's one place where we would fight.

—**Terence Smith,** *editor of the* New York Times' *"Washington Talk" page, on what America would do if the Iran-Iraq conflict were to stop the flow of oil from the Middle East*

MARCH 6 I think "Star Wars" is for the birds.

—**Walter Sullivan,** *science editor of* The New York Times, *on SDI*

MARCH 9 [Jesse Jackson's] Rainbow Coalition will change the politics of the United States. ...It is estimated that by 2050 one of every two Americans will be non-white.

—**William K. Wolfe,** *director of the Urban League of Greater Cleveland, on Jackson's strategy for winning the Presidency*

APRIL 24 [Democratic front-runner] Walter Mondale may promise industrial renewal, but Carter-Mondale delivered bail-outs, Band-aids and industrial decline. Workers pleaded for aid, as steel and rubber plants closed in Akron, Cleveland and

Gary Hart

Maureen Reagan

throughout this state. Carter-Mondale did nothing and Walter Mondale was silent.

   —**Gary Hart,** *Democratic senator from Colorado and presidential aspirant, arguing for tax incentives for corporate modernization*

   Q: What real differences are there between you and Mr. Mondale besides the age disparity?
   Hart: It's the outlook disparity.

JULY 12   Democratic presidential nominee Walter Mondale taps New York congresswoman Geraldine Ferraro to be his running mate.

SEPTEMBER 7   The time is now for black people to stand on their own. The door to freedom and viability is open. White civilization no longer feels the need to exploit cheap black labor. ...Whites no longer feel it necessary to hold blacks down. ...On the other hand, they absolutely feel no obligation to lift blacks up. ...However, whether we stand still, slip backward or move ahead will be entirely determined by what members of the black race do or fail to do. ...The responsibility for the black race lies squarely in the hands of the black race itself.
   —**James Meredith,** *the first black student to enroll (under U.S. Marshal escort) at the University of Mississippi, now a professor of black studies at the University of Cincinnati*

SEPTEMBER 14   We did exactly what the American people said they wanted done. They wanted government contained, they wanted more money in their pockets, they wanted an opportunity for the future and they wanted lower inflation. ...We haven't seen an inch of Soviet expansion in the last four years.
   —**Maureen Reagan,** *the President's daughter and special consultant to the Republican National Committee*

SEPTEMBER 27   The liberty to keep the product of your labor and not give 40 percent of it to the federal government. The government steals the earnings of people in this country. Many people feel the Internal Revenue Service is the closest thing we have to a terrorist group in this country.
   ...Freedom from the risk of war. We need a sensible foreign policy which deals realistically with world problems. If I am elected, I will invite [Soviet Foreign Minister Andrei] Gromyko here to Utah, Montana or Nevada, to watch us take out of the ground or a silo a nuclear missile and witness it being dismantled. I would then go to Russia and put the Russian leadership to the same test.
   —**David Bergland,** *Libertarian Party presidential candidate on the ballot in at least 42 states, outlining his party's stated platform*

OCTOBER 16   Nobody has to tell the people of Cleveland how

1984

dangerous the deficits are. After coming so far and working so hard to get back into the bond market, this city should not be punished by deficits that are out of control. ...We need a President who will stop putting our money where his mouth is.
—**Geraldine Ferraro,** *Democratic vice presidential nominee*

OCTOBER 18 Ronald Wilson Reagan has no right to quote John Fitzgerald Kennedy.

Ronald Reagan was a Democrat for Nixon in 1960. He opposed President Kennedy's civil rights bill. He opposed President Kennedy's test-ban treaty and, at a rally only days before the 1960 election, he attacked John Kennedy and introduced Richard Nixon in glowing terms for a national television speech. So I have a simple question: I wonder why Reagan doesn't quote Nixon now?
—**Edward M. Kennedy,** *Democratic senator from Massachusetts and brother of the slain President*

OCTOBER 23 *In the early morning hours in Beirut, two Islamic Revolutionary Movement assassins drive trucks loaded with explosives into a compound where American Marines are sleeping. More than 200 men die in the attack.*

OCTOBER 25 I expect that the high deficits we now have will be taken care of through more people working and paying taxes.
—**Margaret M. Heckler,** *secretary of health and human services*

OCTOBER 29 Can you imagine the predicament of Joseph, Mary and Jesus under Reagan? They would have been in the stable, without weather-stripping. There would have been no breakfast or lunch program for Jesus in school.
—**Jesse Jackson,** *criticising the Reagan administration's cuts in public education, housing and welfare*

NOVEMBER 2 National party convention delegates were once selected at state party conventions run by politicians, by people who understood politics, by people who felt their job was to find a candidate who not only represented their general, mainstream party, but also who could win. Now they are chosen in state primaries where you have people out there voting and working in campaigns who basically are zealots. They're single-issue people or they're kind of out on the fringes of their party. That change is affecting, I think, the kind of candidate we wind up with, which is why you poor Democrats are stuck with Walter.
—**Lyn Nofziger,** *former Reagan assistant for political affairs, now an adviser to the Reagan-Bush campaign*

DECEMBER 28   If you were to walk among them with your food-filled luncheon plate they would not grab for it nor take it unless you offered it to them. I have never seen such dignity. I have seen a chicken walk among the starving and nobody made a grab for it. [Here] in Cleveland, if you have an earthquake, you have to call out the National Guard to keep people from looting.

—**Dick Gregory,** *comedian and political activist, giving an eyewitness account of his recent tour of refugee camps in Ethiopia as he plays a tape recording of the cries of starving babies*

1985

On January 28th, 22 months into his tenure as superintendent of Cleveland schools, Frederick Holliday commits suicide. He leaves behind an open letter to Clevelanders asking that they "use this event to rid yourselves of petty politics, racial politics, greed, hate and corruption. The city deserves better. The children deserve better." The City Club immediately puts together a special forum on "What Politics Does to People in Cleveland."

FEBRUARY 1   **Kucinich:** George Forbes and I had a battle going for the better part of 17 years. When you consider the intensity of that battle, you're right, it affected the community. ...Here are two men who, at one point in their careers, almost destroyed themselves and almost destroyed this city.

But we found a way. We see in each other decent human beings who are trying to serve [their] constitutents, each in his own way. We let [the past] go to try and heal this city. George, if there's a way for us not to continue the war, to slowly find a way to bring peace to our community, then I think others can do it as well.

Forbes: [The Holliday] suicide has nothing to do with the City of Cleveland. It was a tragic incident that involved the destruction of two lives: [school board member and Holliday opponent] Ed Young and Fred Holliday. And that is the last time I will publicly speak about this.

—Panel discussion by former Cleveland mayor Dennis J. Kucinich and Cleveland city council president George Forbes

...The forum was called to make some sense out of our system of power—a system that's been criticized and held tangentially accountable for the death of Frederick Holliday. The city needed to see these two leaders in the flesh and hear something calming or reassuring from them about the future.

What the audience got was hardly reassuring. What they heard in the "citadel of free speech" was hardly even professional. Two men, public officials, speaking on a serious subject before an audience of Clevelanders and, by radio network, beyond, simply "winged it." Nothing was prepared. The two spoke in predictably self-serving ways, telling us nothing new about how things work or how they'll work better.

1985

Forbes swaggered and Kucinich preached. It would have been laughable had it not been so close upon tragedy.
—Edition *editorial*

MARCH 8 From as far back as I could talk and think about not being a free person, I was very vocal. But people didn't care to listen. They thought I was insane, and that there was no such thing as defying the white power structure in the deep South, in Alabama especially, the cradle of the Confederacy and the heart of Dixie. I felt that, if we were in a free America, that all should be free, and no skin color or national origin or religious belief or nothing should prevent one person from having the opportunity of another.

...When the 1954 Supreme Court decision was handed down to end racial segregation in the public schools, I felt a ray of hope. However, that was soon dashed because we couldn't find enough parents in Montgomery to sign the petition to put before the board of education...so therefore the schools remained as segregated as ever.

...On December 1st [1955]...I was arrested and placed in jail because of my refusing to stand up on the orders of the [bus] driver for one white man to sit down.... On the evening of December 5th, we had a meeting at the...Baptist church.... The church was as full as any building could ever be. I could almost not get in. ...And there were thousands on the outside. Loudspeakers were set up to hear the proceeding of the meeting. ...The people were so enthusiastic and they were so willing that when a vote was taken (that was after the speakers, Reverend Martin Luther King, Jr., Reverend [Ralph] Abernathy, Mr. E.D. Nixon and many, many people spoke...) there was not one dissenting vote as far as voices could be heard for blocks away against our remaining off the buses.

...This attracted so much attention that people came from everywhere, from all over the country. They sent money, they sent clothing, shoes—we had more shoes in Montgomery in our little storehouse than I think they had in the stores downtown— food and everything. And they sent enough money to purchase several station wagons through the churches. All of this went to make up what was considered the first mass movement in the South for freedom in a nonviolent and peaceful way....

—**Rosa Parks,** *whose refusal to give up her seat on a Montgomery, Alabama, bus to a white man launched the civil rights movement*

SEPTEMBER 5 *We didn't feel [the mayoral primary] was enough of an issue.*
—*Alan Davis, explaining why the City Club had decided to cancel its traditional pre-primary debate by Cleveland mayoral candidates*

I think it's a shame the people of Cleveland will not have a chance to hear the issues debated [so] I once again call upon the

Rosa Parks

Dith Pran

mayor to come into the neighborhoods and defend his record.
—Gary Kucinich, Cleveland councilman, Democratic candidate for mayor and brother of Dennis, reacting to the news of the City Club's decision

SEPTEMBER 6   *Apparently the public has been heard. I look forward to meeting the mayor on the political battlefield.*
—James W. Barrett, former city safety director and one of Voinovich's three opponents in the primary, commending the City Club for reversing its decision to cancel the primary debate

[The City Club has] sort of gone national. They figure that people in Oshkosh, Wisconsin, are not as interested in local Cleveland politics, so let's have people speak on national issues and concentrate on [pleasing] our radio audience. ...In terms of what I'm interested in that's a minus.
—Seth Taft, in an interview with the authors

SEPTEMBER 23   ***Ronald A. Boyd takes over as superintendent of Cleveland Public Schools.***

OCTOBER 4   Cambodia during peaceful times was a country that could survive without foreign assistance. They have a relaxed life. The farmers work only six months a year and can live the whole year. They keep six months to relax. They have so many festivals. ...I feel very sad and sorry for my people. They lost all their culture and tradition.
—Dith Pran, *former assistant to former* New York Times *foreign correspondent Sydney H. Schanberg, whose relationship was examined in the book and movie,* The Killing Fields, *on life before the communist Khmer Rouge ruled Cambodia*

OCTOBER 11   ***Four U.S. Navy fighters intercept an Egyptian 737 carrying the four Palestinians who had that week seized the Italian luxury liner Achille Lauro, killed one passenger and held 400 other persons hostage. The fighters force the airplane to land at an American Navy base in Sicily, where the Palestinians are turned over to the Italian government to be tried.***

You don't have to study law to know that it can't be lawful. If it is, then might makes right. I don't mean to say that we don't have to address horrible murder; we do, wherever we see it. But we don't have to start a war [whenever there is a] transgression against an American citizen. ...We cannot police the world.
—Ramsey Clark, *terming the intercept illegal and provocative*

OCTOBER 18   The "Other America" described two decades ago by [author and Democratic Socialist Party leader] Michael Harrington is a changing neighborhood. Men are moving out, and women, many with children, are moving in.

1985

...Two decades ago women maintaining households accounted for 36 percent of those at or below the poverty level, while today they account for almost half of all poor families. ...Not only are women and their families more and more of the poor, they are poorer. Half of all families maintained by women [have] incomes of 50 percent below the poverty level. ...Moreover, the poverty experienced by women tends to be longer lasting, more persistent.

...That is the "feminization of poverty."

—Diana Pearce, *sociologist who coined the phrase for this phenonenom*

One of the reasons Nancy [Cronin] encouraged me to join was that she was actively seeking women.... She talked to me about how the women who were active in the City Club wanted to fight for women's speakers, women's representation on the board, and that until we reached the point that we had some decent numbers as members they were going to have a hard time arguing for a program component that was responsive to women's concerns.

...My sense is that women, in the program component, still are not heard from or planned for to the degree that men are. ...Sandra Day O'Connor was the last luncheon speech that I was there for, and what surprised me about it was how many women were present in the audience that day. ...My overwhelming impression was, "This audience has got to be 80 percent women; isn't this fantastic." ...It makes me think that the City Club is successful when they do address women's issues or have important women speakers, so maybe we should have them do it more often.

—Mary O. Boyle, Cuyahoga County commissioner, in an interview with the authors

NOVEMBER 8 I think I can cross all lines because I want nothing and only need help and support from businesses, universities, corporate people—those are the kind of politics I will be playing.

—Ronald A. Boyd, *superintendent, Cleveland Public Schools*

1986

The population of the United States numbers some 240 million as immigrants from poor and war-torn countries seek work in America's service industries. More and more people have left the city to enjoy the good life of the suburbs, and the major urban centers they left behind are choked with slums, poverty, disease and racial and ethnic intolerance. Nationwide, heart disease and cancer are by far the leading causes of death.

In Cleveland, the population has fallen to little more than half a million, making it the 19th largest city in the country. With the decline have come problems never before encountered, but one place where the issues are

debated is a venerable organization of concerned men and women—the City Club of Cleveland.

JANUARY 10 What do we find when we turn over the stone of so-called "constructive engagement"? I think we find a long-term policy of strategic involvement of America in the subcontinent—not only South Africa but of all the neighboring states to South Africa—which is posited upon the pivotal position of white-run South Africa, the most secure local representative and agent and ally of United States interest. Despite lip service being paid to the just and humane campaign against apartheid, I do not believe yet that there has been any profound change in thinking amongst those who formulated this policy.

 —Breyten Breytenbach, *Afrikaner author of* Mouroir: Mirrornotes of a Novel, *a description of his seven-year imprisonment in South Africa for "terrorism," giving the first in a City Club series on racism*

JANUARY 14 Isn't it amazing how arbitrary...all of the articles of faith really are? And how ludicrous it is that we have sent out missionaries...in order to do the good work which we feel needs to be done...which is significant and important to us but may not yet be significant or important to the people upon whom we are imposing ourselves.

 Utterly, racism isn't a matter of calling people derogatory names. Racism isn't a matter of depriving people of positions in jobs and in buses and in public places. Racism is a matter of depriving people of the right to be themselves, whatever that might be and no matter how certain we are that what it is they are is unsatisfactory.

 —Jamake Highwater, *American Indian, public television documentary writer/producer and author of* Songs From the Earth

JANUARY 21 Nazi Germany is gone.... I faced another reality when I visited East Berlin. On...a boulevard now dominated by the Soviet embassy and other communist governments, I passed huge propaganda window displays commemorating the 40th anniversary of the end of World War II. Enormous posters celebrated the end—and now I'm quoting—"of mass murder in the concentration camps, the end of terror against communists, democratics and all anti-fascist, democratically minded people, the end of the explusion of humanistic writers, artists and scientists." The word Jew was never mentioned.

 ...How extraordinary that even I needed the persuasiveness of personal experience to reconfirm a fact that I had long known: that the threat to Jews from the right, from the anti-Semitism of Nazis and fascists, had been superceded by the threat from the left.

 —Lucy Dawidowicz, *historian and author of* The War Against the Jews, 1933-1945

1986

JANUARY 24   America's always had in its mind a concept of white men's jobs and black men's jobs. ...Now the sin that Jesse Jackson committed in 1984 was that he dared to aspire for the Number one white man's job in the country. He offended quite a few people; they began to look for weakness to attack him and knock him off this heady perch. It seemed as though the weakest link was [black Muslim leader and Jackson supporter Louis] Farrakhan.

Now Louis Farrakhan, in 1984, hadn't said anything that he hadn't been saying since 1959, but for some strange reason suddenly what he said became a media event. The fact of the matter is that most blacks in America would not have been aware of Louis Farrakhan had not the media made such hay of his being a black bigot. The white liberal establishment started demanding of blacks that they denounce Farrakhan and start apologizing for him. ...I'm certain that most blacks didn't feel any sympathy for Farrakhan or didn't empathize with him or share his convictions or his prejudices, but to have another group come out and tell you that this is what you had better do..., dictating the behavior and even the feelings of the black community..., I don't think they were aware of how insulting it was.

    —Claude Brown, *author of the autobiographical* Manchild in the Promised Land

JANUARY 31   The origin of the idea of race is American, and it came about as a result of the abolitionists of Europe.... The slavers had to find [an] answer [to abolition] which would justify their continuation of...the trade in slaves...and they did. I have read many of their books and many of them are brilliantly written.... They found lots of reasons to show why it was ordained by God that there should be different races and that some of these races should be the servants of the white man. ...What they said was...that the blacks...were benighted heathens; that it was difficult to teach them anything; they couldn't read or write; and that there was [no improvement] to be hoped for.

    —Ashley Montagu, *anthropologist and author of* Man's Most Dangerous Myth: The Fallacy of Race

    There hasn't been really more than a handful [of black members]. I think the primary reason is that most blacks don't have the kinds of jobs which would free them up to come to the City Club. Secondly, they don't have the kinds of income that would allow them to come and eat a lunch at the price you pay here.

    ...Still, I would hope that the City Club would find a way to engage the interests of the minorities to a greater extent than it has. They've got to find a way to make it possible for minorities to come in here and participate and to find a role that they can play. I'd like to see [an issues] table here that's a black table—"black" in the sense that we discuss issues that impact on the black community, pick them out of the larger issues and

Ed Asner

say, "Well, now how does this play in the black community?"
Not to be exclusively attended by blacks, but by anybody [who
wants] to learn more about how all these instances, political,
economic, et cetera, impact on the black community.
　　—Bertram E. Gardner, former president of the City Club,
in an interview with the authors

FEBRUARY 11　What it does is put weapons at risk, not
people. How much more moral can you get?
　　—George Bush, *vice president of the United States, on*
SDI

FEBRUARY 28　I believe along with James Madison that there
have been more instances of abridgement of the freedom of the
people by gradual and silent encroachments of those in power
than by violent and sudden usurpation. The only way to guard
against those stealthy thieves who would rob us of our proud
heritage is by a constant, unflagging vigilence. For while the cat's
away the Meese will play.
　　—Ed Asner, *former president of the Screen Actors Guild,*
on Attorney General Edwin Meese's campaign against pornog-
raphy

MARCH 7　Washington is manifestly not meeting its responsibilities. Gramm-Rudman [the law mandating that the federal
budget be balanced by 1991, passed the previous year] is an
amoral abdication of government and civic responsibility. The
Democrats and Republicans who voted for it said they've lost
the ability to choose. They've said that a dollar for a sick child
is no different than a dollar for the Nixon library.
　　—Bruce Babbitt, *Democratic governor of Arizona and*
possible presidential aspirant

MARCH 19　Before 1914...the movement for the independence of Ireland—which at the time was totally...directed from
Britain—had reached a position of authority and strength. ...The
British Parliament had ratified the policy of home rule for all of
Ireland. [In 1918] the Irish people voted on the question...and
85 percent of the Irish people, peacefully, democratically, by use
of the ballot box, sanctioned and supported the British
Parliament position. ...Why did it not happen? ...Ireland's
national minority, the Ulster loyalists...located in the three
northeastern counties...objected to and resisted the democratic
decision of the British and Irish people....
　　Leading right-wing conservatives in the British Parliament...[decided] to "play the Orange card." ...They raised the
slogan "Home Rule is Rome Rule," and it began immediately to
create religious intolerance and religious fear.
　　...A very bloody war of independence was fought [against the
British] from 1918 up until 1920-21. ...The British terms for
ending the war were that the 26 counties who had voted for
independence would be allowed to secede...but the three

1986

northeastern would be allowed...to remain in the United Kingdom. That was the treaty that was signed.

The boundary commission...very quickly established that there was no viable economic base to form the state, so three other counties were forced into it. ...Of necessity, the [Ulster loyalists] built the institutions of their state to exclude these people who frightened them, and our problems started there.

—**Bernadette Devlin McAlaskey,** *Catholic rights advocate, on the roots of the continuing conflict in her native Northern Ireland*

APRIL 4 There is no machinery for the system to change, except from the top. It is a monolith, and every cell in it is related to the next cell, from top to bottom. And who will change it from the top? I think no one will, for those are the people that have all the privileges.

—**Vladimir Ashkenazy,** *symphony conductor, pianist and Russian emigre, on his homeland*

APRIL 29 *The Soviets ask the West for help in evacuating thousands from an area 60 miles north of Kiev where an explosion has ruptured the Chernobyl nuclear reactor.*

MAY 9 It is time to start treating the Soviet Union as a country with grave problems, bureaucratic, changing.... [Instead] we build up these threats [from them] to an absurd level and no one yells, "Nonsense!" When Reagan says a $4.8-billion "Star Wars" defense system is needed, no Democrat is getting up to protest it will never work and doesn't deserve a nickel. At best, the President's opponents will say, "I don't know if it'll work. Maybe $2.5 billion is enough."

—**Archibald L. Gillies,** *president, World Policy Institute*

JUNE 30 *Under pressure from the school board, Ronald Boyd resigns.*

SEPTEMBER 19 There is absolutely no doubt that far more people will die from that accident than [from] what happened at Hiroshima and Nagasaki.

—**Harvey Wasserman,** *nationally known nuclear power opponent, on Chernobyl*

OCTOBER 22 *Governor Richard Celeste squares off against an empty chair, when his opponent, James Rhodes (who has come out of retirement to make one more run for governor), declines the City Club's invitation to debate.*

One of my early experiences [with the City Club] was one of embarrassment. The questions were very direct and hard-nosed. No one stood on ceremony. Some of the questions were almost

Bernadette Devlin McAlaskey

insulting, they were that blunt.

However, as time went on I began to appreciate almost the demand *for answers, for reckoning: "If you are a senator, if you are a member of Congress, if you are a judge, if you are an advocate for some special cause, why...are your policies this, and if they are this, and I disagree with them, I want an answer as to why you shouldn't agree with me?" Very contentious were these questions, and many of them were preceded by statements despite the fact that there is a constant injunction from the chair that you should not make speeches.*

...I realized I was in the presence of something very unusual, something I had never experienced before. ...I have sat in on some very epic moments as a newspaperman, but the most memorable ones, the ones that gave me the best feeling about being a member of this community, of being a citizen and trying to think as a decent person, have come out of the City Club.

...Now you may ask: "What in particular is there about it?" I can't break it down into microscopic details; I can only give you generalities.

A special chemistry takes place. Its members, especially its regular members, appreciate it almost to the point that it becomes a narcotic. You feel bereft if you don't go to one of the forums. There is this feeling of camaraderie with the people with whom you're sitting at a luncheon. And coming away from these meetings feeling that you've filled another cup within yourself.

I can remember sitting at City Club forums where you could hear a pin drop. But without losing your attention of what's being said, your eye would turn to someone else who was equally as wrapped up, and [it's] as if you've reached across and touched that person, a special chord in his or her psyche. A lot of this sounds so damn romantic and flowery, but that's the City Club.

—Herb Kamm, in an interview with the authors

Index

Photographs courtesy of: City
Club of Cleveland (pages 34, 235);
Cleveland *Plain Dealer* (125,
137, 145, 154, 157, 166, 177,
182, 184, 187, 193, 197, 200,
201, 206, 208, 213, 225, 230,
233, 238, 239, 242, 243, 247,
248); Cleveland *Press* Library and
Collections, Cleveland State
University Libraries (27, 29, 31,
39, 40, 41, 44, 45, 49, 54, 55, 57,
58, 61, 62, 65, 67, 70, 72, 77, 79,
83, 86, 89, 90, 92, 95, 97, 100,
102, 105, 109, 110, 112, 114,
116, 118, 120, 123, 124, 126,
128, 129, 132, 135, 138, 140,
144, 147, 152, 164, 168, 170,
174, 178, 189, 204, 211, 219,
222); Cleveland Public Library
(80, 107); Western Reserve Historical Society, Cleveland, Ohio
(25, 36, 50)

BOOKS OF INTEREST FROM OHIO PRESSES

Photocopy this coupon to order additional copies of *America's Soapbox: 75 Years of Free Speaking at Cleveland's City Club Forum* — or any of these other popular titles.

YES! Please send me:

Quantity

_____   *America's Soapbox: 75 Years of Free Speaking at Cleveland's City Club Forum,*
by Mark Gottlieb and Diana Tittle, Citizens Press, $17.95 hardback

256 pages, illustrated; foreword by David S. Broder

_____   *Superman at Fifty: The Persistence of a Legend,* edited by Dennis Dooley and
Gary Engle, Octavia Press, $16.95 hardback

192 pages, four 4-color plates

_____   *The Ultimate Benefit Book: How to Raise $50,000-Plus for Your Organization,*
by Marilyn E. Brentlinger and Judith M. Weiss, Octavia Press, $22.95 hardback

232 pages, including a variety of adaptable forms and planning aids

_____   *Halle's: Memoirs of a Family Department Store (1891-1982),* by James M. Wood,
Geranium Press, $29.95 hardback

224 pages, duotone photography and graphics

Please add $1.50 postage and handling for one book, 50 cents for each additional book.
Ohio residents add 6.5% sales tax. Deduct 10% on orders totalling $50 minimum before
shipping and applicable sales tax.

☐ Payment enclosed   ☐ Please charge my: ☐ MasterCard

☐ VISA   ☐ American Express

Account no. _____   Exp. date _____

Signature _____

Name _____

Address _____
(no P.O. Box numbers, please; we ship UPS)

City _____   State _____   Zip _____

Send form to: Octavia Press
3546 Edison Road
Cleveland, Ohio 44121